W9-BVG-924

Heterick Memorial Library
Ohio Northern University
Ada, OH 45810

AN UNCOMMON FRIENDSHIP

AN UNCOMMON FRIENDSHIP

. . .

*From Opposite Sides
of the Holocaust*

BERNAT ROSNER & FREDERIC C. TUBACH

with Sally Patterson Tubach

University of California Press   Berkeley Los Angeles London

University of California Press
Berkeley and Los Angeles, California

University of California Press, Ltd.
London, England

© 2001 by
The Regents of the University of California

Library of Congress Cataloging-in-Publication
Data

Rosner, Bernat, 1932–
   An uncommon friendship : from opposite sides
of the Holocaust / Bernat Rosner & Frederic C.
Tubach; with Sally Patterson Tubach.
      p. cm.
  ISBN 0-520-22531-7 (cloth : alk. paper)
  1. Rosner, Bernat, 1932– 2. Tubach, Frederic C.
(Frederic Christian), 1930– 3. Jewish children in
the Holocaust—Hungary—Tab—Biography.
4. Holocaust, Jewish (1939–1945)—Hungary—
Tab—Personal narratives. 5. Tab (Hungary)—
Biography. 6. World War, 1939–1945—
Children—Germany—Biography. 7. World
War, 1939–1945—Personal narratives, German.
8. Holocaust survivors—California—Biography.
9. Germany—Biography. 10. California—
Biography. I. Title.

DS135.H93 R67 2001
943.9′7—dc21   00-053207

Manufactured in the United States of America
09 08 07 06 05 04 03 02 01
10 9 8 7 6 5 4 3 2 1

The paper used in this publication meets the
minimum requirements of ANSI/NISO Z39.48-
1992 (R 1997) (*Permanence of Paper*). ♾

TO OUR CHILDREN

. . .

Michael Rosner

Andrew Rosner

Owen Rosner

Karen Tubach

Michael Tubach

Contents

. . .

. . .

Foreword

Two European boys from small villages, one Jewish Hungarian and one German, grew up on opposite sides of the deadly divide constructed by Nazi Germany. One barely survived his imprisonment in several concentration camps, while the other attended meetings of the Jungvolk (Pre-Hitler Youth). The father of one was exterminated at Auschwitz, while the father of the other was a counterintelligence officer in the German army. After the war, both youths followed their luck and drive, each in his own way, to leave Europe and cross the Atlantic. The transformative power of the United States liberated them from their particular European fates. It gave them the opportunity to define who they were, with careers and families far from the traumas of their youth. Two Europeans became Americans, even as the turbulence of the past left marks on their souls.

As adults Bernat Rosner and Fritz Tubach met by chance in the San Francisco Bay area and became friends. But it was more than a decade before they began to talk to each other about their pasts and made the decision to record their stories. In order to keep his past life as victim at a distance, Bernie preferred that his story as an Auschwitz survivor be told in the third person, as a narrative by his German friend. The daunting task of writing the story of his Jewish friend helped Fritz confront his own past in Nazi Germany along with that of his family and childhood village. Both Bernie and Fritz believed that their lives in rural Europe before the Holocaust also needed to be revisited for the sake of the dead, the living, and the innocent, and because of the guilty.

Ultimately, both men refused to allow Hitler's agenda to define their lives and prevent their friendship. Their stories are about bridge building; they stand in opposition to the ethnic strife generated by "blood and soil" legacies. In these double memoirs Bernat Rosner attempts to come to terms with a past long suppressed; for Fritz Tubach, there is a search for redemption through narrating the story of one of Nazi Germany's victims together with his own.

But let the two stories, joined here, speak for themselves.

SALLY PATTERSON TUBACH

. . .

Acknowledgments

Many friends, colleagues, and acquaintances have helped us
along during the adventure of writing these double memoirs. We
not only had the benefit of strongly held opinions but also expert editorial advice on how best to tell our stories. From Fred
Amory, who was the first to read a tentative draft of an early chapter, to our University of California Press editor, Stan Holwitz,
whose insightful and comprehensive view informed the finished
manuscript, our work was encouraged and aided by many:
Martin Ebel, Dr. and Mrs. Paul Erdman, Christa Karpenstein-
Eßbach, Wolfgang Eßbach, Gerd and Kirsten Hillen, Marty
Markinson, Shelley McEwan, Susan Rosner, Johan Snapper,
Christa and Gerhard Wolf, and Martha Patterson Wynegar. We
are also grateful for the help and suggestions of Leonard Nathan,
Julie Christensen, Eli Katz, Susanne Lowenthal and the Staats-
archiv in Wertheim. Others at the University of California Press,
whose work and expertise were indispensable in turning our
manuscript into a finished book include Sheila Berg, Diana

Feinberg, Barbara Jellow, Steve Renick, Amy Torack, and particularly Suzanne Knott, our project editor. We owe a particular debt of gratitude to Charles Merrill, Jr., and to Mark Magowan and Peter Magowan for their close and engaged reading of the manuscript.

To German friends who helped organize our 1997 tour and provided many insights into contemporary Germany, we also owe our thanks: Manuela Bayer, Bernhard Holl, Ursula Strozynksi, Kurt Schüssler, Manfred Zink, and Alfred Ernst and Erika zu Löwenstein. We are also grateful to the Cosmos Club at the University of California at Berkeley and to the German Wirtschaftsgilde e.V. under its president, Hansjörg Weitbrecht, which provided us with forums to present preliminary excerpts of our joint enterprise in public readings and discussions.

We would like to give special thanks to Carol Sanger for her critical and productive line-by-line reading of the manuscript. Her commentary prompted us to rethink some key aspects of the work when we had thought it near completion and became crucial in bringing this project to a successful conclusion.

For whatever faults that remain and whatever controversies the book may engender, we alone are responsible. We have not written these memoirs to be paradigmatic of any particular political stance or to endear ourselves to a particular readership. We are motivated primarily by the desire to tell our *personal* stories, the stories of Bernie and Fritz. We are grateful to have had the encouragement and support of so many people in a project that turned out to be more difficult than we had initially imagined. They have enriched an experience we will never forget.

Finally, in an endeavor in which two life stories are combined, particularly ones partially shaped by a fateful divide, an extra measure of cooperation and sensitivity is required of the authors. Each of us would like to add some individual acknowledgments.

．．．

I, Fritz Tubach, believe that it was Bernie's extraordinary openness and flexibility that brought forth his story, allowed it to be told in my narrative voice, and set the tone of the project. It was the simple faith of one human being in another that served as the guiding principle of our work.

Beyond my friendship with Bernat Rosner, I owe the most to two people who gave me the inner strength to live up to the confidence he placed in me: one from the past, my stepmother, Maria Tubach, née Zink, one of the very few people I knew as a child and teenager who had the courage to oppose the Nazi hysteria; the other, from the present, my wife, Sally, who provided me with the professional distance and steady presence I needed for an endeavor so close to me. She polished my rough-hewn prose, and her collaboration was crucial in all phases of the project.

．．．

I, Bernat Rosner, would like to give credit to the impetus provided by my friend and partner in this venture, Fritz Tubach. For most of my adult life, I prided myself on traveling with a minimum of baggage. I now realize that this was one of the mechanisms I subconsciously adopted to cope with the past. This project has helped me to see that the human experience cannot be fully lived and appreciated without fitting the past into the mosaic of the whole. The form into which the project finally evolved was originally Fritz's idea, and his and Sally's enthusiasm, dedication, and initiative gave me the needed push to overcome my inherent inertia.

Some readers may wonder why my story is told in the third person, by a different narrator. This is in large part because the "Bernie" of the story is not the same person that I am today. Each survivor has a different way of coping with the past. My way has been to pretend that all the horror of the past happened to someone else. Having Fritz tell my story in the third person is part of this same coping mechanism.

By training and makeup, I am passionately devoted to accuracy and truth. I wanted the story that I told to be true and accurate because, in the end, truth, accuracy, reason, and logic are the only reliable yardsticks by which any human experience, including the horrors of the Holocaust, can be judged and understood. Even though I tried to keep emotion out of this work as much as possible, I am unable to do so with respect to the following point: what has happened to me since the war and what I became could not have happened in any country other than this one. This country means more to me than I could possibly express.

Finally, it will become clear in these memoirs what Charles Merrill, Jr., has meant to me and my life. There is no way that I could ever begin to repay him for his generosity, kindness, and, above all, courage for taking into his home and family a homeless urchin wandering the byways of postwar Europe who could have been a totally damaged human being. What he did for me and for so many others demonstrates that a single human being *can* make a difference.

ACKNOWLEDGMENTS

ONE

· · ·

The Return of the Past

We humanize what is going on in the world and
in ourselves only by speaking of it, and in the
course of speaking of it we learn to be human.

HANNAH ARENDT

The end of the journey came five days after the train left Kaposvar. People spilled out of crammed cattle cars onto the platform of the Auschwitz-Birkenau concentration camp on a foggy
morning in July 1944. The bodies of those who had died were
left behind in cars whose heavy sliding doors had been barred
shut the entire trip with iron and barbed wire. The only light
had filtered through narrow ventilation slats, and the terrified
victims now blinked in the daylight, looking for friends and
family members on the platform. They shouted out names in
Hungarian—Pista, Jozsi, Sanyi, Kato. But SS guards ordered silence, striking with rifle butts anyone who was too slow to stop
searching for a familiar face or calling out names.

Twelve-year-old Bernat Rosner was unloaded from a cattle
car together with his father, mother, and younger brother. Bernat tried to hold onto the family's small pile of possessions and
to keep it separate from the others. He caught a brief glimpse
of his Uncle Willy and of Jenö, one of his older cousins and

1

playmates back home. But then he lost sight of them in the crowd.

All of those who had been designated car "leaders" before their departure by the SS crew in charge of the deportation were ordered to report to the camp authorities. As the leader of their freight car, Bernat's father did so, and disappeared—forever. Bernat and his ten-year-old brother, Alexander, soon joined the men and boys, but not before their mother admonished them to stick together. Then she too vanished forever, like their father had just a short while earlier. Now the two brothers stood in a group of males on the platform in the camp—a desolate, flat place surrounded by a heavy chain-link fence, topped with coils of barbed wire.

. . .

In summer 1983 I was invited to dinner at the home of Bernat Rosner, Auschwitz survivor and husband of my wife's high school friend. Sally had run into her friend again by chance after twenty years. When Susan Rosner asked us for dinner at their house, I reflected on the fact that most Germans of my generation and younger had not known any Jews personally— or, if so, only fleetingly—because when we were young in Germany, the Jews among us were removed from our midst and exterminated. As a German American, I returned to the United States, studied and worked at the University of California, and lived among Americans, some of whom were Jewish.

During my years in Berkeley, I met only a few concentration camp survivors. One such encounter took place in the staging area of an academic procession near the campanile on campus. I paired up with a Czech lecturer waiting in a crowd of professors for a march to the Greek Theater, where a graduation or a visiting dignitary was to be celebrated. The woman, in her late thirties and with chestnut hair, was a friendly colleague on the fifth floor of Dwinelle Hall. My office was in the German Department, and hers was around the corner in the Slavic Department, which we both referred to jokingly as "the Polish corridor." There, at the base of the campanile, we were all wearing our academic robes and mortarboards, and the atmosphere was festive. I was shocked when the San Francisco Bay breeze suddenly raised the sleeve of her gown to reveal a concentration camp number on her arm. It contained, among other digits, a seven, with the characteristic German side cross over the down stroke. Looking back, I have sometimes wondered whether I offended her by asking where and when she was so marked. Her answer was simple: "Auschwitz." Then she continued to talk about other things in a casual manner. She also bore a deep half-moon scar on her chin that might well have been inflicted on her by a jackbooted guard; but at the time I couldn't bear to put the two things together in my mind.

I felt apprehensive about the upcoming evening with my wife's old schoolmate and her husband. It would have been easier to watch a documentary film or to participate in an academic discussion on the rise of Nazism and the Holocaust. This dinner for four could be attended by uninvited guests — any of the dead members of his family or of mine. Perhaps my distant uncle, who had been an SS officer in charge of a refugee camp near

Würzburg and hanged by the surviving inmates at the end of the war, might appear. Or perhaps my own father in his Nazi Party uniform would join us for dinner, or my host's father and mother as they emerged from the ashes of the crematorium.

When I was introduced to Bernie, as he now called himself, I was convinced that he was older than I. He looked worn out from his job as general counsel of the Safeway grocery chain headquartered in Oakland. His days at the corporate head offices were obviously more hectic than mine as a professor at the university in nearby Berkeley. No wonder. The revolutionary days of the 1960s and 1970s had passed. The campus atmosphere was more "academic," though Berkeley never became a tranquil place for quiet contemplation. But Bernie was the lead attorney in a field where the financial stakes were high. We had our battles at the university, too, but as Henry Kissinger once described the paradox at Harvard, university turf wars were fierce because the stakes were low.

Although the subject of concentration camps didn't come up over dinner, I couldn't help thinking about it. I noticed that Bernie had light blue eyes. Words from the "Todesfuge" (Death Fugue) of the Jewish poet Paul Celan, an Auschwitz survivor who later committed suicide in Paris, crowded in on me: "Der Tod ist ein Meister aus Deutschland sein Auge ist blau" (Death is a master from Germany his eye is blue). I repeated them several times to myself, re-creating in my mind the ritual intensity with which they are repeated in the poem. As a child I was told that I had inherited the blue eyes of my mother, who died before the war, when I was three years old.

From these self-absorbed reveries, I looked again at our dinner host and decided that perceptions were a result of the moment. Now it seemed to me that he had the upturned mouth of Frank Sinatra and could easily pass for his first cousin, if not his brother. No hint of Auschwitz there. I noted that he and I, both on the short side, were just about the same height. He was slight and wiry, while I had to watch my weight. What little hair he had left was sandy brown, while I had all my dark but graying hair. I probably looked more "Jewish" than he did to those who saw people as stereotypes. My mind drifted to my father, who told me once of being terribly afraid of a barber in Germany who had asked if he was Jewish. My father denied it, insisting that appearances can be deceptive, but he had the feeling the barber didn't believe him and would have liked to have cut his throat with the straight-edged razor he used to shave him. The dinner conversation with the Rosners escaped me for a short time, but no one seemed to notice my silence. And my free associations about blue eyes, appearances, and barbers faded away. In reality, Bernie is a year younger than I am.

As it turned out, the hours passed quickly during that mild summer evening in northern California, when the setting sun suffuses the air with a pale yellow tinge. World War II was two generations behind us. The past seemed far away. We stayed late to sip cognac and watch a sampling of Bernie's video collection of grand opera. The Rosners had a large-screen television, and with several remote controls Bernie could tune in the finest arias of Mozart or Verdi. Classical music enveloped the living room as we listened to excerpts from Strauss's *Der Rosenkavalier*.

Who, at our age, would not be touched by the Marschallin's musings on time as a wondrous thing—"Die Zeit ist ein sonderbar' Ding." Wouldn't it be best for both of us to just surround our pasts with the detached glow of great music?

. . .

After this first dinner, I didn't know whether we would see the Rosners again. But when we reciprocated the invitation and they accepted, we began to develop a pleasant, if superficial, suburban friendship. At first our wives encouraged and held it together. They had shared an upper-middle-class background in southern California and had some common friends from the high school they attended in Pacific Palisades in the early 1960s. As couples we had similar interests—in good food and wine, tennis, travel, culture, and contemporary affairs. When it came to our pasts, Bernie and I could easily talk about our early childhoods. It turned out that we both grew up in European villages. Bernie was born and raised in the Hungarian village of Tab, located southwest of Budapest, where his parents cultivated and sold fruit and walnuts. And although I had been born in San Francisco, I also grew up from the age of three in a village— Kleinheubach, on the Main River, about 75 kilometers southeast of Frankfurt. We both knew the lazy days of summer when nothing moved during the midday heat aside from the swallows that swarmed with high-pitched screeches over red-tiled roofs or flew low over the cobblestones to signal the arrival of a late afternoon thunderstorm. Growing up in a village gives you a special sense of place and the physical appearance of things: the polish of smooth-worn stone steps; the penetrating smell of wax and Lysol in the school buildings; the fierce look of the scarecrows that were supposed to protect the cherries on the neighbor's trees but instead frightened small children far more than the pesky, ever-present sparrows.

Though small, the villages of our youth were connected to the outside world by trains that stopped several times a day. This limited traffic didn't prevent weeds from growing up between some of the tracks. Because we knew the train schedule, we could use the tracks as a shortcut to the nearest fishing pond, thereby avoiding the dusty roads. Our villages had few lights, so that day and night were sharply demarcated, as were the seasons. A quiet life characterized our early childhoods.

But the parallels in our lives ended abruptly one day in spring 1944 when the SS and their Hungarian Nazi henchmen arrived in Tab and deported the twelve-year-old Bernie, his family, and the other Jewish inhabitants to Auschwitz. In the summer of that same year in Kleinheubach, when I was thirteen, I was a member of the Jungvolk and slated to become a Hitler Youth. My father, a full-time employee of the Nazi Party, became a lieutenant in the German army. Most of my family, including my father, survived the war. Bernie's family perished. He is its only survivor.

.   .   .

When you emigrate to America, you turn the pages of your life quickly. If you don't do it yourself, the country will do it for you, or you'll be "history," as they say. This is America. In contrast, a contemporary German writer recently stated that not a day had passed since Auschwitz. That is Germany. As our acquaintance deepened into a friendship, Bernie and I were caught for more than a decade between our European pasts and our American present, and neither early childhood memories nor the many things we now had in common were enough to bridge the divide that had existed between us during the years when Hitler was in power.

. . .

Bernie's experience of Auschwitz and the disappearance of his family and my German upbringing and Nazi father couldn't be discussed over dinner. I couldn't just say, "How was it?" or "Tell me about it, Bernie." There was no adequate way to broach the subject. But neither could we ignore these facts; they were close by, somehow, whenever we met. The Holocaust had become an important topic of academic research, but in spite of all the insights that have been gained, the distance between the trauma itself and present reflections on it has inevitably become greater. Once, during a cocktail party at our home, I happened to hear a well-known Berkeley professor mention to Bernie that he had just returned from a conference on Auschwitz in Hamburg. Bernie replied, "I was there—at Auschwitz, I mean." For a moment silence ensued, and then my learned colleague changed the subject. The gulf between the Auschwitz victim—an uncommonly articulate man—and the normally communicative scholar, well versed in the current academic discourses about the Holocaust, was striking. These two party guests had little to say to each other.

After I had known Bernie for a year or so, Auschwitz drifted into our conversation inadvertently. But Bernie was reluctant to dwell on it. He told us, as he has told many people in America over the years, that he had lived two different lives—a childhood in Europe and an adulthood in America—and that the first life had nothing to do with the second. He obviously wanted to leave it at that.

. . .

At the end of one of our dinners—in fall 1989—the Rosners mentioned that they were planning to visit Hungary and Bernie's village, Tab, the following summer. They suggested that we join them, and we agreed. I was going to be on sabbatical in Europe, and we already had plans to see Hungarian friends in Budapest, so the timing was right. We decided to meet in Budapest and drive to Tab.

When Sally and I reached Budapest in the late afternoon on the appointed day, we were delighted to find that our friends had arrived safely and were already in their room at the Hotel Buda. The next morning we spread a road map on the hood of our rented car and plotted the route from Budapest southwest to Tab. Sally, our designated driver, negotiated the Hungarian traffic while Bernie navigated us toward his native countryside. On the way we caught up on each other's lives. Bernie must have thought about it, but until we arrived at Tab, it seemed as if the rest of us had given little thought to the fact that we would be visiting not just the village of his childhood but also the village from which he and his family had been forcibly torn by

Nazis. Much later I realized that in proposing this trip, Bernie had emphasized the tourist aspects, since at that time he kept his life as Nazi victim far away, if not entirely from himself, certainly from the persona he presented to the outside world, including his friends and family. For Bernie and me, however, it turned out to be the beginning of a journey that took us far beyond the one-day trip to his native village.

About an hour and a half out of Budapest, we approached Tab. Small side roads to orchards, plowed fields, and groves of trees, marked the rolling landscape. Once in Tab, we parked the car near the railroad station, and Bernie became our guide. Our vacation mood changed, and our animated conversation faded as the reality of Bernie's past came into focus. We walked slowly down the main street as if picking our way through a minefield laid down by history. Bernie oriented himself by identifying places where particular houses had stood many years ago. At the end of the street was a tavern of the type one finds all over Europe, filled with men who, over a late morning snort, tell each other how things are with the world. They hardly took notice of us as we entered to use the rest room, except to tell Bernie the way to the Jewish cemetery when he asked in his halting Hungarian.

We walked up the dirt road that led past a row of modest houses. Between two of these houses, Bernie pointed to a broad flight of stone steps that stopped abruptly at the top of a slope where the synagogue had once stood. Now there was nothing — no memorial, no sign — just these steps, crumbling, deformed, and partially covered by clumps of grass. We made no effort to climb them. As a boy, Bernie must have trod them many times on his way to and from the building that had once stood there. I thought of the railroad tracks in *Shoah* that stopped at the entrance to the Treblinka extermination camp, tracks leading to a dead end, like these steps that now led only to an empty plot of earth and grass.

We walked on, saying little. Gray clouds shifted over the distant fields. At the edge of the village we continued beyond the last houses on a dirt path that led to the Jewish cemetery. Enclosed within a rickety fence and partially bordered by trees, it was abandoned and overgrown with weeds. We forged our way through the surrounding hedges and a hole in the fence. Tall grass, still damp with morning dew, hid many of the grave sites. Bernie looked for names he might remember, names of family and friends, and found a few. Reading the stone slabs, he told us the profession of this or that person and related a few anecdotes in a matter-of-fact way—fragments of life from his normal childhood, before things changed. At one edge of the cemetery, almost hidden beneath the trees, we came across an abandoned coffin and cart that had been used to transport the deceased from the village to their burial place. The cart had been sturdily built, so that even with the passage of more than forty-five years the wooden planks were only partially rotted. Bernie became animated, as if he had made an archaeological discovery. He knew people who had been taken on this cart to their resting places. I felt an aversion to this smug Hungarian village for neglecting the cemetery, for allowing the coffin and cart to lie abandoned and exposed to the elements, for forgetting its former citizens and letting the weeds grow over their graves.

Bernie asked us to leave him alone for a while in the cemetery. So Susan, Sally, and I made our way out through the broken fence, down to the main road, and headed back in the direction of the village below the constantly shifting clouds in a sky that was beginning to clear. We walked slowly so that Bernie could catch up with us. He seemed small and alone as he approached us from a distance. I realized that he may have been the only one of his people to have survived and to have revisited this village. To my amazement, he was striding lightly when he rejoined us. His step had an unexpected buoyancy. We talked about wholly different things, and I suddenly had the feeling that four American friends, whose present lives had hardly anything to do with this place, walked like tourists back toward the main street of Tab. I now know that Bernie wanted it that way.

We made another stop at the tavern. The same men were still talking and drinking. Again, they seemed to take little notice of us. Would they have cared had they known why we had come to Tab? A couple of them might have been old enough to have known the twelve-year-old Bernat or his ten-year-old brother or his mother or father before they were taken away. Why weren't they more curious when they heard this foreign tourist speaking in broken Hungarian?

The walk back down the main street seemed long. I thought of the three burial grounds in my childhood village of Klein-heubach—the Protestant cemetery, the most prominent and the one closest to the village center, the Catholic graveyard, next to a main road that used to be about a ten-minute walk beyond the last houses, and, finally, up on the east slope of the Odenwald, the Jewish cemetery, located in a forest, not unlike the graveyard in Tab. On my last visit to my village, I had taken a walk past the Jewish cemetery. Partially hidden behind high walls, it was locked up tightly. A German sign posted on the gate read, "Anyone defacing this cemetery will be punished by law." This warning was signed by a former mayor of Kleinheubach, Herr Lippert, who had been a member of the Waffen-SS during World War II.

The main street of Tab brought us back to the railroad station. A semideserted, two-story building, its paint was peeling. Cobwebs hung across some of the doors. Printed signs were yellowed with age. This country station, which looked abandoned like so many train stops all over rural Europe, came to life even in 1990 only twice a day. As we approached, the station appeared quiet and forlorn. Just as in Bernie's youth, the building was inscribed with the word "TAB" in capital letters. Our car stood where we left it. The only sounds were the electric humming of summer crickets and the buzz of low-hanging telephone wires. The clouds were gone, and the sun beat down. Nothing moved. Silence enveloped us for a long moment. Cameras ready, the four of us stood there wondering what pictures to take before our departure. We decided to photograph ourselves, in front of the station and next to the partially overgrown railroad tracks.

After the picture taking, I noticed that Bernie's eyes were fixed on a couple of run-down brick buildings dominated by a tall chimney near a stand of trees to the west. He didn't move except to raise his hands to shade his eyes from the glaring sunlight. Suddenly he said, "That's the brickyard. That's where the horrors began." No one spoke. As we climbed back into the car and drove away from the village, the fleeting remark hung there in the summer heat.

. . .

After our visit to Tab, various bits of conversations I had with Bernie about his past would run through my mind over the next few years. Despite this visit, I still had only fragmentary knowledge of his early life. He had never told his entire story to anyone, preferring to think that the Nazi terror had happened to a "Bernie" in quotation marks, a different Bernie. Would he someday trust me enough to tell me more? Perhaps our suburban California lifestyle was not conducive to such communication. Or was my German background an unspoken barrier? Yet his untold story, the "other side" of him that was closed to me, did not let go. He wanted it that way at first, because it helped him support the division he had made between his present and past lives. I, however, was left with a desire to build a bridge but few means to do so.

. . .

When you are twelve years old you feel immortal. Bernie and I both felt that way then. He had told me that much. I remember looking through an open air vent on the tiled roof of my grandparents' house, feeling invulnerable as I watched low-flying American Mustangs strafing the countryside. I asked myself whether Bernie felt fearless, even invulnerable, while he was being transported to Auschwitz—at least before he came in close contact with the death machine. Is that sense of immortality a privilege of youth, no matter how great the dangers? The danger to his life was incomparably greater than the danger I faced. After all, no one was out to get me, personally. No one forced me to go up to the attic to watch American planes during air raids. And air raids didn't continue indefinitely. But the threat to Bernie's life was ever present. A chance decision by a guard or a general order involving the group of inmates to which he happened to belong could have meant his death at any moment. Or he could have been chosen to become a human guinea pig in the bestial experiments of the camp doctor, the infamous Josef Mengele.

How did this twelve-year-old live his daily life in an extermination camp? In another brief allusion to his past, Bernie had compared his experience as a camp survivor to that of a barnacle attached to an underwater rock. I was struck by this metaphor, the hard jagged shell that protects the animal inside. Do analogies help one to understand the life of another person, in particular a life lived inside a factory of death? His analogy was distilled out of his experiences. I drew inferences from what he said, but they were not enough for me to understand the catastrophe that befell him and his family, notwithstanding my years of training as a professor of German and the textbook I had written on the Nazi period.

It wasn't until the 1990s that I became aware that Bernie had searched for links to his past, to that other life from which he claimed to have cut his ties. In the course of putting down our stories, he told me that before his first trip to Israel in 1995 he had thought long and hard about contacting Simcha Katz, his concentration camp buddy of fifty years before. "Without a buddy you couldn't survive," Bernie told me after this trip. "With a buddy your chances for survival were a little better, because you could help each other." But instead of elaborating on their friendship and dependence on each other in the concentration camps, Bernie stressed how the intervening years had distanced him from his former partner. They had corresponded for only six months after Bernie's arrival in America. After much soul searching, Bernie decided to reestablish contact with his old friend as part of his visit to Israel. The result was an emotional reunion at the Jerusalem Hyatt, dampened, however, by trouble communicating. Their native Hungarian had grown rusty, and Simcha spoke no English. Bernie's spoken Hebrew was minimal, and neither of them was fluent in Yiddish anymore. They talked to each other through a Hebrew-English interpreter.

Simcha had immigrated to Israel after the war and raised a family. He made his living as a self-employed paving contractor, and the Rosners had tried to downplay how well off they were in comparison. Although I wanted to hear details about the "buddy system," Bernie told me more about present matters—Simcha's current life and the Rosners' impressions of contemporary Israel. Simcha did not want Bernie to talk about their experiences in the concentration camp. The pain, as Bernie told me, remained too raw for him, even after so many years. I, for my part, began to ruminate on this glimpse Bernie had allowed into the buddy system and what might have happened to them decades ago behind the watch towers, barbed wire, and electric fences. Too much time had passed, too much had changed for these two concentration camp inmates to find their way back to the days when they both needed each other for their survival.

I thought about my own childhood buddy, Ludwig Bohn, with whom I played chess in summer 1944—at the time that Bernie was deported to Auschwitz. We played our game behind shuttered windows to keep out the heat and humidity. Ludwig and I would take long walks through the countryside, and on several of these forays we searched for a specimen of Goethe's *Urpflanze*, the ideal prototype of perfection in the plant world. We convinced ourselves that we found the *Urpflanze* in the form of a particularly tall pine tree in the English gardens of the Prince of Löwenstein's castle at the edge of Kleinheubach. I lost track of Ludwig when I came to the United States. But I found out that he married a woman of German descent in Namibia, a German colony before World War I, and I also heard rumors that he had become an anti-Semite.

Shortly after Bernie told me about Simcha, I dreamed that I telephoned Ludwig in Africa and tried to question him about these rumors. In the dream I reminded Ludwig that we had boycotted some of the meetings of the Jungvolk, the pre–Hitler Youth organization we had to join, preferring to play chess, collect stamps, and look for Goethe's perfect plant. We had considered ourselves better than the clods who ran the Nazi youth meetings. I asked what had happened to him. Why had he changed? But the answer to my repeated questions over the phone was silence. In my dream he did not reply.

I sometimes thought that Bernie and I should just let go of our pasts. I reasoned that if we would simply forget, we wouldn't be suppressing anything. We were the buddies now, but not to survive a death camp or to search for an *Urpflanze* in a princely park. Why not just have another glass of wine and listen to music, or discuss philosophy or European literature? After all, the 1990s were not 1944. We might just as well take advantage of suburban American life and the easy escape from history it provided.

One day, as we lounged at his pool, I was amused to learn that Bernie could barely swim. He not only admitted it but also thrashed across the shallow width of his pool to demonstrate his uncertainty in the water. I told him about my own water shyness and how as a boy I used to tell my grandmother that I'd been in the Main River all the way up to my neck, when in fact I'd barely gotten my swimming trunks wet. We both had a good laugh. Wasn't communicating such intimate trivia of the past enough? Isn't it exactly the shared *bons moments* in life that deepen a friendship? Although we enjoyed this pleasant status quo, I wondered whether it could be sustained. Lurking just below the surface of this everyday, after all, were events that remained never more than a nightmare or a phobia away for both of us. Without our being completely aware of it, the walls we had raised around these events had already begun to crumble. As it turned out, something unexpected happened that brought the walls crashing down.

On a business trip to the East Coast not long before his retirement in 1993, Bernie visited the Holocaust Museum in Washington, D.C. The museum was crowded, and when he received a number that would have allowed him to enter too late in the day to make his afternoon flight back to the West Coast, he informed museum personnel of his predicament and of the fact that he was a concentration camp survivor. They immediately allowed him to enter.

In the museum Bernie looked up the Nazis' records of the arrivals at the Mauthausen concentration camp. He had been transferred from Auschwitz to Mauthausen in September 1944. His reaction to these documents took him by surprise. He told me that his heart began to pound as he started to turn the pages on the microfiche machine to the date of his own arrival. When he finally reached the relevant page and ran his finger down the entries, there it was, his name, in an old German typeface: "Rosner Bernat." Thus he came face-to-face with his experience at Mauthausen. He told me that as he stared at his name, all the steps he had taken in his life seemed to lead nowhere but back to the horrors of that past. He was shaken, and he decided there in the museum that the time had come to confront his concentration camp experiences as directly as possible. These bureaucratic documents that stood for events that he had believed no longer would touch him convinced him to do so. Not only did he want to tell his story now, but he wanted to tell it to me. I felt moved by his decision, yet uncertain about what it would mean.

It became clear that our suburban get-togethers with our wives, our casual poolside or dinner table conversations accompanied by good food and wine, were not the appropriate framework for the telling of his story. So we decided that just the two of us would meet, beginning in fall 1995. By then we were both retired and no longer had to focus our energy on present tasks or on long-term professional objectives. I think that this slight slackening of the will—which Thomas Mann considered crucial for gaining insights into the past—also helped us to bring our histories out of hiding.

. . .

Our working method was simple. I took notes of Bernie's oral accounts and rendered them into narrative form. I wrote up my own story in conjunction with his. My wife, Sally, a freelance writer, then worked on organization and English style. After the draft of a section was written, we got together for a reading and discussion, and Bernie made additions and corrections. This matter-of-fact chronicling of how we proceeded, however, conveys little of the difficult path we had chosen to travel together. For one thing, even after Bernie decided to tell me his story, we drifted toward these memoirs, or rather, we backed into them gradually. We had no preconceived notion of a "final product." That early unselfconscious, naive phase of our joint efforts, when we gathered memory fragments, wrote them down, and discussed them, was crucial for the emergence of the eventual memoirs. And at the outset, we had no idea what obstacles and limits we would encounter on our way—obstacles in Bernie, limits in myself.

The story emerged in twists and turns. At first it seemed

enough to listen to Bernie tell me about his concentration camp experiences in a deliberately detached and factual manner. His initial recollections emerged well thought out and usually presented without hesitation. He was an attorney, after all, accomplished in articulating conflicts and complexities. His verbal facility helped to put me at ease and allowed me to approach a life very different from my own. It helped that we had a silent agreement about the limits regarding what needed to be or should be articulated. But then, sometimes a year or more later, heartrending facts would surface when he made new "stabs into his memory bank," as he called them. I slowly learned that "sticking to the facts" and recounting them as rationally as possible was also Bernie's way of not seeing that these facts had inflicted wounds. It took him time to admit this.

To maintain the separation between his two lives, during our visit to Tab in 1990 Bernie had downplayed the trauma he had experienced there. And true to his American persona, it was late in our work that he admitted to me his compulsive desire during one period of his adult life to return to Tab, to revisit the places where his parents had lived. During this period, he even purchased a detailed map of the region and memorized all the train stations between Tab and nearby Siofok.

As for me, I narrated my story believing that my good memory and grasp of details in their historical context would be a reliable guide to my own past. I learned, however, that what one puts in and leaves out—what one likes to remember or prefers to forget—also tells a story, one that is difficult and occasionally impossible to narrate. But over time, as I saw Bernie struggle with his own past, it was natural for me to look at myself, at who I am now and what made me this way. Bernie encouraged me to do so.

. . .

Someone asked me why I wanted to know Bernie's story at all. For one thing, because the German crime of the Holocaust never lets me go. But wanting to know about Bernie's "first life" was only part of what motivated me. I also wanted to link it to my own story. To do *both*, to tell his story *and* mine — the Hungarian Jewish boy and the young German villager trapped on opposite sides of a mortal divide, who come to America where their paths cross and they can work and play together — this new undertaking came to form the crux of what was important to me: bridge building. I simply refused to accept the fact that the deadly barbed wire erected by Adolf Hitler and his henchmen half a century ago would forever mark us off from one another in a fundamental way, that Hitler would have the last word in how we could relate to each other. The murderous events had been too horrendous to ignore in our emerging friendship, but I didn't want to grant the Nazis the power to perpetuate that divide indefinitely into our present lives.

It was Bernie's desire to have his story told in the third person, thus making it accessible to my narrative voice. I approached this role with apprehension. My narrative voice would be that of an outsider to the Holocaust, a German one at that. Would this constitute a sacrilege? Should I have maintained a discrete distance from one who had "returned from a descent into hell"? Should I have urged Bernie to tell his story in his own voice? He did not want it that way. He wanted us to look at our pasts together, because he believes that reverence for the extraordinary trauma he experienced can sometimes have an exclusionary effect; it can bar entry, define outsiders and keep them at a distance. It can create an inner circle of empowered narratives that renders the past less accessible to others. Toward the end of our work, I asked Bernie what had persuaded him to undertake this perilous journey with me. He said it was our common European cultural heritage, with its utopian longing for a civil society and the shared experiences of great art, and as for the rest, we agreed with Peter Ustinov's dismissal of ethnic and religious identity: one should have one's roots in civilized behavior and leave it at that.

TWO
. . .

Two European Villages

In this dream, summer was all year round,
our land a map of child-like colors. . . .
But if you held this map up to the light, you could see other lines,
not roads or streams, but tiny cracks suddenly opening under shaky
towns. . . .

LEONARD NATHAN

Tab, the village of Bernat Rosner's birth and childhood, is located in the open countryside south of the Danube River and Lake Balaton, about 120 kilometers southwest of Budapest and 90 kilometers north of what is now Croatia. To the west, about 130 kilometers away, lies German-speaking Austria. The parameters of this rural world were broken by Germany's designs on Europe.

Despite the presence of a few radios in Tab, one of which belonged to a neighbor of the Rosners, the village was far removed from the outside world before World War II. News as we know it, broadcast first by radio and later by television, did not yet exist. To be sure, the people of Tab learned about Hitler's invasion of nearby Czechoslovakia in 1938 on the radio and in the local press. And Bernie remembers the occasion when half the village crowded around a neighbor's radio to listen to the announcer's jubilant description of Hungary's Regent Horthy, astride a white horse, as he led his troops into Kassa (Košice, in

Czech), the capital of the province returned to Hungary after Hitler's dismemberment of Czechoslovakia. But such an exciting event receded into the background, drowned out by the predominant sounds of everyday village life with its domestic rituals. Like so many other European villages at that time, Tab was encircled by a wide geographic band of near-perfect silence, a silence that provided illusory protection from the catastrophe unfolding around it.

Only two villagers owned cars, the doctor and the count, who was the largest landowner in the area. But there were trains—two trains, to be exact—one in the morning from Siofok, the nearby lake resort, on its way to Kaposvar in the south and another in the afternoon that followed the same route in the opposite direction. These trains captivated the young Bernie's imagination as far back as he can remember. They gave him the sense of a horizon with wondrous things beyond it. As a small child, whenever he got lost his parents always found him at the train station. At home he loved to construct trains out of wooden blocks that were later chopped into kindling for the stove.

I believe that something more than curiosity made trains so central to Bernie's early life. His body and mind were always on the move, never at rest. Still true to the nickname, "Zizi kukac" (wiggly worm), he earned as a child, the perpetual motion that enlivens his memory is evident now as he gesticulates while telling his story.

But there is something else Bernie wants to communicate to me about trains and that railroad station, and he continues rapidly and with obvious urgency. During his early childhood, the station was a thrilling place where he could watch the trains depart to what he imagined were the distant and enchanting destinations that made up many of his daydreams. The Tab railroad station was also the starting point for the most exciting events of his childhood—the annual visits to his grandparents in Kiskunhalas. But in contrast to those early exciting adventures, at a later stage in his life the station came to connote something sinister, as when, shortly after the Nazi takeover of Hungary in spring 1944, he witnessed an elderly, bearded Orthodox Jew being beaten senseless there with the butt of a guard's rifle, for no other reason than that his distinct appearance annoyed the oppressor.

I wait for him to elaborate on what must be his most dreadful memories of this train station in Tab—the place, after all, from which he and his family were deported to Auschwitz. But he doesn't. More time had to pass before these particular memories emerged. Instead, he relates another nightmarish incident that occurred at a much later time in his life.

In 1971, when he was well established in his American life, Bernie, with his late wife, Betsy, revisited the village of his birth for the first time since he left it twenty-seven years before. After an emotionally wrenching daylong pilgrimage through Tab, they had come to wait on the station platform for the late afternoon train—the same train that played a major role in his youthful fantasies—that would take them back to Siofok and Budapest. A number of local inhabitants were also waiting at the station. Suddenly and without warning a grubby and obviously drunken old man approached Bernie and his wife and began a loud diatribe. Because of both the man's slurred speech and Bernie's by then poor grasp of Hungarian, he couldn't fully understand what the man was saying or the cause of the unprovoked outburst. He did, however, understand enough to realize that the harangue was filled with obscenities and anti-Semitic insults. The crowd waiting at the station immediately distanced itself from the ugly scene, leaving the two hapless foreigners to cope with the confrontation alone until the train arrived to take them away. For Bernie, it was a dreadful moment in which he recognized the same townspeople who had watched in silence as their Jewish neighbors were taken away so long ago. At the time, this episode also seemed to him still another variation on a theme—reminiscent of the same image in Tolstoy's *Anna Karenina*—in which the Tab railroad station served as a haunting landmark punctuating the turns and twists in his life.

. . .

Every year Bernie's mother took him and his younger brother, Alexander, born in 1934, to visit their maternal grandparents at Kiskunhalas. Although it was less than 200 kilometers, the train trip, with many local stops and an hour's wait at Kaposvar before the transfer to their final destination, lasted from 7:00 A.M. to 5:30 P.M. Sometimes they took an alternate route via Budapest, the home of Bernie's aunt Rebecca, the sister closest to Bernie's mother in age and friendship, where they would spend a day or two before continuing. These visits to Kiskunhalas were the high points of Bernie's year.

Beyond the train rides, Bernie loved the time spent with his grandfather. But on each occasion he first had to get past his fierce maiden aunt, Libby, the dragon of the family, whom he compares to the Wicked Witch in the "Wizard of Oz." Because the grandparents were elderly, Aunt Libby met the boys and their mother at the Kiskunhalas station. From the moment of their arrival, she monitored their behavior relentlessly and sternly corrected each transgression, no matter how minor. Bernie would say his prayers in Hebrew, and in one prayer—according to Aunt Libby—he mispronounced a word. However, this was the pronunciation he had learned from his mother, and he stuck to it whenever Aunt Libby was out of earshot. Not only his prayers but also his eating habits fell under her scrutiny. Knowing that Bernie hated sweet noodles, Aunt Libby made sure that he finished every bit of this dreaded concoction that was placed on his plate every Tuesday.

On one occasion, Bernie's spinster aunt even went so far as to turn Bernie into an unwilling accomplice in a scheme to postpone the marital bliss of one of his uncles. The day after his wedding, this uncle Schimi had brought his bride to Kiskunhalas to present her to Bernie's grandfather. Bernie usually slept in a particular cubbyhole near the pantry when he visited his grandfather's house. But on this occasion, Aunt Libby ordered him to sleep in the same bedroom with the newlyweds, frustrating any passionate hopes they might have harbored for the night.

Bernie's relationship to his grandfather, the assistant rabbi of Kiskunhalas, left a deep mark on him. The old gentleman lived a dignified existence in a world of books and reflection. Bernie remembers his grandfather's long flowing beard and the two to three hours devoted to the study of mathematics and the Talmud that he spent with him every morning during vacation. He idolized this learned mentor.

As Bernie recalls his early years of calm and tradition, he conjures up a sensual link to these fleeting weeks in his grandparents' house, with its scents of furniture polish and dried flower petals. Hoping that this elderly scholar had died a natural death before deportation, thus being spared the horrors of Auschwitz, I ask Bernie about his fate. But he does not know.

Religion determined the rhythm of daily life in the Rosner family. Tab had two synagogues, a large one for the moderately religious Jewish community and a small one for the few ultra-Orthodox. Bernie's family were members of the latter, and rituals were strictly observed. There was a prayer for everything, as Bernie recalls, one for eating and one for drinking, one before meals and one afterward, even one for full meals and one for snacks. At the age of three, Bernie's hair was shorn in Orthodox custom, and he began to learn the Hebrew alphabet. The letters of the alphabet were described by Hungarian words to serve as a bridge between the visual signs and the pronunciation of the letters. By the age of four, Bernie was able to read both Hungarian and Hebrew. When I ask him how he learned the German he still knows today, I am surprised at his answer. I had assumed he learned it in the concentration camps. In fact, German was the foreign language required in schools that he attended as a boy. Eager to read everything he could, he even tackled at an early age the German translation of Ibsen's dramas that his literate mother had purchased for their home. The family also owned a Yiddish translation of the Book of Leviticus. But Yiddish, a language for daily communication, was not used by the Rosners.

Each day began at 7:00 with a half hour of prayer at the synagogue. From 8:30 to noon Bernie attended the secular school that was run by the local Jewish community. He returned home for lunch but then went back to Hebrew school, or Heder, for religious instruction. These sessions began at 2:00.

The half-hour break at 4:00 Bernie remembers even now with a sigh, as if after all these years he still feels the need to pause for a brief respite before continuing. The midafternoon break was followed by more excruciating religious instruction that lasted from 4:30 to 6:30, five days a week. During these interminable two hours, Bernie rode his imagination out of the confines of the classroom to places beyond Tab, to Kaposvar and Kiskunhalas, and beyond the reach of the train journey he knew. And when the longing for escape became particularly intense, he imagined himself following the sun on its path to more distant places.

By 7:30 during the summer, everyone was back in the synagogue for the evening prayers before the appearance of the first star. In winter nightfall came earlier, and so did the evening prayers. In summer supper was eaten between school and the evening prayers; in winter it was eaten after the evening prayers. An hour of homework assigned by the teacher of the secular school finished the day's duties. The only free time during the busy week was on Friday afternoons. Even this interval was filled with chores left undone during the week or with preparations for the Sabbath, which commenced at sunset on Friday. Nevertheless, the absence of school on Friday afternoons and the relief that the drudgery of the week had been left behind lent those few hours a magical sense of exhilaration.

Bernie associates the beginning of this short period of respite with the Friday lunch that his mother prepared for the family: potatoes spiced with paprika and crispy fried chitterlings. Friday afternoons were also punctuated by the weekly bath and sunset attendance at the synagogue to celebrate the arrival of the Sabbath. At the end of prayers and after their return home, the Rosners' religious rituals continued with a blessing by Bernie's father and a sumptuous meal of fish and chicken and the traditional Sabbath eve soup prepared by his mother. This meal was followed by the recital and singing of traditional prayers. Young men from the Yeshiva—upper-level students whose homes were not in the area—were invited to the meal, to pray with the family, tell stories of their lives, and accompany the Rosners in song. These young men also joined the family for several other meals during the rest of the week and became part of the ritual life of Bernie's Orthodox family.

The Sabbath day started at 9 o'clock with an extended service at the synagogue that lasted until almost noon. On the way home from the synagogue the Rosner brothers stopped at the baker. There they picked up the casserole made of beans and a goose neck filled with a delicious spicy stuffing that their mother had prepared on Friday afternoon and that the baker had baked on Saturday morning in his large oven.

Saturday afternoon from 2:00 to 4:00 was examination time, when children were tested on what they had learned the preceding week. These examinations were conducted by learned men of the Orthodox community. Bernie's father was not a learned man and was chagrined that he was not qualified to examine his own sons. Following the Sabbath exam, the Rosners often took a walk up the "hill of a hundred stairs." The stairs were made of railroad ties, and Bernie recalls that on one of these traditional walks the adults talked about how the Germans had just invaded Poland.

This austere schedule might suggest that Bernie's childhood was a time of unremitting tedium. But that is not the way he perceives it now. The little bits of free time—the Friday afternoons, the several half-day holidays at Passover and Succoth, and the visits to his grandparents—were, because of their scarcity, all the more enjoyable and precious. And an intelligent boy could infuse even the most disciplined days with his own imaginative escapes. On the 2-kilometer round-trip he made several times a day between his home and the village center where the school and the synagogue were located, he would run at full tilt and shout, "I'm the train on the way to Siofok." On snowy winter days, a farmer would permit Bernie to ride to school on the runner of his horse-drawn sled, the only means of transportation during the Tab winters. These winters were enveloped by an aura of pristine innocence when he trudged home through the deserted, snow-covered streets with a candle enclosed in a glass lantern. At times he would take imaginary excursions to Andocs, the village where the Rosners' housemaid lived.

Bernie did not feel close to his father, Louis Rosner, who was born in 1892. But the son enjoyed the stories the father loved to tell and remembers that one of them was called "The King of Claws." It had something to do with a cat, tiger, or lion, but the plot has faded in Bernie's memory. As Bernie and Alexander grew, their father became less involved with them and more absorbed in the changing fortunes of his business growing, processing, and wholesaling walnuts and other produce.

The Rosner ancestors had been wealthy. On walks through the village, Bernie's father would show his boys the property once owned by the family and drop hints about some disaster that had radically reduced the Rosner wealth and about the paternal grandfather who deserted his family to go to America. As young boys, Bernie and Alexander were told two different versions of the grandfather's fate—one that he was dead and the other that he ended up in San Francisco. The family was not poor at that time, however, and their fortunes improved during Bernie's childhood, so that in 1940, when Bernie was ten, they were able to move into a better house.

Louis Rosner, a redhead, had an emotional side that ill tolerated the impertinence of his eldest son. Their frequent quarrels were caused by a "lack of subordination," as Bernie describes his own behavior, assuming a fatherly tone himself. At one point, Bernie's interest in learning and books got him into trouble. A prayer book belonging to one of the pillars of the community sat on the shelf right next to Bernie's customary seat in the synagogue, day in and day out. Bernie coveted that marvelous, leather-bound book so much that one day he stole it, took it home, tore out its pages, and deposited the cover, now devoid of its spiritual content, back in its customary place. Bernie was the prime suspect. When accused of the theft, he denied everything, prompting the owner of the book to comment sarcastically that perhaps an angel had taken it and removed its pages. The boy's insistence on his innocence gained him the nickname "Angel Tralala." As the full wrath of his father was about to descend on Bernie's head, a minor religious miracle occurred. The owner of the book, the man who had dubbed him Angel Tralala, pleaded that the boy not be punished, since his transgression proved a genuine interest in reading and in matters spiritual. Thus the anger of the father was diffused, but the nickname stuck to Bernie for the remainder of his life in Tab.

Little Angel Tralala felt closer to his dark-haired mother. Bertha Rosner, née Schwartz in 1893, was the spiritual bridge to Bernie's grandfather in Kiskunhalas. She was a sensitive person who cried easily, and Bernie suspects that his mother was a hypochondriac with an imagined "bad heart." She was the emotional font for him and his brother. An articulate storyteller, she was also the inspiration for his enduring love of books. He still remembers how beautiful her handwriting appeared in the letters she read aloud to him when he was very young. As he found out, these were the letters she had written to his father during their engagement. With a teaching credential, Bertha Rosner was the most educated member of the family. She was the one who made sure there were books in the home, even though the volumes often had batches of pages missing. Bernie remembers how frustrating it was to arrive at page 15, only to find pages 15 through 34 gone, so that he had to use his imagination to bridge the gap. Bernie's mother was also an expert seamstress and a good cook. She baked delicious sweets—cinnamon swirls, jellied rolls, and the kind of cakes that showed that Tab and its inhabitants were not far from Vienna and its elegant pastries.

Bertha Rosner instilled in her boys a sense of duty to take the straight and narrow path. This Hungarian mother employed old-fashioned educational methods in vogue all over Europe—unadorned scare tactics. When confronted with a disobedient son, she threatened him with the gypsies who roamed the landscape: "If you don't behave, we'll hand you over to the gypsies, who will take you away."

How many times was that admonition used to reprimand European children, and in how many languages? I remember the gypsies in my village who knocked at our front door to beg. I hid behind my grandmother's skirts, fearing they might take me away whether I had misbehaved or not. The very gypsy wagons that moved in and out of villages struck fear into every child, since these wandering people played a sinister role in the pedagogical arsenal of European parents. In Bernie's mother's case, this disciplinary arsenal also included the *Scherenschleifer*—as he told me in German—the knife sharpener, who appeared periodically to sharpen the knives and scissors of the villagers. I remember that this same apparition, the quintessential outsider, wearing ragged clothes and a broad-brimmed hat, descended on my village as well.

The scarecrow of village life, par excellence, for both of us was the chimney sweep, with his black suit and small, hooked shovel slung over his shoulder. The broom and metal ball at the end of a thick, rolled-up wire cord became the emblem of this mysterious figure who would move in and out of houses to remove the soot, a service for which he was paid. I was convinced that my grandparents gave money to this dark specter to get him to stop damaging our chimney and go away.

But not all fears were induced by the outside world. Many came from within. When he lay in bed at night, Bernie was terrified of a nearby window that appeared brighter than the walls of the room. He thought that a corpse would enter through this dimly luminous square and seize him. I, in turn, felt the ominous presence of thieves, cutthroats, and night owls in the dense forest right next to the house of my favorite aunt in the Odenwald. During overnight stays, I dared not breathe too loudly for fear of attracting their attention.

The nucleus of Bernie's family—father, mother, and two brothers—was part of a large, extended family. Bernie's mother was one of twelve siblings, and his father had two brothers with sizable families of their own living in Tab. There was a paternal spinster aunt, who, in contrast to his maternal spinster aunt— the strict Aunt Libby of Kiskunhalas—was a gentle woman. Uncle Willy had a limp. He also had a daughter with artistic talent who helped Bernie with an assignment in his drawing class. Unlike his brother, Alexander, Bernie couldn't draw, so this cousin sketched a steam engine for him, and Bernie received a high mark for her efforts.

Uncle Joe, the troubled member of the family, had several

children. His house was in constant disarray, and he frequently had to be bailed out financially. Bernie remembers that a family council was once convened to discuss the miserable state of affairs in Uncle Joe's household. Nevertheless, one of Bernie's first adventures into the world of marketing involved one of Uncle Joe's sons, Jenö. Bernie was hired by this older cousin to serve as a distributor for his tiny candy business. Angel Tralala was unceremoniously fired from his job, however, when he ate the candy he was supposed to sell, or "consumed the inventory," as he puts it today.

Despite his tightly scheduled days and the inescapable role assigned to him in the religious rituals of the Orthodox family, Bernie was keenly aware of the Hungarian world around him. Most of the non-Jewish villagers were poor sharecroppers who survived on a subsistence diet of homegrown food. Whatever cash they earned, these men spent on alcohol. On Sunday afternoons, Bernie recalls, their wives' and children's cries could be heard as they were beaten by the drunken, angry patriarchs. The black eyes and welts on women and children revealed the violence typical of these poor village men. In the street and stables, the animals—cows, horses, goats—became victims of physical abuse as well. And like any other village in Europe, Tab had its town drunk—Pista Krocsek. Unlike the fathers and husbands who were drunk only on Sundays, Pista Krocsek walked around in tatters in a continual daze. He became the inspiration for Bernie's first poem (which rhymes in his native Hungarian):

Pista Krocsek walks on the street,
Under his arm, he carries a big ax,
And what does he do with that ax?
He chops up little kids.

Tab also had some wealthy inhabitants. From the vantage point of his front porch, Bernie admired these "beautiful people" in white outfits who carried tennis rackets under their arms as they made their way to the local court. He yearned to be one of them, to join their relaxed ways of leisure and plenty. But there was a figure the eight-year-old Bernie admired even more than these tennis players—the second lieutenant of a Hungarian military detachment housed near Bernie's home. A well-groomed officer, in his tailored uniform he represented "the absolute epitome of grandeur," as Bernie told me. It was the first time uniforms played a role in his life.

Jews who converted to Christianity were also among the upper stratum of village society, but interactions between the rest of the Jews and the Christian community surrounding them were generally hostile. Such antagonism had a history in Hungary that had affected Bernie's family long before his birth. His mother used to break down in tears when she told about the fate of a brother who was killed after World War I. Following the communist Bela Kuhn regime, counterrevolutionary "whites" took over and blamed the loss of World War I and the ensuing "Red Terror" on the Jews. During their "white reign of terror" they wanted to settle scores, and Bertha Schwartz's brother was on their list. They broke into his house and arrested him. When he asked, "Why am I arrested? What am I accused of?" they replied, "You're a Jew, and that's enough." He was taken away and executed.

Although he was outgoing and communicative, Bernie had no Christian friends in Tab. For one thing, the strict Orthodox family rituals that structured his everyday life prevented friendships from developing. Even more important, the instilled hostility of the non-Jewish children created a barrier to friendly encounters. Gentile children often bullied and even threw rocks at Bernie and Alexander, targeted because of their Orthodox side locks, especially when they walked unaccompanied through the village. Bernie still remembers one particular tormentor and his frequent daydreams about beating him up. This bully grew up to volunteer for the Hungarian army, and Bernie recalls being pleased at the news that he had been killed in battle.

On March 15, 1944, the Hungarian National Holiday, a group of Jewish boys from his school who were carrying a Hungarian flag joined the parade through Tab. The other villagers taunted them as impostors with no right to participate and said that they were defiling the flag. They jeered and chased them away from the celebration. Bernie remembers it was usual for the hostile encounters with non-Jewish kids to deteriorate into fistfights and to end with the flight of the Jewish kids, who had not been raised to resort to violent actions or to fight back.

But the Jewish community had its own defense against such hostility. They would sing Yiddish songs for each other that were unintelligible to the Hungarian-speaking villagers. When I asked Bernie what kind of songs they were and whether he remembered any of them, he asked me to wait while he excused himself for a few minutes. When he reemerged from the downstairs of his home, he carried a tape recorded off a scratchy old record that contained some of these Yiddish songs. When he played one of them for me, I could catch no more than a few words at first. Bernie also had difficulty understanding the text of this melodious, seemingly plaintive song, sung in a minor key. Only after he replayed it did I realize that the message of the song was anything but plaintive. It told in a subtle, almost insinuating way about Christians who behaved violently and got drunk in taverns, in contrast to the Jews, who were pious and hardworking and attended synagogue regularly. We had a good laugh over this subversive piece of musical resistance that had been languishing for years in a bottom drawer. The only other contacts between Jews and Christians took place between poor Christian villagers and the Jewish households who employed them as servants. In Bernie's home, these Christian servants had the task, among other things, of switching the electricity on and off during the Sabbath so that the Rosners could live up to the Orthodox tradition of not working on the Holy Day.

All villagers, rich and poor, shared an everyday communal life that changed only with the seasons. In springtime the various fruit crops were harvested—cherries first, plums later, followed by apples and pears. Walnuts developed in their soft green outer shells until ripe for picking and peeling toward the end of summer. The threshing season started in August, first with the wheat and afterward, the rye. Sharecroppers would bring their loaded wagons to the threshing machine that ground on all day and into the night, separating the kernels from the chaff. Sacks were attached to one end of the machine, and by moving a lever, they were filled with the ripe grain. According to a certain rhythm and accompanied by an incredible racket, the tightly packed straw would emerge in neat bundles at the other end of the big machine.

During midsummer, a fair was held in Tab. Large tents were erected for this rural spectacle. Animals, crops, peasants, and merchants all shared this special time that obscured the general poverty. Bernie was forbidden to go to the fair but found the opportunity to sneak away nevertheless and watch the activities.

Early winter was the season for slaughtering pigs. From sunrise to sundown, the squeals of dying pigs were heard all over the village. Blood was collected from their neck arteries, and sausages were cooked in a huge pot at the end of the day.

In midwinter our footprints marked the snow as we carried lanterns to light the way home through the dark night. And in the morning, after a night of heavy snowfall, the village was transformed into an enchanted landscape. Timeless moments of the seasons, with no beginning and no end. These memories of the boy from Tab are also the memories of the boy from Kleinheubach.

But these times came to an end. They ended for Bernie in early spring 1944, when the seasonal rhythms were replaced by the shouts of Nazis. Those harsh new voices disrupted life as the Jews of Tab had known it, and in less than three months ordered their deportation and extermination at Auschwitz. There, or in other camps, most of the Jews of Tab were killed—Bernie's literate mother, who thought she had a bad heart, and severe Aunt

Libby of Kiskunhalas, and Uncles Joe and Willy and their children, and Bernie's father, preoccupied with his work, and the nice spinster aunt of Tab, and Bernie's own little brother, Alexander, a talented drawer of horses, and, if he lived that long, the wise and learned grandfather of Kiskunhalas, and the devout Orthodox Jew from the next pew in the synagogue whose book Bernie stole, who pleaded with Bernie's father for leniency. And...and...and. There is no end to this list. The only survivor among family members, friends, and acquaintances was Angel Tralala.

. . .

Located southeast of Frankfurt in the Main Valley, the village of Kleinheubach was one of the few Protestant enclaves in an otherwise Catholic region of northern Bavaria. Many of the family names still have Huguenot origins: Dauphin, Zink, Willared. In the early 1930s, news in the modern sense, as in Tab, was still in the process of being invented. Few villagers had enough money to buy the newspapers that existed. And after Hitler's rise to power, the press was anything but free and objective. The village was roused out of its rural slumber when the wealthier families acquired a radio, or *Volksempfänger*, the so-called people's receiver. Promoted by the Nazis, it was sold at low cost so that villagers could begin to partake in the events of the wider world—operettas by Franz Lehar from Vienna, soccer matches from Rome and Amsterdam, Hitler's speeches from Berlin, and Nazi propaganda about Germany's noble past and the murderous designs of its enemies.

During Hitler's speeches, village activities almost came to a stop, as if by command of an invisible wand. Scurrying home through the deserted streets, one could hear the Führer's staccato voice blasting out through open windows here and there or even through the walls of some houses. His voice seemed to be everywhere while families hovered around their radios listening to heroic stories of World War I and ominous assertions about outsiders ready to destroy the "German soul." One place villagers might read about Nazi Party opinions was in *Der Stürmer*, a weekly that was posted publicly in a vitrine on a wall on Main Street. Everyone knew the reputation of its editor, Julius Streicher, the quintessential Nazi anti-Semite. Printed in Nuremberg, the paper was full of venomous propaganda against the Jews.

Hitler had come to power on January 30, 1933, and in the fall of that year my father moved my mother and me from San Francisco back to Kleinheubach. Though a German citizen, in California my father had worked as a professional violinist in Bay Area movie theater orchestras. But the depression was in progress and the talkies had made theater orchestras obsolete. I was three years old, and as my father once explained, he returned to Germany, not to become a Nazi, but to feed his wife and son. Other family stories told of how he was moved by letters he received in California from family and friends that extolled the bright future being shaped for all Germans ready to participate in the Nazi movement.

By the time we arrived in Germany, the Ermächtigungsgesetz (law of empowerment) had put the power of the

German state into the hands of Adolf Hitler, all opposition parties had been forbidden, all unions had been disbanded, all non-Aryan bureaucrats had been fired, and Jewish professional activity had been severely curtailed. Moreover, the first concentration camps had been erected in Dachau and Oranienburg.

In that year, 1933, Kleinheubach had 48 Jewish citizens—23 men and 25 women—at least 4 of whom were sent to the Dachau concentration camp.[1] Three of them, Adolf Sichel, Theodor Weil, and Ernst Sichel, who was nicknamed "Judenernst," were arrested together in March and jailed. Without a trial or sentencing, they were sent to Dachau. Fritz Sichel was arrested and sent to Dachau in a separate action in May. He was released toward the end of 1935 and in 1937 was able to emigrate to America. Ernst Sichel was released after sixteen months and later emigrated to Argentina. Theodor Weil was imprisoned for six years before his release and emigration to the United States in 1939. Adolf Sichel was also released but never made it out of Germany; in 1942 he met his death in the concentration camp at Maydanek, Poland. As I grew up during the next nine years, until April 23, 1942, when the last 3 Jews were deported to extermination camps, 8 Jews died of natural causes and were buried in the Jewish cemetery, 16 moved elsewhere in Germany between 1935 and 1941, and 19 managed to emigrate to Palestine, the United States, Venezuela, and Argentina. The fates of 2 are not in the record.[2]

The year I turned five, the Nuremberg Laws forbade Christian-Jewish marriages and Jews lost their German citizenship.

．．．

On our arrival in Kleinheubach, we moved in with my paternal grandparents and my father found his first job playing the piano in a hotel. Soon he landed a better job working for the Nazi Party. A Nazi who worked for the DAF (Deutsche Arbeitsfront, the worker's wing of the NSDAP, or National Socialist German Workers' Party) had learned of his musical talent and asked him to work in the KDF (Kraft durch Freude, or Power through Joy), a division of the DAF involved in organizing social events and vacations for workers to wean them from socialist leanings and bind them to the Nazi Party. My father was eager for a better job, and when this Nazi bureaucrat learned that my father was not a Nazi Party member because he had recently returned from America, he arranged to take him in retroactive to March 1933, a date that increased my father's seniority. Germans who had joined the Nazi Party before Hitler came to power enjoyed enhanced status as the "best," most reliable Nazis. This elite of so-called Alte Kämpfer (old warriors) also generally attained to the most prestige within the party.

Whereas Orthodox Judaism structured the everyday life of Bernat Rosner's family, politics had a major impact on mine. The adults in our house were always in an uproar over faraway events, village rumors, and even opinions expressed within the narrow family circle. My family was politically split. Frequent verbal altercations were led by Uncle Ernst, a convinced communist, on one side, and by my father, on the other. My grandfather, a conservative who still had loyalties to the monarchy, insisted that the fights be kept *zwischen den vier Wänden* (within the four walls)—a frequently used phrase. Even someone as talkative as I was as a child quickly learned to *Mund halten* (keep quiet) when it came to political opinions outside the confines of our home.

One of my earliest memories of family life involved these heated arguments among rival brothers. If the subject wasn't politics, they competed over who could more quickly identify the composers of the music broadcast over our newly acquired radio. My youngest uncle, the quiet and retiring Ludwig, who usually shied away from the political fights, used to win these music contests. Although the political split in the family was severe, all the adults agreed with the Nazis about the "dark days" of unemployment and cultural decadence in Weimar Germany. I remember pamphlets in the house critical not only of the high crime rate of the Weimar Republic but also of its "degenerate" art. The Tubach family members were without exception antimodernist defenders of classical art and music (*hohe Kunst*) and felt threatened by modern trends. I recall my grandfather Tubach's pun on the name of the composer Hindemith: "Hindemith, her damit, weg damit," which meant roughly, "Hindemith, take him and throw him away."

Regardless of the nature of the disputes or alliances that formed in the verbal trenches, my grandmother, who raised me after the death of my mother, kept everyone fed—primarily on my grandfather's meager World War I invalid's pension. During the depression that lasted into the mid-1930s, my uncles and my father added whatever else they could bring home from their various jobs to this steady, if small, source of income. As an employee of the Nazi Party, my father always had more money than the others.

I took it all in and was fascinated by the excitement that the outside world caused in our household. Because I was good at mimicking people, I was frequently asked to imitate Hitler or the Protestant parson of the village, Pfarrer Wagner, for the amusement of the assembled family members. I had a keen eye for personal mannerisms, and everyone in our house, monarchist, Nazi, or communist, would break up over my Hitlerian speech or my version of a pastoral sermon. But I was under strict orders *never* to reveal this skill outside our four walls. Once I broke the rule, causing my father great distress. On a visit to my father's sister, my aunt Gretel in Nuremberg, my father took me for a walk through the Reichsparteitagsgelände, the Nazi Party parade grounds, where he pointed out to me the concrete podium from which Hitler spoke during the rallies. It was too great a temptation for a small boy. I dashed up the steps and started my Hitler imitation. My father bounded up after me, yanked me away, and disappeared with me in the Sunday crowd that was strolling through the arena.

Many village men ran around in uniform, alternately angry or elated for reasons I could not understand, but their actions had an aura of importance. At one point, meek Uncle Ludwig had the opportunity to participate in the main Nazi Party rally held every year in Nuremberg, and I remember how he returned home glowing, transported by an enthusiasm quite uncharacteristic for his timid nature. The entire family joked about

Ludwig's *innerer Reichsparteitag* (internal party rally), a phrase that gained widespread use during that period to designate any happy experience or emotion. Although my father worked for the party, he was disdainful of Ludwig's temporary transformation and ridiculed him for it. In fact, he had a keen eye for Nazi bathos and enjoyed making fun of it, from goose-stepping soldiers to Hitler's theatrical antics. My father once happened to meet Julius Streicher, the Nazi leader of the province of Franconia and editor of *Der Stürmer,* at a meeting in Nuremberg. At one point in the evening, Streicher spread a map of the moon out on a table and in all seriousness discussed its eventual colonization by Germany. My father found this hilarious and thought that his superior was crazy.

My father had lived a musician's life in the big open world of the 1920s and early 1930s in America and enjoyed telling everyone how considerate Americans were. He wanted to please his Nazi superiors for the sake of his own advancement, but he also liked to impress those around him with his savvy cosmopolitanism.

While the men tended to fluctuate in peculiar ways, my grandmother remained steady, always the same, always kind. My grandparents' house was the most stable element in my young life, as long as my grandmother was inside it. When she left the house for even a short trip, I felt lost and uncomfortable. To reassure myself, I would stare at the huge photograph of her as a beautiful young woman that hung in the living room. When I left the house, I loved to hear her voice ring out, calling me home for a snack. I knew I would get my favorite liverwurst sandwich if I begged. When I had a toothache, she would grind up some nutmeg to apply to the painful spot. One day during one of the endless, hot summers of my childhood, I saw her approach rapidly up an unpaved street that accentuated her stumbling gait. With her hand she shielded something from the sun, and when she approached, gave me the melting vanilla ice-cream cone she had carried home for me. If she had a personal fault, it was that she loved to buy fine clothes, to the consternation of my grandfather.

The few trips I took with her, proposed to me as an adventure, in actuality frightened me, especially because the first one turned into a mishap. On our way to her father's village near Würzburg—Königshofen, where he had been mayor—we took the wrong train and ended up in Walldürn, a well-known site for Catholic pilgrimages. After an hour of negotiation with the railway authorities, we were put onto one of the stifling pilgrimage trains, crowded with hundreds of people reciting Catholic prayers. I was forced to stand among the praying strangers, unable to move even as far as the WC at the end of the car, while outside a landscape moved by that was alien to me. Only after several transfers did we finally arrive, shaken and exhausted, in her native village. I much preferred her to stay home, and to stay home with her, where things were familiar and safe.

My grandparents' house was close to the railroad station, a marvelous and forbidden playground. Surrounded by shrubs, trees, and tall grasses, the station grounds provided ample hiding places from the station master, who would emerge from time to time to chase me and my small friends away. My grandfather had been a railroad engineer, and he told me stories of troop trains he conducted to Russia during World War I. A head-on collision with another train ended his career and left him nearly blind. One day he took me to see a locomotive that had stopped on one of the side tracks of the station. I was allowed onto the conductor's platform, where the engineer opened the heavy metal door to let me peek inside the roaring furnace in the belly of the engine.

The sound of steam engines starting off from the train station was as much a part of my everyday life as was the ticking and chiming of the grandfather clock in the living room, or the cackling of chickens in the backyard. In contrast to Tab, all kinds of trains stopped at Kleinheubach—not just passenger trains but also trains filled with Catholic pilgrims on their way to Kloster Engelberg, the monastery on the other side of the river, or trains organized by the Nazi Workers' Party for outings. Some of these latter trains were festooned with flags and swastikas and carried workers from the industrial regions of Germany to the Main Valley for a few days of parading, speeches, and relaxing in the countryside.

Music played an important role in our household. In 1900 my grandfather had founded a men's choir in the city of Mannheim. One of his brothers, my godfather and namesake, was a violinist who played his way from the resort town of Baden-Baden to the movie house orchestra of the Golden Gate Theater in San Francisco during the 1920s. It was he whom my father had followed to San Francisco, where they both played violin in the same orchestra, as well as in the Paramount Theater Orchestra in Oakland. My cousin Lore was a brilliant piano and harpsichord student at the conservatory in Nuremberg. I was pitted against her during one of our dreaded competitive family recitals. She played Chopin's "Minute Waltz" with ease, while I managed only a halting version of Mozart's "Rondo alla turca." Enraged at my incompetence, my father told me that I had embarrassed both of us in front of the entire family. After that I came to detest piano practice even more than I had before.

Though he was usually absent, my father loomed large in my mind. He was not just another peasant villager huddled at the radio listening passively to the happenings of the outside world. Rather, he was an active participant in "important events," organizing visits of workers to our rural region in his KDF capacity. He came home on weekends and tried to make up for his lack of paternal presence during the rest of the week by intensifying his surveillance of my progress in grade school. I usually fell far short of his expectations without ever really understanding what he wanted of me. There were so many things I did not understand, and no one, including my father, bothered to explain them to me. I couldn't understand, for example, why the letter *q* was not independent like the other letters and always had to be accompanied by a *u*. When I was told to sing *zweite Stimme* (second voice), I thought I was to somehow split my voice and sing two different tones at the same time. My teachers couldn't understand why a musician's son was so lacking in talent.

I remember once misspelling the German word for "little tree"—*Bäumchen*—three times, and my father began to rave that I would never amount to anything. Lessons with my father very often ended up in a beating. When I finally began to read a little, he arranged for my second-grade teacher, a friend of his, to give me a primer full of anti-Semitic stories. By the time I was seven I could read enough to see that all twelve verses—one for each month of the year—on our sentimental kitchen calendar began with the word "Deutschland." When I asked my father why none of the verses began with "England" or "Frankreich" or "Italien," he replied, "Das kannst Du nicht verstehen" (You can't understand that). As I had already done in relation to music, now, in relation to my schoolwork, I withdrew into my own fantasy world where I could control what happened.

When I was nine years old, six years after my mother died, my father decided to remarry. He discovered that the respected village blacksmith, Heinrich Zink, had an unmarried daughter. When he married Maria Zink in 1939, the comfortable intimacy I had enjoyed with the kind grandmother who had raised me for six years came to an end.

For about nine months after the wedding and while my father had civilian work in the small village of Trennfurt downriver, the three of us lived together as a family—patriarch, wife, and son. I was very unhappy. My thirty-four-year-old stepmother and I developed a kind of statistical game in which we tallied the evenings my father spent with us at home versus the number of evenings he went out, not to return until long after we were both asleep. I remember our findings: for every ten evenings he was absent, he spent one with us at home. Although he was no longer a full-time employee of the Nazi Party, he remained friends with his Nazi cronies, some of whom I knew by name. They spent their evenings carousing in local taverns, well-known Nazi hangouts. I knew that my stepmother despised his friends, and because of his absenteeism, I began to grow disillusioned with him. Later, when I was older, my disillusionment came to encompass the political and moral spheres as well.

Despite the free time he granted himself carousing, my father must have decided that his life was too domestic, because he volunteered for the German army in 1940. Before he left, he arranged for my stepmother and me to move in with her family back in Kleinheubach. Then, except for an occasional appearance during his military furloughs, my father disappeared for the next seven years.

The move with my stepmother, whom I called "Mama," to the small house of the village blacksmith changed my life. My stepgrandfather Zink arrived in Trennfurt to pick us up driving a wagon pulled by two cows. We loaded our belongings onto it, and the slow journey of about 8 kilometers up the valley to the blacksmith's house took the rest of the day. Once settled in my new home, the seasons of the year organized everyday life. I learned to work in the Zinks' fields, cutting and baling hay in the springtime, weeding potato fields, picking blueberries in the forest—a backbreaking chore—and harvesting rye and wheat in early summer. In the fall we picked apples and dug up potatoes with hoes. We used hoes for this task because my stepgrandfather believed that a cow-drawn plow would damage too many potatoes.

Despite the hard labor in the fields, all went well with my new extended family. I was completely accepted and well treated by the Zinks. My stepmother, much younger than my grandmother, was better able to continue the task of my up-bringing. It is clear to me now that my father married Maria Zink so that she would raise me, but she never communicated to me any resentment because of it. Quite the opposite: she was loving and kind. Although I provided my new family with an additional farming hand, it was my stepmother more than anyone else who urged me to study hard in the *Gymnasium* (the equivalent of a college-preparatory high school) I entered in nearby Miltenberg, a few kilometers upriver.

More important to my upbringing than their interest in my education, this new family of mine was politically opposed to the Nazis. The Zinks' opposition to Hitler's regime was clear and at times openly communicated with family members and their closest friends, but never outside a carefully circumscribed circle. They loved to tell anti-Nazi jokes in their down-to-earth lower Franconian dialect. I remember one that my stepgrand-father told, one for which he could have been arrested:

Question: "Was hod der Hitler dem Mussolini g'sacht?" (What did Hitler say to Mussolini?)

Answer: "Wenn's schepp geit mit Pole,/duschd du widder mauern und isch widder mole." (If things don't go our way in Poland, you can go back to masonry and I to painting.)

The Zink family had a long memory. Feuds with other families were never forgotten, but neither were the misdeeds committed against the Jews. I remember that when a particular Nazi thug returned from the war with his left arm amputated, my stepgrandfather maintained that it had been the very arm the thug had used to tear the sheets out of a ledger that listed his debts to a Jewish store. He had seen him do it from the other side of the street. The Zinks were righteous people who attended church on Sundays but did not pray during the rest of the week. I shared a room and a double bed with my stepgrandfather. Every night after getting in bed next to me following his hard day's work in the blacksmith shop downstairs, rather than say a prayer, he uncorked a bottle of prune brandy, took a big swig, and started snoring almost immediately.

There was a maiden aunt in the Zink family who wore several petticoats. For some reason, known only to her and her brother, the blacksmith, they never spoke to each other. She was cloistered in a room apart from the rest of the house that no one was allowed to enter. Through her curtained window I could see the dried herbs, flowers, and fruits that hung from her ceiling and walls—preparations that were earmarked for use against every conceivable ailment that might befall family or friends. Aside from practicing her herbal arts, she wrote poetry and over the years produced more than a hundred pages of neatly handwritten poems that celebrated every feast in the family and village. At the end of each poem, she signed off with the words "Heil Hitler!"

To the irritation of her fastidious brother, this aunt had her own plot of land just outside the village that had the appearance of a jungle compared to the neatly plowed fields that surrounded it—the perfect place for children to play hide-and-seek. This *Schloßtante*— "Castle Aunt," so called because she had worked for the Prince of Löwenstein, whose ancestral castle stood near the edge of the village—was beloved by every child in Kleinheubach. Her pockets were always filled with candy. I felt privileged to be part of the family of which *Schloßtante* was a member. She would take me on walks in the late evenings and teach me the names of the constellations, everything from the Big Dipper to the Pleiades. She had dialect names for some of these constellations, animal names such as hen, horse, or cow, that replaced the more erudite Greek terms. For her, the Milky Way was the road outlined in the sky by God so that the good people could find their way to heaven. I am sure she believed that everyone in Kleinheubach would get there, except for her brother. After the war, she took care to cut the "Heil Hitler!" inscriptions neatly off the bottom of her countless poems with a pair of scissors.

. . .

About the time my father left for the German army and my stepmother and I moved to her parents' house, I turned ten and was drafted into the boys' division of the Nazi youth movement, the Jungvolk. Precursor of the Hitler Jugend, or Hitler Youth, membership was required of all non-Jewish boys. Gentile girls had to join the Jungmädchen and then the BDM (Bund deutscher Mädchen). During my early teens, I developed an interest in singing, a skill encouraged by the Jungvolk. When I was thirteen and a half, I knew more German folk and marching songs than any of my peers and was rewarded for this accomplishment with the post of *Singführer* (song leader). On rare occasions when I still touched the piano, I played passages I liked very slowly and rushed through those I didn't. I tried to teach such fluctuating tempi along with the lyrics and melodies of the Nazi songs to the boys in the Jungvolk. But because we were supposed to march at a steady pace while singing these songs, my idiosyncratic "rubato" style was not welcome. As quickly as I had been promoted, I was disqualified and demoted to simple marcher.

My demotion was not due to my erratic tempi alone. My buddy Ludwig Bohn and I had such a bad attendance record in the Jungvolk that we were accused of undermining the morale of the entire group. Ordered to defend ourselves at the Hitler Youth headquarters at Miltenberg, we arrived in our everyday clothes and were immediately reprimanded for not wearing uniforms. When we were asked, "Do you place any value on your ranks?" Ludwig, completely intimidated, became flustered and answered, "We place no value on our ranks whatsoever!" When the group leaders angrily mistook his confused answer for impertinence, Ludwig quickly corrected himself to maintain the opposite: "We place enormous value on our ranks!" The budding Nazis in charge decided that we were too young to be punished, but they threatened to punish our parents instead and demanded the address of my father. They already knew Ludwig's father's address. I said, "My father is away fighting the war."

My insolent answer infuriated the bullies all over again, and they literally pushed us both out the door and down the long flight of stone steps. But this was the end of the matter. There were no repercussions for Ludwig or me or our families.

Once a week we had to show up for roll call, or *Appell*, as it was called, which was followed by Nazi indoctrination, marches, and paramilitary field games. Everybody did exactly the same thing—sang in rhythm, marched in rhythm, shouted in rhythm, and recited quasi-religious cant about the high points of Hitler's life. There was hardly time left for my usual fantasies. Just to insert a contrary element into these rigid routines—and for no deeper reason than that—I once took the tiny American flag my parents had brought back from the United States in 1933 and stuffed it behind my Nazi brown shirt, so that it was concealed there during the Jungvolk exercises. I had removed the flag from its small, gold-tipped, black wooden pole, and the silk material from which it was made felt soft to my skin. My tightly cinched belt prevented it from slipping down and out through my pant legs. I reveled in the feeling of difference this hidden object produced. I was well aware that I had been born in San Francisco, but somehow I knew that my secret game with the American flag was dangerous, perhaps not to me but to my family for owning it.

Nazi politics and the war also insinuated themselves into my schooling. My teachers at the *Gymnasium* in Miltenberg were either very good or very bad. Some of them had been transferred from major cities to this provincial outpost as punishment for reasons unknown to the students. I held one teacher, Professor

Schwegler, in particular esteem. He had been a tutor in France, and he had a gentle way of looking at literature; it seemed to exist for him in a world quite apart from the one guided by the controlled hysteria in which we all lived. He was different, and that is why I revered him. After his only son was killed in the war, my entire class brought flowers to school. The dignified, frail old gentleman lowered his head and wept—an unbelievable sight in the hierarchical atmosphere of the *Gymnasium*.

Although he wore the same clothes year round and never washed or shaved, our chemistry instructor was another good teacher, passionately devoted to his subject and nothing else. He justified his appearance by claiming that God wanted him to look unkempt and he was not about to interfere with divine will. But for the most part, the *Gymnasium* seemed like a milder version of the Nazi youth meetings. Rigid performance was demanded; no real questions asked, no real answers given. I withdrew further into the world of my own fantasies and, as I grew older, into a world of books.

Although I now lived with the Zinks, I would often visit my Tubach grandparents on the other side of the village. In one room of their house, books were stacked on the floor in the corners rather than lined up on bookshelves. One day, when I was looking through one of those piles, I came across Schopenhauer's *Aphorismen zur Lebensweisheit* (Aphorisms of Wisdom) and began reading it. An adolescent at the time, I internalized what I read about pessimism and renunciation without fully comprehending it. Schopenhauer was a great boon to my budding intellectual introversion. Once I tried to call on the inner reveries inspired by this philosopher in a composition assigned in school entitled "Roads to Self-Knowledge." I committed myself to the topic and spent hours formulating my thoughts. I promptly received an "F" for plagiarism. The teacher maintained that I could not have written it. After that I quit trying to produce anything original.

Another problem I had in school from kindergarten all the way through *Gymnasium* was my inability to sit still, a trait I shared and still do with my friend Bernie. The description *zappelig* (fidgety, restless) and all its variants crept continually into my report cards. It was no different at home. My grandfather, a man given to verbal extremes, once told me in exasperation, "Once you die, they'll have to beat your mouth and feet to death separately before they can bury you."

. . .

Festivities marked the seasons in Kleinheubach, much as they did all over Europe. On New Year's Day women baked huge soft pretzels as "large as a barn door" (*Bredzel wie e Schaierdoah*) or so the ditty went in the soft, drawn-out dialect of lower Franconia that we heard as we walked through the village to pay visits to friends and family. I remember a fine New Year's Day, a crystal-clear cold morning with the sun glinting off the new snow as I made my way to my grandparents' house—a timeless moment in the mind. The carnival season, which brought wagons laden with masked fools on the way to local parades, interrupted the winter. Festivities as old as the village itself: celebrations in hastily erected tents, in the streets, and in homes open to everyone for the occasion. Winter would give way to spring and then to the long summer, with children's games in cornfields and, when we were older, work in the same fields. There were my favorite cousin's visits from Nuremberg. In the fall, there was the harvesting and the making of hard apple cider and sour white wine, since the village did not enjoy the southwest exposure necessary for growing sweeter wines. Finally, winter would come again, and once more, as Bernie also remembers, you carried glass-enclosed lanterns to light your way home through the dark night.

Other rituals marked the passage of time on an irregular basis: funeral processions with horses draped in black pulling the coffin-laden wagon. The gravedigger was a one-eyed man who held the job until he was in his nineties. I never wanted to get too close to him, because I knew he must have dug the grave that my mother lay in.

All of these ageless village routines ended for my family, too, although differently than for Bernie's family since we lived on the opposite side of the fateful divide. Uncle Ludwig was drafted on the first day of the war. My grandmother cried for days over this favorite and late-born son, the gentle butt of his brothers' jokes. He became a soldier in the German divisions heading for Moscow. Uncle Willy—whom we kids loved because he would rather fly kites with us than tend to his watchmaking—volunteered for the army, preferring, as he said, to fight and make history than to repair stupid watches. Then there was Uncle Ernst, a mechanic and a communist, who somehow avoided the draft and remained a civilian repairing tractors. My father joined the army to become a counterintelligence officer. As the men disappeared into the war, the mailman became the most important inhabitant of Kleinheubach. This messenger began to bring news of the fates of its sons who had left, whether they were alive, wounded, dead, or missing in action. This news meant nothing to the Jewish villagers of Kleinheubach, because, by mid-1942, all of them were gone. These neighbors of ours, with their own traditions, had been a part of village life for more than two hundred fifty years. Now they were rarely talked about, and then only in whispers.

THREE

. . .

The Loss of Innocence

The hair of my mother would never turn white.

The early spring of 1944 was cold. While much of Europe went up in flames, rural life in Tab, even for the Jews, went on relatively undisturbed, with its timeless, seasonal routine. The fortunes of war were shifting. As the Soviet army approached from the East, Hungary slowly became a battlefield. In Tab the guns were still too far away to be heard, but fly-overs of the American and British air armadas on their way to Germany or to the oil fields of Rumania had become more frequent. On a clear day such orderly flight formations looked like swarms of bees except for the contrails they left high in the sky.

As they continued their ritualized daily lives, Jewish villagers in Tab began to whisper to each other their hopes for an Allied victory. The local newspaper provided them with a small window to the outside world. On March 19, while Bernie was at school preparing for his Bar Mitzvah, the newspaper appeared for the last time. At seven o'clock in the evening as Bernie returned home, a neighbor woman asked him, "Have you heard the news?"

He had not heard the news. How could he? During the strict hours of instruction, only the world of the school existed and nothing else. But while he had been concentrating on his lessons, the Hungarian government had been replaced by a Nazi puppet regime. This was the last news reported by the paper, and its announcement became grim reality in the streets of Tab within a week as anti-Semitic laws were put into effect. A decree forbade Jews to travel, and thus the first boundaries—still invisible—were drawn around the Jewish community. "Stuck in Tab," as Bernie puts it now. The opportunity to escape vanished. Some Jews, including one of Bernie's cousins, had left Tab for Palestine before the doors were closed. But few could afford to go far away, and as villagers with strong local roots, they had no idea where they should go. Most simply waited in the hope that staying in familiar surroundings would somehow protect them against the outside forces that were closing in on them. This hunkering down shaped the behavior of the Jewish community. It was their undoing.

By mid-May, Jews were ordered to wear six-pointed stars on their shirts, coats, or jackets. Made of yellow cloth, this identification mark had to be of a precisely prescribed size. Bernie's mother purchased yellow material and fashioned the stars for her family on her Singer sewing machine, a brand found in households all over Europe. All Jews—even those who had converted to Christianity—had to wear this star, with the result that the price of yellow cloth went up. Just a short time before, Bertha Rosner had sewn smart sailor outfits for her two boys. Unfortunately, the suits, with ties in the front and bibs in the back, were ruined when the boys were caught in a downpour on their way home one day. The blue and white fabrics were not color-fast, and they ran in chaotic patterns, ruining her labor. She did not have time to replace them. The six-pointed stars were the last items Bernie's mother sewed for her sons, herself, and her husband.

Now the Jews were forbidden to enter the main square of their village unless they displayed the yellow star. The public space within which they had moved as naturally as they had breathed the village air was radically transformed. The paths connecting school, synagogue, home, baker, and railroad station that had been engraved in the mind through everyday repetitions were distorted. New paths were beginning to form, with uncertain contours at first. But their evil nature was to become apparent as the weeks went by. In village life a person's identity is not only defined by family, personal traits, religion, or social status. One's dwelling place, and particularly its location relative to the rest of the village, is also one of its crucial elements. Many European family names derive from the places where people made their homes, marking thereby the origins and uniqueness of one family as distinct from others.

As one area of the town was designated an official ghetto, Tab became two distinct villages. One remained rooted in its established social context; the other, under the control of outside forces, was rendered unstable and marked for elimination. This geographic division created a radical break between Jews and non-Jews that became more and more insurmountable as the weeks went on. Where there had been commerce, personal contact, myriad one-on-one interactions, both hostile and friendly, now there developed an ever-increasing division.

Jews who did not already live within its confines were ordered to move to the ghetto. The extended Rosner family of Tab whose homes lay outside came to live with Bernie's family, whose house, located at the edge of the village, was within the ghetto boundaries. About a dozen people now occupied the house that Bernie had always shared only with his parents and brother. The life Bernie had known collapsed around him. No longer was it the voice of his mother that set the tone for daily life, or of his father, or of the rabbi or the neighbor with the news of change to come. What for the Jews had been a village-based governance under Hungarian law changed to rule by edict, proclaimed by the unfamiliar voices of Hungarian Nazis.

A group of these Nazis arrived and convened a Jewish council composed primarily of elders. The Nazis passed instructions on to this council, threatened its members, and used them as a conduit for their message of fear to the rest of the Jewish community, now crowded into the ghetto. It was not clear to the disoriented Jews exactly what legitimized the Nazis' authority. These thugs wore no uniforms and belonged to no discernible Hungarian state organization. Apparently, they felt no need to prove their legitimacy. They simply gave orders and spread fear, and this was enough. The victims in the ghetto were made to submit, and the non-Jewish inhabitants of Tab stood by in silence or cheered openly.

A bright boy of twelve, quick on his feet and adept at languages, Bernie was chosen as a runner to carry messages from the town hall to the Jewish council and various other organizations involved in administering the slow destruction of the Jewish community. He was present at some of the meetings of the Jewish council run by the Nazis. The tone set in these meetings still rings in his ears: "You Jews are traitors. Before we go, you will go. If you don't give us your hidden treasures, you'll be tortured and shot." Threats and humiliation were often directed against individual council members.

Increasingly isolated from the rest of the village and marked by the yellow star, the Jewish community was gripped by a paralyzing fear. People, including non-Jews, particularly those with communist affiliations, started to disappear. Soon rumors raced through the ghetto that whole families were vanishing. One day, without advance warning, close friends of the Rosner family were suddenly gone. When Bernie heard this news, he went to the synagogue and sobbed.

By the beginning of June, the rumor spread that Jews would be deported. No one knew whether to believe it. Then a Hungarian in a captain's uniform arrived and ordered the Jewish council to convene a ghetto meeting. He spoke to the assembled Jews and tried to calm their fears with promises and advice: "You'll be fed. Keep your noses clean. Everything will be fine. You'll be given work to do." His speech suggested in vague terms that an official relocation was being planned.

Nazi authorities designated Tab, which had the largest Jewish population in the area, an assembly point for the deportation of all the Jews of that region. Jews from villages in the vicinity began to arrive and were added to those already at Tab.

Many of these new arrivals not only had converted to Christianity some time ago, but they were well-to-do and thoroughly assimilated in Hungarian society. As they were marched into the ghetto, they made a point of acting relaxed, making light of what seemed to many of them some kind of huge joke. After all, they were converted Christians by choice and baptism as well as respected members of the Hungarian middle-class establishment—men and women of the world with good educations, money, and an enlightened outlook on life. Yet, in the Nazi revolution, all distinctions of social class—education, talent, accomplishments, quality of character—were rendered meaningless. The only distinction that mattered was the one made between Jew, as defined by the Nazi racial laws, and "Aryan." Thus, "blood" became the deadly metaphor for a new kind of human typology. And this new human typology was the logical complement to the changes in village geography that made the ghetto borders in Tab ever more impenetrable. Finally, the Nazis erected a gate that cut the ghetto off from the rest of the village altogether. To make sure that all the Jews of Tab had been corralled inside the ghetto, the Nazis relied on village knowledge of longtime Jewish residents. In the case of Polish refugees who had recently settled in Tab, the test was simple. Nazis ordered men and boys to drop their pants and reveal their genitalia. If they were circumcised, their fates and the fates of their families were sealed.

As a messenger, Bernie still retained more mobility than most inhabitants of the ghetto. He was allowed to pass through its gate and cross over the newly drawn boundaries. From the town hall to the Jewish council, from the ghetto to the main street, he scurried from one assignment to the next. On the main street of Tab one day, an assembly of high-ranking German SS officers arrived in their military vehicles, presumably to inspect this ever-growing collection site for the Jews of the region. Seeing their elegantly tailored uniforms and neatly polished high jack-boots, the boy immediately realized that these Germans were important people. They all wore the *Totenkopf* skull emblem of the SS on their hats. One displayed the four-star insignia of an SS *Obersturmbannführer* (lieutenant colonel) on his lapel. These uniforms impressed the young Bernie even more than that of the Hungarian lieutenant in Tab, and today Bernie is still able to draw for me the insignia of the top SS brass exactly as I remember them, either from sight or from the primer of Nazi military ranks that I and my young German compatriots com-mitted to memory as members of the Jungvolk. It was clear to Bernie which of these high-ranking officers was in command, because he gave orders to the officers of lesser rank. At one point, this commanding SS officer turned toward the young ghetto messenger, patted him on the head, and said, "Kleiner Bube" (little boy). His picture was unmistakable; Bernie saw it in newspapers after the war. The officer with whom he had come face-to-face was Adolf Eichmann, chief transporter and executioner of the European Jews. (The historical record puts Eichmann in Hungary at this time, directing the transport of rural Hungarian Jews to Auschwitz and other camps.)

A few days later, with the Hungarian police and uniformed special forces in command, the order came down that everybody was to be ready, with a minimum of belongings, to move out of their homes the following morning for "relocation." No one was surprised. "Tomorrow is the day," they said to each other, knowing only that their exodus into an unknown future was at hand. On the evening before leaving their homes forever—it had been a bright, sunny day—they saw a squadron of Allied bombers heading south high in the sky. The setting sun illuminated the vapor trails they left behind with a brilliant glow. Some saw in this a sign from heaven signaling their deliverance.

. . .

At this point in his recollections Bernie says, "It's coming," the use of the present tense wrenching both of us away from his evocation of the past. It is a signal, a subtle linguistic marker of what I know to be the most difficult event for him to recount. He closes his eyes in a characteristic manner as he begins to tell me about the unfolding of that day.

. . .

At about 9:30 in the morning, the Jews of Tab, who had assembled in front of their homes as ordered, were herded from the ghetto to the Catholic parochial school. Each person was allowed to carry one suitcase or package. Because it was unclear where meals would be coming from, the Rosners carried some food in their bags. Bernie remembers that his parents packed, among other things, a jar of goose fat. An old woman who had brought several more jars of goose fat gave the Rosners some of her own treasure. I asked Bernie how he felt having to leave his home and their settled rural life on less than one day's notice. He replied that the speed, force, and direction of events unfolding around him were such that he had no time to contemplate how he felt and what it meant. He remembers that his family concentrated on what would be best to take along into an uncertain future. Fear was not an overriding factor but rather expedient decisions and actions. Fear came later.

As the Jews were marched through their village, some of the non-Jewish onlookers jeered, while others were visibly upset at this unprecedented sight. Most remained behind closed doors and windows, however, preferring not to watch or be seen. Those villagers who witnessed the march were not allowed to talk to their former Jewish neighbors as they proceeded to the schoolhouse, the place where, over the next couple of hours, the nightmare began, as Bernie tells me, his eyes still almost closed. There, in this Christian school building, the incident that became the first station of his family's suffering took place. Bernie had hinted at it during our summer visit to Tab while we stood at the railroad station, looking west toward the brick buildings, five years before we decided to write down our stories. I had often wondered what had taken place during this first day of relocation but had never pressed him on it. Even after we began work on our project in earnest, I didn't want to be the one to bring it up. I began to shrink away from whatever it was, to protect him from having to recall a part of his story that was obviously very painful to him and also to protect myself from having to hear it. Even now, it is difficult for me to commit this recollection to paper, although the facts are perfectly simple.

After their arrival at the Catholic school, the Jews were taken to a classroom and everyone was ordered to strip—men, women, and children—all in view of everyone else and of their oppressors. Right in front of him, Bernie's mother was forced to take off all her clothes. He had to watch while, naked and helpless, she was searched by the hands of a hostile Nazi thug. One might argue that Bernie had to endure worse atrocities later at Auschwitz and beyond, but he was only twelve, and he had never seen an adult, much less his own mother, naked. The evil mix of the forced nudity, the public humiliation, and the physical molestation converged to form an enormous emotional shock for him that symbolized a loss of innocence as well as the beginning of unimaginable horrors to come. For a brief moment, Bernie's mother was stripped of her social persona, her family status, and turned into a hapless creature subjected to the crude hands of an anonymous oppressor.

Toward midafternoon, the Jews were herded from the schoolhouse to the brickyard located near the train station. Everyone carried bedding, and they were ordered to settle down on the bare ground, because they would be spending the night there. They were not fed. It was a Friday, and as evening fell, they tried to arrange an impromptu Sabbath service. When a frail woman in her eighties stood up and started to recite her pre-Sabbath prayer, a Nazi silenced her with a blow to her head. The brickyard sheds had roofs but no walls. As it turned out, they became a holding corral for a few days until the Nazis transported the Jews and their meager belongings to a collection point for ghetto residents of the region established at the provincial capital of

Kaposvar to the southwest. Its railroad station, a stop on the way to Bernie's beloved grandparents, had been turned into a way station for Auschwitz.

These events marked the end of Jewish life in Tab. If the remaining villagers of Tab looted the abandoned homes that were, of course, still filled with possessions—furniture, dishes, carpets, drapes, clothes, memorabilia—their actions did not make it into the history books. On postwar visits to Tab, Bernie found no plaques or monuments remembering the former Jewish community. He discovered the Jewish houses, including his own, still standing and occupied by strangers. How they came into possession of the Rosners' home, he does not know.

. . .

The Holocaust had begun earlier in Germany than in Hungary. In my village of Kleinheubach, the Kristallnacht (Night of the Shattered Glass) of 1938 visibly marked the Jews off from the rest of us. Suddenly, there were two kinds of houses in our village—those protected by law and custom and those owned by Jews that became targets for vandalism. Jewish homes were sprinkled throughout the village, and after the ransacking in the night of November 9–10, they all bore traces of violence. As in Tab, Jews could leave their houses only if yellow stars were sewn to their clothes. I remember these stars on people who passed in the streets. It was no longer possible to separate these people from the stars they were forced to wear.

My eighth birthday fell on November 9, and I vividly remember the moment when the news of the violence against the

Jews reached the home of my grandparents. It was my agitated father who entered that evening to tell us that average German citizens, not the police or the military, were breaking into homes owned by Jews and destroying their property—under police protection. While a musician in San Francisco, he had worked with Jews and counted many among his friends. He dubbed the violence against the Jews "stupid."

I was all ears. Even at that early age, I knew that something extraordinary was happening. Everyone was upset, even my grandmother, who had the uncanny ability to see a positive side to virtually anything. I still hear my father saying, "This is the beginning of another world war." The adults turned on the radio to get the official news, and the tone of the report had everyone in an uproar. It became clear in our house in the Bahnhofstraße (Train Station Street) that similar events were taking place all over Germany. But the destruction of property—and particularly the smashing of doors and windows—had upset the daily village routine. Most of the Gentiles were more upset about the property damage than about the wronged property owners. The Jewish villagers had been victimized not only by decrees from Berlin but also by some of our neighbors. The assault on the Jews was no longer something that took place in the outside world accessible only through the power of the radio or by word of mouth. It had come home. It was happening in our village.

I was not out-of-doors during the Kristallnacht, and our house was located at the edge of the village away from the violence, but many villagers assembled to watch the extraordinary spectacle. Some joined the band of "outsiders" who instigated the attacks on Jews and Jewish property in Kleinheubach. Former mayor Bernhard Holl's local history reports on the events of that night. In the gang that included six or seven "fremde" (strange) uniformed SA members of the notorious Brownshirts, one was recognized as the *Sturmführer* Bertisch from the nearby village of Röllbach. Kleinheubach police commissioner Staab prevented them from destroying the house of Samuel Wetzler by arguing that it had already been sold to a Christian family. Staab, known in the village for decades as a stalwart policeman with a sense of order and justice, came too late to prevent destruction elsewhere—for example, of the Jewish shoe store and of the windows and interior of the synagogue. The roving gang had entered the Jewish place of worship by ramming the door with a tree trunk. They broke all the windows and destroyed the interior, but when they tried to set the synagogue on fire, a neighbor, Fritz Abb, a glazier by profession, intervened and ordered them to extinguish it before the fire burned down the houses next door. This they did before leaving to ransack elsewhere. Commissioner Staab wrote after the war that some Kleinheubach residents joined in the violence, while the majority observed passively and were only willing to aid the victims in secret. After the war, my stepmother was proud to have in her possession one of the few extant copies of this police report.[1]

"Why are they doing this?" still rings in my ears as an unanswered question that evening. If I had been sophisticated enough, I could have answered it by opening the primer I had been given by my grammar school teacher the year before. It contained pictures with captions in large print that contrasted

Jewish with "Aryan" ways of life: the "Aryan" butcher shop, for example, with its meats and sausages neatly displayed and its slender butcher carving cuts to order for smiling blond, blue-eyed customers. On the opposite page was the Jewish shop with a fat, ugly butcher, bloody handprints on his soiled apron. A cat tugged at a large chunk of meat that lay on the dirty floor. The customers, extravagantly dressed in flowing silk dresses, scowled, with somber miens.

What had been discussed in our home only behind closed doors and secure walls I now saw on my way to school on November 10, the morning after the Kristallnacht. Still etched in my mind is the figure of Frau Sichel, a heavy-set Jewish woman who had the habit of swinging her left arm out to the side when she walked, as if to propel her body forward more efficiently. I saw her when she emerged from the basement of the grammar school—where Jews were permitted to retrieve some of their vandalized belongings—to make her way back to her ransacked house. I remember that she was desperately trying to act normal, as if nothing serious had happened, as she sauntered up the village street, swinging her arm out in her familiar gait. I don't know whether I felt ashamed of something I did not understand, or whether I picked up from this middle-aged woman, whom I knew, her shame at having been humiliated by thugs. Kundera is right when he says that the transformation of a person from subject to object is experienced as shame. I had not seen the thugs who had done this to Frau Sichel. All I saw and experienced was her altered demeanor, a reflection of her altered status. It was unsettling at the time. Even as an eight-year-old, I understood that certain fundamental rules had been broken and that this gentle woman had been robbed of something more important than her material possessions. Frau Sichel had changed in my mind into someone unusual, someone exposed to a nameless dread. It remains a visual memory, one on one, of the eight-year-old boy and the middle-aged woman. I do not recall that I ever saw her again. Years later, at a reception of the German consul general in San Francisco, I met a wine merchant from Darmstadt named Sichel who turned out to be a cousin of my Frau Sichel. She had not survived.[2]

On my way home from school a few days after the Kristallnacht, I saw an empty house in the Baugasse that belonged to Jews, who were now gone. Halfway torn from its frame, the front door hung open. Most of the windows in the two-story house were smashed. Glass, papers, and books were strewn about outside. Feather beds had been slit open and thrown around so that goose down had floated out the second-story windows to blanket the street like a thin layer of snow. I thought of the figure of Frau Holle in a Grimm's fairy tale, who was said to make it snow by shaking her feather beds out of the windows. I hesitated for a moment but couldn't overcome my curiosity to enter the empty house. I walked up a flight of stairs and came upon a scene of chaos in what had been the living room. I was alone, and suddenly my curiosity turned to fear. I ran back down the stairs to the street, then stopped and stared at the house. Something on the cobblestones in the gutter caught my eye—a long, white, unused candle. I picked it up, brushed off the dirt, and took it home with me. I remember the act very clearly but cannot recall any feelings related to it. Did I think at that moment that I was stealing or saving something? It was years before I understood that I had committed a theft against the owners of that house in the Baugasse.

. . .

In the "orderly" days of prewar Nazi Germany, the Jews were not collected in a public square and marched out of the village in plain view of the other inhabitants, as happened later in Tab, Hungary. By January 1942 when the "Final Solution" was conceived at the Wannsee Conference in Berlin, most of the Jews had already left Kleinheubach. Holl's record relates how on March 27 the Gestapo ordered local authorities in Würzburg to "evacuate and relocate" (*Wohnsitz verlegen*—a term that implied a move to a new domicile) one thousand Jews from the area. The gendarmerie of Kleinheubach distributed eleven pamphlets, with ten copies each to the three Jews who still remained in Kleinheubach—Frieda Freudenstein (b. 1884), Gerson Freudenstein (b. 1899), and Regina Sichel (b. 1893). Seven additional documents described in minute detail all the instructions to be followed by both the authorities and the evacuees, including the amount of food and clothing Jews were to bring on the journey, the type of suitcase allowed, and even how to empty the garbage, turn off the gas, electricity, and water, and extinguish the fires in the ovens of their homes. The records show that on April 23, 1942, the orderly deportation of the last three Jews of Kleinheubach was completed.[3]

I had not known Jewish children growing up. Because the

number of Jewish children had dwindled, the Jewish school was closed in 1923.[4] The Jewish teacher left town with his family, and the few remaining Jewish children were integrated into the Protestant *Volksschule*. I have a photograph of my second-grade class of 1937, when I was seven. There are no Jewish children in it. As a child, I knew who some of the Jewish adults were, and I do recall the last Jewish man, Herr Freudenstein, by sight. He tended his garden and went about the village, passing our house to walk in the nearby forest. I never saw anyone speak to him, but I remember that family members started rooting for him "to make it," to be overlooked by the Nazis. In the minds of many, he stayed an individual villager and in this way escaped the deadly metamorphosis into a *Jude* for a time. But he, too, was gone before summer 1942.

Although I have no visual memory of him, I remember that people frequently talked about "Judenernst," who left his mark as a village personality. Bernhard Holl's local history tells something of his story. Born in 1896, Ernst Sichel was a bachelor and an active member of the Communist Party who survived sixteen months of *Schutzhaft* (protective custody) in Dachau in 1933–34 only to be accused of *Rassenschande* (racial disgrace or defilement, a Nazi term used for sexual relations between Jews and Gentiles) and imprisoned again for three months in 1936. When authorities failed to prove this accusation, he was released and eventually managed to emigrate to Argentina. By all accounts, he was young, fearless, and flamboyant. A butcher by profession who specialized in poultry, he was said not to have been particularly strict about following ritual Kosher methods.[5]

And, according to village lore, before his departure he swore to return to take revenge. After the war, everyone wondered whether he would return to fulfill his promise, but he never did.[6]

Once the Jews were gone, and as time passed, conversations about them retreated behind closed doors and opinions about their fate were voiced only in whispers. Thus were our neighbors, who had been a living and breathing part of our village life, transformed into the *Judenproblem,* an abstraction. After a time, the houses of the Jews of Kleinheubach had new occupants, some of whom were especially devoted Nazis.

. . .

Sometimes it is difficult to stay in the narrative flow of a story. The story of Bernie's mother in the Catholic parochial school of Tab does not let go of me. A friend to whom I mentioned the incident replied with the predictable comment that worse things happened during the Holocaust. I know this, but this knowledge does not free me to go on. I must try in another way. I have to think of my own mother.

She died in Germany, on October 5, 1934, when I was almost four. She was of Eastern European origin. It was never clear to me exactly what caused her death. A heart attack was the official pronouncement of the country doctor. On the day of the funeral—I knew something dreadful had happened to her, but I did not know what—I was standing in the Jahnstraße when the village midwife, Frau Herrschaft, walked up to me. She told me she had just come from the cemetery where my mother now was, and she asked me if I had seen her soul fly up to heaven. I had seen nothing.

After my mother's death my father broke off with her family, and I never tried to contact them after the war. I had been too young when she died to have more than fleeting memories of her. And, at the end of the war, Germans, young and old—and notwithstanding their individual fates—only looked to the future. The fate of Bernie's mother brought me face-to-face with the past, not only my own, but that of my generation of Germans as well. All Germans suffered a fatal loss of voice because of the crimes they committed or allowed to be committed in their names.

. . .

In the Jardin du Luxembourg in Paris stands a white marble statue of a nude woman that I've passed by many times. On rainy days, the drops that run down her face look to me like tears. They collect around her neck and shoulders and continue in rivulets down her entire body to the stone base and steps below.

FOUR

. . .

The Maelstrom:
To Auschwitz and Beyond

Der Tod ist ein Meister aus Deutschland...
PAUL CELAN

On Monday, July 3, 1944, a train left Kaposvar, Hungary, for Auschwitz, Poland, via Budapest. It was filled with Jews from the rural regions of southwestern Hungary, Polish Jews who had fled their native country in 1939 in advance of the German invasion to seek refuge in Hungary, and Jews who had converted to Christianity. Marked with a sign that read "Suitable for twelve cattle," each wagon of the freight train was crammed with forty to fifty people, men and women, boys and girls, of varying states of health, wealth, and social status. The heavy sliding doors were tightly locked and entwined with barbed wire. The outside world was visible to the human cargo through narrow slatted openings originally designed to provide enough air circulation to keep cattle alive for the slaughter-houses of Europe. There was no way for the imprisoned passengers to open up the wagons from the inside for ventilation, for relief of bodily functions, or for physical mobility. Escape was impossible. Pressed into one of these freight cars were Bernie, his father, Louis, his mother, Bertha, and his younger brother, Alexander.

Before their departure, the Rosners and the other Jewish families of Tab had spent an entire week in an open field in Kaposvar. The food doled out was so horrible that most ate only what they had carried with them from their homes. Each family spread out the blankets and clothing they had brought in an attempt to mark off their own little plot of ground and preserve, at least symbolically, a sense of privacy. A woman screamed intermittently in desperation. A doctor who had brought medicines along attempted suicide. Bernie's mother tried to distract her young sons to shield them from their surroundings. But Bernie saw and remembered. This was the only time he thought seriously about escape. He told no one, not even his family, that he studied the positions of the German and Hungarian guards around the campsite to find an escape route—in vain. Once on the train to Auschwitz, all possibility of flight vanished along with the last vestiges of private space.

Bernie's solitary plan to flee raises the frequently asked question of why there was no widespread effort to escape, no general resistance. For both of us, the answer seems simple, quite beyond the overwhelming physical force that controlled these Jewish captives and the psychological cliché of their collective denial of the fate to come. Voting with your feet may be an American cultural heritage, but it was not a ready-made response for most European villagers faced with danger during this epoch. Where would they have gone? How would they have gotten there? Who would have received them? The immensity of the genocide into which they were about to be drawn was also beyond human imagination, and therefore beyond denial. Only the bestial and prescient could have had an inkling of the crematoriums that lay ahead.

. . .

July 3 started off hot. But rain fell in the afternoon, cooling down the stifling wagons and preventing the occupants from suffocating before their arrival four days and 400 kilometers later at the Auschwitz-Birkenau concentration camp. There was little food or water, minimal space to move one's limbs, and only a couple of buckets to serve as toilets. While the train was temporarily stopped at Budapest, a woman handed an orange to Bernie through the barbed wire, saying it was from "someone who cared." Bernie remembers that his father spoke little on the train and that his mother prayed a great deal and made sure that he and his brother had something to eat. Alexander developed a slight fever but claimed that he felt all right. When someone encroached on the family's small space on the floor of the cattle car, Bertha Rosner protected it. Time passed. Shortly before their arrival at Auschwitz, as they watched the passing countryside through the air slots crisscrossed by barbed wire, Bernie remembers that his father turned to him and said matter-of-factly, "It's all over."

Like so many others, Bernie's train arrived through the turret-topped gatehouse and stopped at the unloading platform inside the Birkenau section of the camp. That notorious entrance gate and platform are still vivid in Bernie's memory, as are the two lifeless bodies of acquaintances who were left in their freight car after the living exited. Several in his wagon had lost their sanity during the journey to Poland. One was a young woman, Martha Banoczy, known in the Rosners' native village for her beauty, who pranced around the platform babbling incoherently, clad only in a short fur coat that failed to cover her pubic hair. Her family, assimilated into Hungarian society, had converted from Judaism to Christianity long before these events. After all these years, Bernie's voice bears a trace of sadness for this beautiful young woman and the catastrophic transformation she underwent during their common journey, displayed for the eyes and ears of the other villagers as well as the SS guards.

Decades later, Bernie still hid the terrible images and details of these memories in the recesses of his mind, only to look at them through the blurred vision of one who tried to think that they had happened in some other life—the stench in the air, the terrified milling crowd, the faces of his uncle Willy and his cousin Jenö, familiar names shouted in despair and hope, the disappearance of his father, the admonition of his mother before she too disappeared, taken away by the murderous arms of death on a gray day in July.

What about the others in the cattle cars? And not just on the Rosners' train but on 170 trainloads over three months in all that brought some 475,000 Jews to Auschwitz from Hungary alone? An enormous mass of humanity—475,000 individual lives—yet only a fraction of the numbers ultimately devoured in the Holocaust. Most of them perished, with their lives not lived out and their stories never told. How did the old people manage to move their stiff limbs to climb off the cars? Was Bernie's learned grandfather somewhere among them? Did some of them collapse when they reached the open air? How did their eyes adjust to the sudden brightness? Was the height of the platform level with the interior floor of the cattle cars? Why did some people go mad while others did not? Is "madness" really the right term to describe their state? Could there have been a "normal" reaction to this four-day transit to hell?

· · ·

Bernie continues his recollection with the utmost precision. As he and the others waited on the platform, everyone was aware, victims and Germans alike, of a major Allied air strike in progress at the nearby industrial plants that were part of the Auschwitz complex. But this event did not alter the daily routine. Above the noise of the distant attack, orders were barked in German: "Ruhe, schweig' still, Schweinehund." A rifle butt struck the head and back of a urinating man, and a boot knocked in the teeth of an inmate to whom a guard had taken a spontaneous dislike. Yet, at this point in the disembarkation, the violence remained primarily verbal. Too much individually directed brutality would have constituted an inefficient waste of time and energy; the agenda was, after all, mass extermination. Processing human beings through this destruction machine was itself the ultimate manifestation of violence. The Rosner family had arrived in the eye of the maelstrom that was devouring the Jews of Europe and other Nazi victims.

As the "leader" of their cattle car, and without time for good-byes, Bernie's father was the first of his family to disappear from his life. I presume that by removing the potential leaders first, the Nazis could more easily manipulate the remaining victims for efficient extermination or assignment to holding barracks or slave labor.

Men and women were then ordered to separate, ostensibly for showers and delousing. Bernie's mother wanted her sons to stay with her. Some very young children were allowed to remain with their mothers. But twelve-year-old Bernie didn't want to shower with the women. His mother admonished him to stay with his little brother. Everything happened with breathless speed. Bernie saw panic in his mother's face as they were separated from her. Now he and Alexander were among the men; and Bertha Rosner disappeared forever.

Without their parents now, the Rosner brothers were moved along the paved part of the disembarkation ramp in a line of males. At the head of the line stood two SS officers dressed in their military uniforms who divided the column approaching them, sending some to the right and others to the left. They didn't know it at the time, but those moved to the left were earmarked for immediate extermination, the others for slave labor or later extermination. Bernie's brother, in front of him in the column, was moved to the left—he was ten years old and, in the minds of the SS guards, clearly not considered worth keeping alive. Bernie, remembering his mother's admonition, tried to follow his younger brother. For an instant, the SS officers watched passively, but after Bernie had taken two steps in his brother's direction, one of the SS selectors took him by the scruff of his neck and shoved him the other way. In this first cut, the Nazis apparently considered Bernie, who was two years older, a candidate for slave labor. He could always be eliminated later. As it turned out, this was Bernie's last view of his brother. As Bernie was herded in a different direction, he didn't realize that his entire family was now gone.

His column slowly made its way past an enclosure that he later learned contained the gas chambers. He noticed how guards forced some stragglers inside the entrance and closed the heavy wooden barrier behind them. Bernie recognized an old woman from Tab in this group and heard loud noises and screams coming from inside after the barrier had closed. At that point he had no explanation for these terrible cries, and his group simply moved on. Bernie's group was marched past these barriers to a brick building where they were shaved of all body hair, deloused, and given showers. Bernie was then given clothing, including a jacket with a characteristic piece of striped cloth on the back that marked him as a concentration camp inmate. The yellow stripe painted across the front designated him as a Jew.

Bernat Rosner, twelve and a half years old, the sole survivor of his family, shorn of his hair, showered, deloused, and clothed in a concentration camp uniform, started his days in Auschwitz. He was assigned to barracks 34, *Lager* (camp) D, Birkenau, which was also called the *Zigeunerlager*, because it was used in the early summer of 1944 as a "quarantine" camp for gypsies. Within a few weeks of Bernie's arrival, the remaining gypsies were removed from the site, gassed, and cremated. Once, as a truckload of gypsies passed by his barracks, Bernie remembers a particular gypsy who caught his eye and drew his flattened hand across his neck, indicating that he expected to be killed. Bernie began to get used to the constant acrid smoke that rose out of the chimneys of the crematorium—located less than a kilometer from *Lager* D—blowing the ever-present odor of death through the camp.

Each barracks had a chief Kapo and several subordinate Kapos, inmates charged by the SS to maintain order. Some of these Kapos were Jewish. They had the power to further brutalize inmates or to alleviate their misery to a small degree. Each prisoner was to receive a quarter loaf of bread per day. In reality, the Kapos in charge of Bernie's barracks first cut a piece for themselves out of the middle of each whole loaf, thus reducing the size of the remaining four portions given to the prisoners. One particularly cruel Kapo beat two boys to death. He had been a pediatrician.

Random beatings were one of the pastimes of many of these barracks leaders. More formalized punishments involved lashes administered with a rubber cable that had a metal wire inside it for added bite. Bernie once was given five lashes for being the last one out of the barracks. The SS in charge of the camp did not administer the beatings personally. Indeed, Bernie recalls, the SS preferred to delegate this dirty work and rarely attended the public floggings.

Each morning began when the Kapos banged on the wooden pallets, covered with thin, smelly straw matting on which six to eight inmates had spent the night. The inmates were ordered to line up outside to be counted. Bernie said that usually everyone got up, because those who did not were sent to the "hospital" from which they did not return. One inmate pleaded with increasing desperation about his need for insulin. The others convinced him that if he reported his illness he would be taken away and killed. As the diabetic grew weaker, fellow inmates continued to carry him outside for the daily roll call and to prop him up for the head count. Soon, however, he went into shock and died. For a few days after his death, inmates let the body lie among them, reluctant to give up even their own dead to the guards.

We know from documentary photographs that over the main gate of Auschwitz the Nazis had affixed the slogan "Arbeit macht frei" (Work Makes You Free). In Bernie's barracks, stenciled on a rafter and adorned with colorful, kitschy flowers, inmates could read the first line of a popular German folk song: "Es geht alles vorüber" (Everything passes). This sentimental song, one of many I learned in my youth, is still sung today in German taverns when the mood is jovial. It promises that after every December, a May will surely follow. The song is usually sung toward the end of an evening of drinking, right before "In München steht ein Hofbräuhaus," when people link arms and sway back and forth in a heightened sense of solidarity. That macabre bit of interior decorating in Bernie's barracks faded at nightfall, as darkness settled in on their cramped quarters, and quite another song emerged, one composed by an inmate in Yiddish. Someone would start to sing it, then a second voice would join in. Soon most of the inmates would be singing. A few remained silent on their pallets, as Bernie recalls, to listen to its desperate cry for deliverance:

> Eykho vi azoy und far vos
> yogstu undz azoi?
> Vi iz, foter, dayn rakhmones?
> Habet Mishomaim Vreh
> Fun himl gib a blik
> Tsu di Yidishe kinder gib a glik
> Lesh oys dem fayer un zol es
> shoyn zayn genik.

> Oh, why and for what
> are you hunting us so?
> Where is, Father, your mercy?
> …
> From heaven give a glance
> To the Jewish children give a chance
> Extinguish the fire—and
> let it be enough.

The first word of this plaint, "Eykho" (how), hauntingly evokes the cry of grief that begins the Old Testament Book of Lamentations ("How lonely sits the city that was full of people!"). And the ending echoes the medieval night watchman's song that exhorted Germans to extinguish lamps and fires to prevent conflagrations from engulfing their towns. In the concentration camp, the ears of the guards keeping watch outside the barracks were closed; the plaint did not reach them. And the God the inmates invoked was deaf.

For a while Bernie nourished his own kind of hope. During his first weeks at Auschwitz, he wrote notes to his mother on scraps of paper and passed them on to inmates who had been selected for the day to work details in other parts of the camp. He never received a reply. As time went on, he simply stopped writing, even though he was still unwilling to accept that his mother was dead.

At one end of the encampment that faced the railroad platform, Bernie would watch the trains arriving with new inmates. The arrivals had become more and more frequent, because, as he recalls, the Germans were evacuating the ghetto in Lodz at the time. When no train was stopped on the tracks, he could see, at a distance of almost a kilometer, a camp filled with women and children. Although this camp was too far away to recognize or to shout to anyone, the sight gave him hope for a while that his mother and his brother might be among them. When inmates would occasionally discuss their chances of survival, Bernie brought up this distant sight of women and children to bolster the dwindling group who clung to hope in spite of the omnipresence of death. Feeding this hope was a semblance of normalcy that camp authorities encouraged in order to maintain tranquillity and thus facilitate the smooth functioning of the death machine.

The SS provided musical instruments to inmates who could play them, and camp concerts took place on Sunday afternoons in an open field. Marches, lilting Viennese waltzes, and German folk songs would fill the air that was also laced with the characteristic odor from the crematorium chimneys. Sunday afternoon concerts were an old German ritual, beloved by the middle class from Vienna to Berlin. One weekday an assembly of a different nature took place on this same field when a Kapo picked youths out of the various barracks and ordered them to collect there. He simply pointed his finger at a youngster and said, "You." If you were chosen, you had to go. No explanation was given. Bernie was among the chosen.

About one hundred fifty youngsters assembled on the field. Many began to wail and sob, some clinging to each other, others looking desperately for a way to return to their barracks. Standing among them, Bernie thought, "This is it. I'm going to be hauled off and killed." Under the watchful eye of the guards, the children milled around for about half an hour. Then, just as suddenly as they had been ordered to gather, they were told to return to their barracks. Bernie has no explanation for the sudden change of orders. Had there not been enough guards available to supervise the killing? Had they run out of poison gas? Had the group of youngsters become too upset and disorderly to dispatch them efficiently to the gas chambers?

. . .

As Bernie recalls this part of his story, it takes on an inexorable, breathtaking progression, a "no exit" inevitability. I ask him if we can take a break. While he goes out to the kitchen, I stand up and look out the large bay window of the den of the Rosners' home into their tree-lined garden. I see that the shadows are growing longer. Even in northern California, early spring days are still short. I become aware of the ticking of a clock. I listen for birds outside to offset the tight grip Bernie's recall has on me. But there is no escape. The death machine has been conjured up in his living room. No time at all has passed since Auschwitz.

At this moment in the present, I understand that no bridge to Bernie's side, to his past experience, can be completely crossed by anyone who was not there. My attempts will ultimately remain inadequate. Nevertheless, I take up the challenge to find something, anything in myself to come closer to this other side, to attempt at least a partial crossing. And I am thrown back on my own experiences for help.

About nine months after the fall of the Berlin Wall and shortly after our visit to Tab in 1990, Sally and I were in East Germany to visit Goethe's Weimar and, a few kilometers outside it, the concentration camp at Buchenwald. The camp was now a museum run by former East German guards in charge of official German Democratic Republic "antifascist memorials." We entered the barracks at one end and then followed the directional arrows from one room to the next, part of a long queue of visitors. When the queue moved, we moved. I found something uncannily mechanical in this inevitable forward thrust of the line, and about halfway through, I simply had to get out. It wasn't the horrors displayed in the exhibits but rather that I suddenly couldn't bring myself to take another step within this slowly moving crowd. I told Sally I had to leave. She understood, and we left the line and moved against the flow of the one-way human traffic. There was room to get by the other visitors, so we didn't impede anyone else's progress. But it was against the rules, and we had to pretend we didn't understand German when the guards barked repeatedly, "Falsche Richtung!" at us. Wrong direction? To hell with that! I *was* going to go against this flow, no matter what they said, propelled by a claustrophobic need to escape. As we were exiting where we had come in, Sally cracked a black joke in English that the guards wouldn't have understood: "What *is* this, a concentration camp or something?"

When we were outside in the sunshine again, I thought about the authoritarian behavior of these guards. Was their response to our unusual motion a vestige of the Nazi mentality that still operated in them, of old Prussia or of communist totalitarianism? Are there cultural patterns and mental habits so deeply and subtly ingrained in a population that individuals fail to see and therefore never change them? Will certain aspects of this mentality inevitably be passed on from one generation to the next, part of a cultural legacy? I fervently hope not, but I'm not sure. I only know that we could reverse our direction in that summer of 1990, in a place that by then was only a museum. But in 1944, Bernie and his family members could not change the direction of the steps they were ordered to take by the SS guards at the Auschwitz death camp.

Bernie comes back and opens the two bottles of Heineken that have been sitting untouched all this time on the low table in front of us.

· · ·

Bernie's story did not unfold quite as easily as this retelling might suggest. Yes, he had decided to tell his whole story to me, and yes, he wanted the facts to speak for themselves. Yet we were two years into the project before he volunteered to tell me about the heartrending plaint in which inmates sang out for God's help in Yiddish from their barracks at Auschwitz during the night. He didn't sing the song—and I didn't dare ask him to do so—but rather dictated the text to me. He agreed to have his recall checked for linguistic correctness by a Berkeley expert on Yiddish, who pronounced Bernie's dictated text "letter perfect."

It took me some time to understand the deeper cause for Bernie's initial silence. I knew that Bernie's family did not speak Yiddish at home, although many of the Orthodox Jewish families in Tab did. The history of pogroms and the Holocaust is woven into the fabric of Yiddish. Bernie has an aversion to telling his own story as victim. He wanted it to be the story of a survivor. He wanted the yellow star that his mother had to sew onto his clothes before their deportation to Auschwitz to remain only on his clothes, not to penetrate to his skin. By rejecting the role of victim, he preserved a freedom he needed later on, but by doing so, he cut himself off from part of his own history. Did I, in turn, wear the swastika on my pre–Hitler Youth uniform only as an external sign, as I believe? And, like Bernie, did I reject that mark of Cain to gain the freedom I needed later to live my life fully? We both believe that the crossing of our paths was only possible by not allowing these symbols to define our souls.

．　．　．

July 1944 had been hot in Germany, too. I remember it well, because it was the last summer before the end of the war, and I was working in wheat fields owned by my stepgrandfather. We took three breaks during the day. Late in the morning we drank coffee from a large tin can. At noon we had a small lunch of bread, followed by another break in the midafternoon. No one wore a watch, so village church bells marked the time of day. Apple trees were everywhere, but we benefited from their shade only when we happened to bundle up the cut wheat sheaves underneath one of them. Only the air raids sometimes allowed us to take a longer break. Then we would stop, gather underneath a tree, watch the passing show, and cool off.

Daylight Allied air raids were a regular part of everyday life all over Germany at this time. In the countryside they took place less frequently than in cities, and then they often occurred when stray bombers that failed to reach their goals unloaded their bombs at random, sometimes wiping out entire villages.

To me, real danger usually seemed far away. The protective shield of immortality that surrounds a thirteen-year-old worked for me. Bernie also imagined that such a shield existed. It became apparent in the way he described his early days in Auschwitz. But, as I was to find out later, when he continued with his story beyond Auschwitz—to Mauthausen, Gusen, and finally Gunskirchen—that protective shield, fragile and imaginary as it was from the beginning, was shattered. Death finally reached directly for his heart, flesh, and bones.

Nothing comparable happened to me. But there was the day when two friends and I were strafed by an Allied plane—a U.S. Air Force Thunderbolt—as we rode our bicycles over open fields. We melted into the ditch next to the road as the plane crossed our path from left to right in low flight. We were not hit, and when, after a few minutes, the fighter plane didn't come back, we broke out in excited laughter. We returned unscathed to our homes to recount our brush with death to anyone who would listen. The danger had lasted no more than a few seconds, not days, weeks, or months. What's more, we were not alone. We had our families, our own beds, and the familiarity of our homes. The odds for remaining alive were infinitely less for Bernie than for me.

On arrival at Auschwitz, Bernie was kept alive by one small movement of an SS guard's hand. What about this SS guard? Was there any difference between him and his fellow henchman with whom he shared the task of splitting the column of people into the living and the dead? Surely there was no difference in their relationship to the death machine they served, but for Bernie the difference between the two anonymous guards was enormous. One of them made a gesture, perhaps a random one, that kept him alive. No, on second thought, it was not random but routine, a routine decision of this guard that was a part of his repetitive job in that well-functioning system. Bernie thinks that perhaps the guard did not like it that the youngster moved left without being told to do so and therefore decided to assert his authority by sending him in the opposite direction.

About the same time that Bernie was deported to Auschwitz, I was sent, over the protests of my stepmother, along with five other students in my *Gymnasium* at Miltenberg, to attend a Nazi training and selection camp. Called a Bannausleselager, it was designed to develop the future leading cadres of the Third Reich, and it constituted a prerequisite for being admitted to the higher-level, so-called Adolf Hitler Schule. My stepmother, opposed to the Nazis, had the courage to protest the decision to the Nazi youth authorities, but she was not successful in preventing my participation.

I left Kleinheubach for almost two weeks of intense physical exams, all kinds of intellectual aptitude tests, ideological indoctrination, and mental grillings that lasted all day and often into the night. Each day started with a roll call. As the camp leader made his appearance to review us, our immediate superior barked out, "Achtung! Stillgestanden! Bannführer, melde gehorsamst" (Attention! Camp leader, I report most obediently). We would snap to attention. Sometimes we were roused in the middle of the night and made to march to nowhere in particular; screamed orders had us drop into ditches on either the right or the left side of the road. We were told to act out imaginary battles against invisible enemies. I have always been claustrophobic by nature (unlike Bernie, I had the luxury of time to reflect on my psyche), so it was no more than an ingrained, knee-jerk reaction to resist the type of rigid discipline to which we were subjected.

Once we had to march out of the camp into an open field about an hour before sunset. We were made to stop, form lines facing the setting sun, and perform knee bends while our leaders strode up and down the columns monitoring us for proper execution. Those of us who began to groan as the unending knee bends became painful were singled out for derision. Others, after more time had passed, started to cry, and a few of us fell down from exhaustion. All of these "weaklings" were moved out of the ranks and made to stand apart in a group of reprehensible failures. As one of the shortest in the group, I avoided bending my knees altogether by simply bending over from the waist. Whenever one of our leaders approached my position in the second row, I performed knee bends, as ordered, but returned afterward to my more comfortable subterfuge. By the time the sun touched the top of the mountain, about an hour after the exercise had started, the ordeal finally came to an end. While most of my compatriots dropped to the ground, I was able to remain on my feet and enjoy a sense of exhilaration for having eluded the watchful eyes of our guards.

Toward the end of the two weeks we were lined up outside the office, actually just a converted bedroom, for "racial classification." When my name was called, I entered the small room and found one camp leader sitting directly in front of me, another at a right angle to my left, and a third, the scribe, in a corner of the room. The fellow in front pronounced me a "Westphalian-Aryan" and gave a thumbnail description of my physical appearance. For him, the shape of my face and my blue eyes qualified me for this category in the Nazi racist taxonomy. Then the fellow at my side piped up and added, "Strong Dinarian features," referring presumably to my prominent, aquiline nose and dark hair. I found out later that these racial taxonomists used "Dinarian" for any German who looked "Mediterranean." More than anything else, this strange ritual struck me as nonsensical. How could their categories refer to me, Fritz Tubach, who had always been proud not to have been born in Hanau, Frankfurt, or Miltenberg but in San Francisco, California? I felt myself to be not this or that; I wanted to defy any categories they would impose on me and be different from everyone else. I had gone so far as to sport a beret with an Edelweiss symbol on it (the symbol of the White Rose resistance group of the Scholl siblings in Munich) and had been ridiculed for it in the village. A Hitler Youth leader who sat next to me in church even accused me of being a member of the resistance and tore my beret trying to remove the symbol. I was not a part of the resistance, but I protested that I had a right to wear whatever I liked.

The camp latrine was a rustic construction with a round hole cut out of a wooden board. The rim of the hole was soiled, and I hated using the latrine. But on the last day of camp, when I had to go, I climbed up on top of it to avoid making contact with the repulsive wooden board. When I unbuckled the belt of my uniform and squatted over the hole, my dagger, adorned with a swastika and an oak leaf, slipped off and fell into the pit of human waste. There was no way to retrieve it, and when, after my return home, I told my stepmother that I had lost the dagger in the latrine, she laughed and said good riddance. She never replaced it for me. My father would have.

My father and stepmother had opposite reactions to my uniform. He associated many of his ambitions with Nazi emblems. Once he fantasized that after the war was won, all members of the Nazi Party would be given white uniforms. He looked forward to this prospect. When he took me on a train ride to Frankfurt during his last furlough, he decided that we both should wear our uniforms, he his officer's regalia with pistol holster and I my Jungvolk uniform and dagger. The upholstered first-class compartment was unoccupied, so we both had window seats. My father encouraged me to stand up most of the way to look at the landscape sliding by but also to be seen whenever the train pulled into a station en route to Frankfurt's *Hauptbahnhof*.

In November 1942, when I was almost twelve, my stepmother forbade me to see a movie about Bismarck that the local Nazi youth authorities had ordered members of the Jungvolk to see, in uniform. I disobeyed her, and when I came home she threatened to spank me. I told her that she could not touch me while I was in my uniform. Her answer was an immediate thrashing. She had strong hands from her work in the fields. In anger I went to my superior, a fourteen-year-old group leader. He showed up in uniform at my grandfather's blacksmith shop to confront him, and only because the boy was faster than my aging grandfather did he avoid a beating, too. The matter was put to rest when the father of this youth, Herr Stahl, who owned a lumber mill, came and thanked my grandfather for putting his son in his place. Until it resurfaced in my own memory work much later, this was a moment I had forgotten, because it did not fit into the cohesive past I had constructed for myself over the years.

To this day I thank my stepmother for her success in preventing my "promotion" from the Jungvolk to the Adolf Hitler Schule. We were called before a Hitler Youth tribunal because she hadn't allowed me to apply to the school even though I had passed the first hurdle of the camp, the Bannausleselager. When she was warned by the Hitler Youth official that she would ruin my career, she replied, "You worry about your career, I'll worry about his." What if she had not been fully in charge of my upbringing at this point in my life but rather my absentee Nazi father or my beloved grandmother, who would have been proud to have her favorite grandson rise in the Nazi ranks? Would I eventually have given up my need to be different and ended up wearing the uniform of death? I refuse to believe so. But I recall a trivial incident that indicates how Nazi indoctrination was not simply hammered into one but was also insinuated into a young mind in a variety of subtle ways.

During the Bannausleselager, one of the twelve boys in my dormitory had brought along a condom. We blew it up like a balloon and floated it out of the window into the courtyard. Camp leaders seemed enraged by this prank. Their investigation traced the infraction to our quarters, and we were grilled for hours, pressured to reveal the culprit, and threatened with severe punishments. At the same time, however, I detected a certain ambiguity in these interrogations, which obviously implied an underlying compliment: "Ihr seid Kerle" (You're real men). We stuck together, refused to betray the instigator, and escaped punishment. The double message of our superiors linked a number of factors—sexuality, transgression, regulations, and male solidarity—that served both to maintain order and to inculcate in us a sense of rebellion and team spirit. They wanted to make us capable of doing anything in service of the grand Nazi design. They encouraged us to develop into a controlled horde, a gang, really, legitimized and led by the greatest tribal chief of all time, who sat in Berlin.

. . .

At this point, Bernie and I wanted to continue our recollections with as few interruptions as possible. His story influenced the present to the extent that it was uncomfortable to stop and pick it up too many days later. It seemed to me almost as if leaving Bernie's narrative on that path to his barracks in *Lager* D added to the length of his stay in the concentration camps. So we met again a couple of days later, this time at my house. Bernie continued recounting his memories in our living room, and I took notes as usual, interrupting him for details of description and chronology. I was amazed at the cool detachment with which he drew with a few sure strokes on a blue-lined sheet of yellow paper a map of the Birkenau section of the Auschwitz concentration camp. He drew arrows to show me how people were moved to the various campsites, to delousing, to extermination stations, or to the outside, either as part of temporary work teams or as permanent transfers to other camps. His precision stunned me. Was it Bernie's clarity of mind that increased his chances of survival against overwhelming odds? Did his mental toughness, of which he is proud even today, protect him from going under psychologically? Or was it the twelve-year-old's feeling of invincibility that kept him sane and flexible, thus increasing his awareness of the few small opportunities that enhanced his chances? It is difficult to weigh these factors, knowing with the benefit of historical hindsight that the flick of a hand of an SS guard could at any moment snuff out any life, weak or strong, any mind, lucid or muddled.

. . .

Bernat Rosner was assigned to *Lager* E, next to *Lager* F, which bore the official euphemism *Hospital-Lager*, where Josef Mengele performed his barbaric medical experiments on living human beings. Bernie remembers the twins who were taken from his section of the camp and assigned to Mengele's adjacent experimentation station. He and other inmates talked to these twins across the fence. When they found out that they were well fed and well treated at that moment, they envied the twins and wished, unaware of the diabolical fates that would follow, that they could join them.

A careful observer, Bernie became aware of the process by which inmates from the "Quarantine Camp," *Lager* E, were selected either for placement in a permanent work camp at Auschwitz or for transfer to other concentration camps. Only inmates selected for placement in a permanent work camp at Auschwitz received blue tattooed identification numbers on their forearms. Since Bernie's initiative led to his transfer elsewhere, he does not bear this mark on his body.

The facilities used for the selection were located in *Lager* E. They consisted of large, elongated blockhouses that were divided lengthwise into two sections by a four-foot-high wall. These barracks were initially constructed as stables, and the wall, hollow inside, served as a conduit for heat generated by a stove near the entrance. A separate door served each half of the barracks.

The process of selection consisted of gathering the inmates outside the barracks and then herding those selected for transport into the righthand side of the divide. As time passed, Bernie noticed that the pool of inmates left behind—the group not designated for transfer—was made up of older and sicker persons and of young boys who were less fit for work. It gradually dawned on him that it would be dangerous to remain behind indefinitely with this group.

One day, when a new selection was under way and Bernie again had not been chosen, he took his chances and decided to jump over the wall to join the inmates on the right side. A guard, positioned to prevent any such crossovers, pinned Bernie's arm to the wall he was attempting to cross with his boot. For a brief moment the guard looked at him while he held him there. Then he shrugged his shoulders and lifted his boot, allowing Bernie to join the group selected for transport. Bernie's desperate decision and the Nazi guard's random act of forbearance removed him for the moment from the immediate grip of the death machine. And because of this leap, a correction needs to be made in the official record of the number of inmates put on a transport on September 17 from Auschwitz to Mauthausen, as recorded in Danuta Czech's *Auschwitz Chronicle, 1939–1945: From the Archives of the Auschwitz Memorial and the German Federal Archives.* The entry in question, recorded for September 17, 1944, lists 1,824 prisoners, among them 1,396 Poles. With Bernie's self-selection, the number of prisoners was actually 1,825.

The more than 400-kilometer transfer to Mauthausen by cattle train took about two days. It was quite a different ride than the one that took Bernat Rosner to Auschwitz several months earlier. There were no women or small children in this group, no acquaintances from his native village, and no members of his family. All the passengers were men in relatively good shape, with Bernie the youngest. The cattle car doors were kept open, and in each car two German SS guards rode with the inmates on their way south. While the train was stopped temporarily in Czechoslovakia near Olomouc, Allied planes dropped bombs near the train but failed to hit it. The pilots must not have known that the cattle cars were filled with human beings. And, of course, the Nazis would not mark such a train to prevent it from being attacked. After the air strike, the train started moving south again. None of the inmates aboard had any idea what their final destination would be.

Bernie started up a conversation with one of the German guards, who took an interest in him. The guard asked Bernie where he came from, and the two of them talked for a long time while the train rolled on. I tried to picture this extraordinary situation, because it seemed so simple and ordinary on a certain level—two strangers who find themselves caught for a couple of days in the same place pass the time in conversation. Bernie interrupted my attempts to interpret this incident by saying that this SS guard was "just an ordinary guy." His remark surprised me. So the guard was just a regular guy caught in unusual circumstances? In other words, he was just doing the job to which he was assigned? We both know this to be a macabre, yet believable, point of view.

The train arrived on the evening of September 19, 1944, at a village on the Danube. The passengers spent the night in the locked cattle cars and entered the camp only the following day. On their walk up the hill toward the high-walled camp, Bernie remembers the intense longing he felt for the everyday life that seemed to emanate from the houses of the village and the fields surrounding it. When they reached the imposing entrance of the camp, with its solid stone walls and huge gate adorned with the eagle and swastika of the Third Reich, they tried to speak with members of work details leaving the grounds but were prevented from doing so by the guards. They had arrived at the concentration camp of Mauthausen. On September 21, 1944, the list of arrivals from the previous day, Bernie's official arrival day, was typed in the camp records, the *Liste der Zugänge vom 20. September 1944.* In this list the following entry appears: "Rosner...Bernat...29.1.27...Budapest...Landarbeiter" (farmworker), and to this was added his number, "103,705," right after Rosenfeld, Ernö (103,704), a Hungarian farmer born in 1905, and before Rotberg, Pinkus (103,706), a Polish machinist born in 1908. The Mauthausen entry contains an important error, again occasioned by Bernie's own initiative—namely, his decision to change his year of birth (1932) on the record to 1927 in order to make himself appear five years older than he was. Although this lie did not assure his survival, it at least gave him a chance to be counted among the work-qualified adults rather than among the younger teenage boys who would almost automatically be eliminated from consideration as laborers.

Mauthausen was divided into three sections. The oldest section, *Lager* 1, was subdivided into thirteen blocks and held German criminals, who, as "Aryans," enjoyed superior status and special privileges. Wearing green triangles on their jackets to signify this status, they were given supervisory roles in the camp. Willy, an Austrian criminal, supervised Bernie's barracks. Polish or Ukrainian non-Jews wore red triangles signifying their lower status. At the bottom of the camp hierarchy were the Jews, who were required to wear yellow triangles. Bernie, the youngest of a group of about twenty teenagers who were part of the same human shipment from Auschwitz, was assigned to *Lager* 2, block 21. Along with the others, he was given a uniform and a haircut called the "Mauthausen-Straße"—their heads were shaved down the middle.

Aside from the Nazi-imposed hierarchy, various group identities developed among the inmates, based on their backgrounds. The Hungarian Jews made up one such subgroup. The one language all groups had in common was the language of their oppressors—German—or rather a kind of pidgin German most had learned in the various camps.

During the daytime, inmates were herded outside, where they usually spent their time standing about idly in the increasingly cold and wet weather of late September and October. They huddled together for warmth, and one of the amusements of the SS guards and the Kapos was to club those standing on the outside perimeter of the group so that the whole group of prisoners would break into a panicked stampede and trample each other. In one of these melees Bernie sustained a slight leg wound that developed into a sore that wouldn't heal. He did not seek medical help, however, for fear his injury would mark him "unfit for work," a death sentence in the concentration camp.

At night inmates were jammed together, often four abreast on a narrow platform bed in unheated barracks. To avoid the almost unbearable crowding that prevented sleep, Bernie made a bargain with his other bedmates for one of their blankets in return for giving up his assigned space in bed. With this second blanket, he hunkered down on the floor below the bunkbeds that were stacked up three high above him. This gave him and his bunkmates a little more space. Bernie gained a partially covered area provided by the bed immediately above him and, most important, another blanket that provided extra protection from the cold.

Beyond the cold, there was hunger. Rations were limited to a quarter loaf of bread per day with either a pad of margarine or a slice of liverwurst, a bowl of cabbage soup that usually contained maggots, and, in the morning, lukewarm brown water that was called coffee. Only non-Jews received cigarette rations, on the rationale that Jews would only use the cigarettes for "profiteering."

As time went on, hunger turned into starvation and many of the inmates began to waste away. The most emaciated among them, the ones who could barely be distinguished as being dead or alive, were given the odd name Musulmänner (Muslims). Teenagers like Bernie worked in the kitchen, where they filled their days with endless reveries about food—about eating meals in warm houses with tables laden down with meats, bread, fruit, vegetables, and sweets of all kinds. The work in the kitchen provided Bernie with an occasional chance to supplement his meager food ration. He made a deal with the other kitchen help that allowed him to smuggle potatoes and onions into his blockhouse. Because his concentration camp uniform was too large for his small body, he could easily stuff it full of the precious vegetables without arousing suspicion before returning to the barracks. On one occasion his pants and jacket burst open as he arrived at his blockhouse, and potatoes and onions spilled to the ground at the very moment an SS officer entered. Both the inmates and the officer broke out in spontaneous laughter. Bernie lost his treasures but suffered no other ill consequences from having taken this dangerous risk.

Vegetable smuggling was not the only survival strategy developed by desperate boys in the camp. Among the relatively more privileged German inmates were a number of homosexuals, and some of the boys prostituted themselves to these men in exchange for food and a degree of protection. It was, in fact, the discovery of one of the boys caught in the act with a Kapo that ended Bernie's and the other teenagers' brief stint of kitchen work, a rare interval during his concentration camp stay when he was not starving.

Every morning and evening a general roll call was held. All the inmates had to leave their blockhouses and line up outside to be counted. The head of the cell block, the Austrian criminal, Willy, would then shout, "Achtung! Stillgestanden, Mützen ab!" (Attention! Caps off!). Then he would turn to the SS officer in charge of the *Appell* and bark, "Herr Oberscharführer, ich melde gehorsamst" (Herr Sergeant Major, I report most obediently). The head count followed.

As the days, weeks, and months at Mauthausen passed, the routine, complete surveillance and total control in the camp established an illusory sense of predictability. At least for a boy of thirteen, it was possible with a bit of luck to increase one's chances of survival to a small degree. After all, as Bernie said in a matter-of-fact way, "In Mauthausen you were killed only if you became sick." (During his internment, he did not know that the laws of murder were different in other parts of this large camp and that Russian POWs housed in nearby barracks were tortured and killed, especially after a major escape attempt.) From his own subjective point of view, the margin of safety seemed to be a little greater around his body here, wider at least than when he lived next to the extermination ovens at Auschwitz. He was spared any significant illnesses that might have been noticed by the guards. So, for a time, his youthful invulnerability worked for him, at least until the day he found himself on the quarry steps.

There was a quarry within the Mauthausen camp boundaries where selected inmates were forced to carry stones, backbreakingly heavy stones, up a long, steep set of stairs from the bottom of the quarry to the top. It was organized for two purposes, one of them being camp construction. But its main purpose was the destruction of human lives. Mere extermination was not enough to satisfy the sadistic urges of the camp authorities, so they devised this ingenious way to torture their prisoners to death on this *via dolorosa* of crude steps. Laden with heavy stones as they ascended the narrow, torturous steps, prisoners were driven continually up and down without mercy, without stopping or rest. These quarry steps existed for Bernie only one day, the day he was forced to work there. Just on the day Bernie worked, half a dozen people dropped around him and died of exhaustion or were killed by the SS guards. The prisoners who faltered, or who failed to move fast enough to satisfy the guards, were shoved so that they tumbled to the bottom of the pit, still clutching heavy rocks to their bodies. Why didn't they let go of the rocks as they fell? Bernie doesn't have an answer and comes back to that question over and over again: Why didn't they let go of the rocks? Half-dead inmates removed the emaciated bodies of the dead like garbage, so that still others, who were already starved nearly to death before they ever reached the quarry, could take their places. Thus were lives turned into dead matter. This was more than a nightmare. For Bernie, it was a day in hell.

. . .

Hours passed, during which the present was obliterated for both of us. But suddenly we realized that we had to end our session of recalling the past, so we left the steps of Mauthausen behind. Bernie had to rush to meet Susan at the Bay Area Rapid Transit station. They were going to San Francisco for the evening. I accompanied him out the front door to his car. He told me he had just taken a bad spill on his bicycle the day before but hadn't been hurt in the least. He looked at me and said, "You know, I must be a very tough guy." I smiled at him and said nothing. As he unlocked his car, he turned to me once more and smiled back with a touch of irony. Then he said, with more insistence, "I'm tough as hell."

It was a long time after he told me about the quarry and even after our visit to Mauthausen that I asked Bernie why he had worked there only one day. I had always accepted this one-day event as self-evident. But, of course, many were worked there repeatedly until they died. It was a particularly cruel form of extermination. Bernie answered me in his usual straightforward, unselfconscious way.

He couldn't be sure, he said, but he had a theory about it. His arrival at Mauthausen happened to coincide with the arrival of the first full contingency of boys. Since there had been no young people there before, it "made news"; it "created something of a sensation," as he put it. The boys were housed in Bernie's block 21, whose *Blockältester* was the Austrian criminal, who seemed to have retained a touch of humanity. Bernie believes that this man knew that people chosen to work in the quarry wouldn't last very long. And when he saw how these youths, including Bernie, looked after their first day at the quarry, he simply decided not to pick them again and had them work instead in the kitchen for a time. The *Blockältester* retained a degree of discretion in making such selections, and Bernie credits him for having made the decision that saved him and certain others from further exposure to the deadly quarry.

. . .

Today Mauthausen is a quiet Austrian town on the Danube River. The charming city of Linz, known for centuries for its *Linzer Torte* pastries and generous hospitality, is not far away. Mozart visited Linz frequently and dedicated one of his symphonies to it. Across the Danube, just a few kilometers away, stands the church of St. Florian, with its finely chiseled baroque decorations and Anton Bruckner's monumental crypt. Its lovingly tended cemetery is full of neat crosses, flowers, and quaint inscriptions on marble tombstones that describe the profession and status of deceased loved ones. St. Florian and Linz have become favorite tourist stopovers for travelers on their way from southern Germany to Vienna, bypassing Mauthausen on the other side of the river.

For Bernie, Mauthausen in autumn and winter of 1944–45 did not connote music, pastries, and baroque architecture but cold, starvation, and steep quarry steps. The Allies moved across the German border in the West while the Russian army reached the German border in the East. The Ardennes offensive in December 1944, launched by the German army to cut off the northern British flank from the Americans farther south, temporarily halted the push of the Western Allies into Germany. This last winter of the war turned out to be very cold all over Europe. Liberation was still far away.

· · ·

About 500 kilometers northwest of Mauthausen, I attended school in Miltenberg, a few kilometers upriver from Kleinheubach in the Main Valley. Today a fast driver can cover the distance between Mauthausen and Miltenberg in less than six hours on the Autobahn. In my village, I knew something about both cold and hunger but nothing about starvation, let alone the stone quarry steps of Mauthausen. Although there exists no equivalence in degree or kind to our fortunes, as World War II in Europe reached its climax and finally came to an end in spring 1945, our individual lives were both caught up in this maelstrom of destruction, Bernie at its center and I at the margin.

Occasionally, when my family wasn't home, I tuned in to the BBC London radio broadcast in German—a forbidden activity—because I enjoyed comparing Allied reports about the progress of the war in France with the reports from the headquarters of the German army. Aside from this "secret knowledge," I and everyone else knew that the German army had performed retaliatory mass executions in villages all over Europe that were suspected of having harbored partisans. These executions were deemed justifiable acts of war, legitimate retaliation for enemy activities behind the German front lines. Beyond that, for years there had been ominous whispers at home about the SS knocking on doors in the early morning hours to arouse German victims and take them away. "Nacht und Nebel-Aktionen" they were called, actions enshrouded in fog and night that shunned the light of day, that were best ignored by "law-abiding citizens." I recall that the actions taken against the Jews in our midst did not meet with the same degree of dread as did these actions against the few Germans who had run afoul of Nazi laws. Even my father, a loyal party member, told us about his near-panic one day when he was visited without warning by the Gestapo, who wanted to know details of a business trip to England he had taken a few weeks before the beginning of the war. The Gestapo was satisfied with his explanation and didn't bother him again, to my father's great relief.

Concentration camps, or *Konzentrationslager* (*KZs*) in German, were not discussed. A taboo against speculating openly about what might go on inside their walls was firmly in place. Any such speculation or questioning was dangerous. With this lack of communication among Germans, it is difficult to find out exactly what was known and by how many. What did I personally know about Auschwitz or about other concentration camps in 1944 when I was thirteen years old? I knew for sure what had happened by May 1945, when I was fourteen and a half, after the victory of the Allies. But what did I know before that time? I was an alert boy who collected the leaflets dropped by Allied planes—forbidden papers that fell from the sky, from another world. I knew I was breaking the rules, but the heady enjoyment in the transgression was too great for me to stop. I don't remember ever reading anything about concentration camps in those leaflets, or, if they were mentioned, I don't recall it. If death camps where millions of Jews were being exterminated in gas ovens had been mentioned, I'm sure almost everyone else in the village would have considered it anti-German propaganda. That describes my limited knowledge of the world as a thirteen-year-old before the Allies arrived. I cannot answer for all Germans.

Hunger came for me in small daily doses, and as the winter progressed, my daydreams became more and more vivid. I was fourteen years old and convinced by then that Germany would lose the war. I kept a typewritten diary of the Allied landing on the coast of Normandy, and when the Germans failed to contain these troops on their beachheads, I decided all on my own that this was a sure sign of eventual German defeat. I reasoned simply that since the British Channel and the German Atlantic wall were breached, there was no impediment to the Allies of that magnitude left between the open French countryside and Germany. The Rhine was a lot smaller, after all, than the British Channel. Anyone interested in geography would know that, I told myself. But I did not share this view with anyone. I kept it even from my grandmother, who surely would have considered me mentally unbalanced. When the war was over, I thought I would return to the United States, the country of my birth, and work in a chocolate factory where I could eat as much candy as I wanted.

Although there was no chocolate to be found in Kleinheubach, potatoes, preserved vegetables, and bread were always on the table. We consumed our small meat rations on Sundays, when, unfortunately, patriarchy reigned at the dinner table. My stepgrandfather would carve up what was invariably a miserable chunk of beef or pork, take the largest portion for himself, and hand out the rest in pieces of diminishing size based on our ages. As the youngest, I received the smallest piece.

In geography at school we were given instruction about northern Europe. The teacher, a large man with a pointed nose and thinning blond hair, stopped in the middle of his lecture and had us recite after him, "In Denmark, there is cheese, ham, butter, eggs, and fresh fish." We eagerly repeated this sentence in chorus, echoing his words louder and louder, as if by conjuring up these appealing culinary images, we might be able to make them appear in front of us.

Our Latin teacher tended toward fanaticism. Once, during an air raid alarm, he refused to let us go to the shelter with the exhortation, "Even if we lose the gun battles, we must be prepared to win the battles of the mind." We, of course, had not studied for the examination he had planned and hoped that the air raid sirens would cancel it. Except for the best student in the class (who later became a professor of Greek at the University of Freiburg), we all flunked that Latin test. For me, school had become a cumbersome diversion. Real life and the war happened outside the classroom.

Nighttime air raids disrupted our sleep more and more. The peaceful walks under the stars with *Schloßtante*, when she had taught me the names of the constellations, were replaced with a different ritual. By the intensity and direction of the glow, we learned to distinguish which of the surrounding cities—Heilbronn, Würzburg, Darmstadt, or Frankfurt—were being bombed. By the end of the war, it was easier for me to extend my arms, with the accuracy of compass points, in the direction of these cities than it was to identify the constellations I had learned earlier.

Months before the war ended, our hunger had become a constant, gnawing presence, like a chronic pain with no relief. Luck had it that a military boat loaded with wheat became marooned in the Main River near Kleinheubach. Villagers scrambled aboard and threw the soldiers who guarded it into the water. Then word went out that the wheat was ours to take. All night we filled every available container. Families with bathtubs were especially fortunate. They were able to store enough wheat for their own use plus some extra for bartering. About 8 kilometers down the river another boat filled with heating oil had been abandoned. This boat was raided, too, and village women tried to render the oil edible by heating raw potatoes in it. (The raw potatoes were said to absorb the residual poison of the oil.) The resulting oil tasted dreadful and made many people sick, but after a time our digestive tracts got used to it. Through such strategies we got by in the village, hungry often but never starving.

I sometimes wondered whether Bernie's lifetime professional association with the Safeway supermarket chain somehow related to his early experience of starvation. But he sees no connection. For myself, I still do most of the grocery shopping in our household because I feel good inside a well-stocked grocery store.

It was very cold in Kleinheubach during the last winter of the war. In our house, only the living room was warm enough to provide some comfort. The bedrooms were not heated. Everyone tried their best to avoid a trip to the outhouse during the freezing nights. On winter mornings, urine was frozen in our chamber pots, and ice flowers covered the windows all the way to the top. I remember that on the coldest days the edge of my blanket near my face had a hoary frost on its surface from my breath. My feet had grown too large for the only pair of shoes I owned and therefore continued to wear. Where the sides of my feet pressed painfully against the leather, I developed frostbite that itched even years later whenever my feet were cold.

To some small degree, I could refer to my own experience of hunger and cold to reach over to Bernie's suffering 500 kilometers southeast of me. But the quarry steps of Mauthausen and the profound impact they had on Bernie remained hidden from me, except during the very moments when he described them to me in my living room in California fifty years later. A surprise recall helped me to comprehend a little better the constant mortal danger he faced.

In 1943 I contracted tuberculosis and was sent for treatment to a sanitarium at Friedensweiler in the Black Forest. During the three months I was there, the other patients and I received routine care and examinations. At one point, however, we were called to our resident doctor's office where he along with two or three uniformed men were present. We were examined by this group individually. I remember that the officers spent more time reading my medical record than examining me. Although I was quite aware at the time that this examination was an odd departure from the normal hospital routine, nothing came of it.

What were these uniformed people doing at our hospital for tubercular patients? A few years ago, I read for the first time a newspaper report that plans had been made to eliminate "unfit" tubercular Germans. In retrospect, I realize that this incident at Friedensweiler, which had been different from anything I had experienced up to that point, might also have been a brush with the Nazi death machine. I have no proof of this, but neither do I have any other explanation for it.

Does my fleeting and vague, after-the-fact anxiety surrounding this strange event help me to understand the quarry steps of Mauthausen any better? Of what Bernie experienced I have only heard his retelling. What do I feel about it all? Sadness and shock, perhaps, because these things happened to him, to my friend. Surprise? No. Sympathy? It's too late. Bernie doesn't need it. I can't experience the physical or emotional pain he went through. Now, with historical hindsight, I can at least understand on a rational level that the same death machine that threatened him continuously may also have crossed the horizon of my own life for a brief moment. I now remember that peculiar incident in my youth with a cold shudder.

. . .

As inmate number 103,705, Bernie had been turned into a manageable and disposable quantity. A transfer to another camp or reassignment to another section within a camp could swiftly become a matter of life or death. The homosexual incident in the Mauthausen kitchen precipitated the transfer of all teenagers from *Lager* 2 to *Lager* 3. There Bernie was assigned to block 27, where the conditions were more squalid than anything he had yet encountered. The campsite was no more than a muddy corral. The origins of the inmates were more varied. Not only Eastern Europeans but also Spaniards, Frenchmen, and even some Americans were imprisoned there. Aside from the diminishing daily rations of bread, the only food was a bowl of soup a day that was almost inedible, topped as it was by a layer of grease that made Bernie sick to his stomach. Such a decline in the quality or quantity of food was a direct threat to survival. The margin was shrinking. The danger of becoming near-dead, of joining the ranks of the Musulmänner, drew closer. A debilitating sickness, a bad case of diarrhea, even if transitory, could mean extermination. Keeping your eyes and ears open came to make less of a difference. But when the margin disappeared, there was still luck. There were random situations that helped Bernie as life in the camp deteriorated further.

It so happened that the *Blockältester* in charge of one of the barracks in *Lager* 3, a German criminal, befriended Bernie, the youngest of the inmates. As his helper, Bernie ran errands, sang songs, and helped clean his living quarters. In turn, this inmate served as Bernie's friend and protector, temporarily increasing his survival chances. For two weeks, Bernie lived, as he put it, "the life of Riley." He was allowed to eat regular food and to bunk down in the warm living quarters of the *Blockältester*. For two weeks he had a name, not just a number. His friend and protector ordered a special identification tag made for him by another inmate who had been a silversmith before internment. The tag consisted of a flattened spoon, fashioned into a little work of art with a design around its edges. A small chain was attached to it for easy wearing, and this oval-shaped amulet replaced the crude official identification tag, made out of a strip of tin can and wire, that was issued to all inmates by the camp authorities. The outer surface of this new bracelet showed his identification number, 103,705, while the reverse "hidden" side had engraved on it his initials, "BR."

. . .

In telling me his story, Bernie hardly mentioned his family after their separation at Auschwitz. When I asked him about this, he told me, "The realization that my family was dead came to me gradually." These were his precise words. He did not say that his family was "murdered" or "exterminated"; rather, he used the language of normal life that includes "death" as a natural event. But his family was *exterminated,* they did not just die, I thought to myself. The everyday task of surviving left him little time to devote to anything else, including reflections on the past or on his family that had disappeared. Their violent deaths in the gas chambers of Auschwitz leave a black hole in his very language that blocks Bernie from capturing these hellish facts in words. And I am rendered incapable of narrating anything. Nothing escapes from that black hole—no image, no cry, no suffering…no language.

. . .

My uncle who was assigned to drive oil trucks in Ploiesti, Rumania, was probably blown up—he disappeared without a trace—but most of my family members survived the war. Uncle Ernst, the communist who escaped service, watched the entry of the Allies into Ludwigsburg from his front door, applauding the victors with glee. Gentle Uncle Ludwig, who had been inspired by the party rally in Nuremberg, had been sent to the outskirts of Moscow and back as a front-line machine gunner. He lost most of his toes, part of his feet, and his mind in the freezing winter near Smolensk in western Russia. When he returned home, he would wake up nights screaming that the Russians were coming to hang him up by his toes, his "innerer Reichsparteitag" over.

My father's fate was quite different. In 1941 the German army assigned him to a job in the British Channel Islands as an *Abwehroffizier* (counterintelligence officer) of the General Staff located at Port St. Pierre on Guernsey. His main problem seems to have been the extra pounds he had a hard time shedding, at least until the German army supplies for the British Channel

Islands were cut off after the Normandy landing in June 1944. I remember a photo of him working up a sweat on a reducing machine. Another photo shows him standing on the steps of the Sacre Coeur in Paris, in the company of an SS officer. What was he doing with an officer of the SS? He told me that while on Guernsey he once ordered an English civilian sent to "a camp in Germany" for having hoisted a Union Jack and for singing "God Save the King" in one of the local movie houses. My father justified his deportation order by saying that the man wanted to be arrested and sent to that camp, to join his girlfriend who was already there. That was the only personal connection with camps to which my father ever admitted.

My father—unlike Bernie—had no difficulties obtaining a visa to come to the United States after the war, despite his Nazi and wartime activities.

. . .

Mauthausen was a center for several satellite camps, including Gusen, in the vicinity of which the German aircraft manufacturer, Messerschmidt, had a factory that built warplanes. In December 1944 Bernie was assigned to *Lager* 1 at Gusen, where he learned to drive rivets and cut out small metal parts used in airplane construction. The work site was located outside the camp, and although Bernie's group was under guard at all times, their march to and from the slave labor encampment gave them some physical movement outside the barbed-wire confines. As they walked through the open Austrian landscape, they could see green mountains, foothills that stretched to the Alps, a different world spread across the southern horizon. Bernie remembers that one day, as his column walked to the factory, an Austrian man working close by in a field dropped a half-eaten apple that Bernie was able to pick up. Bernie is convinced that the Austrian meant for one of the starving inmates to benefit from this piece of fruit. This unexpected bounty was the only piece of fresh fruit Bernie ate during the eleven months of his concentration camp imprisonment.

Those who left the camp on this work detail were considered useful to the German war efforts and less dispensable than the inmates left behind. In spite of their hunger and exhaustion, this group retained some hope and a grim sense of humor to describe their condition. As they were marched to work, they often sang a ditty to the tune of "Lili Marlene" with the lyrics, "Heute nicht arbeiten, Maschine kaput" (Today no work, the machine is broken). The war machine was breaking down, to be sure, but the breakdown had not yet reached Gusen. Fighter planes were still being produced to intercept the Allied bombers in their round-the-clock attacks. Bernie the riveter was forced to do his share to keep the German war effort going.

A second *Lager* reserved for Jews only was situated not far from Bernie's *Lager* 1 at Gusen. There was little contact between these two sections of the camp. After liberation, the survivors of *Lager* 1 discovered that the conditions in *Lager* 2 had been infinitely worse than in their own. It turned out, in fact, to be a horror camp, with regular torture, killings, and deliberate starvation. Few inmates from *Lager* 2 survived.

As time went on, however, the line between survival and death narrowed for everyone at Gusen. The total war that Goebbels had promised the world was beginning to be felt in the camps more and more. Exacerbating the routine brutality and squalor of the camps was the steadily deteriorating state of the overall German wartime economy. Camp conditions worsened as the ground war reached Germany. Not only systematic killings, but starvation and illness caused by the growing scarcity of food and other necessities, accelerated the extermination process in camps all over Europe.

Little more than half a year had passed since the Rosner family had been deported from its Hungarian village. An orange in Budapest on the way to Auschwitz and a partially eaten apple near Gusen on his march to work constituted the only tangible signs of support or sympathy Bernie received from the outside world. Inside the world of the concentration camps, there were the rare incidents of help that came to him from a guard or another inmate. But, above all, the indispensable survival condition for inmates within the camps was a buddy system—a survival unit composed of two friends who watched out for each other whenever possible.

Shortly after his arrival at Gusen, Bernie teamed up with another Hungarian teenager, Simcha Katz, a member of the original shipment of prisoners from Auschwitz to Mauthausen, to form such a survival unit. The ultimate test of this relationship came in mid-January 1945 when Simcha's shoes—the officially issued wooden-soled clogs—were stolen. For two days Simcha trudged to work through the winter ice and snow in his bare feet. If he was going to survive, he would have to repurchase his shoes from an inmate who used thievery as his survival strategy and who offered to "sell" Simcha his own shoes, which the thief claimed he had "found." The ransom for the shoes was two days' bread rations, but such a great sacrifice would have spelled Simcha's death. The only way to save his life was for both boys to go without their bread ration for one day. This they did, and Simcha got his shoes back.

Bernie remembers December 31, 1944, New Year's Eve. The *Blockältester*, the inmate in charge of block 15 at Gusen, turned out to be humane. Bernie no longer remembers the name of this man from Vienna. And he never knew what motivated him. The man obtained some alcohol and invited his compatriots who served in positions similar to his own to a party. Bernie and Simcha watched the drinking bout and celebration through the window from the outside. Right there in the middle of starvation and death, a party took place. Some participated, others watched. What were they celebrating? Having survived so far? Had the news of Allied advances reached them and given them reason to believe that they might be liberated? Was it merely an attempt to escape the horrors of camp life for a while? Had everyday life achieved some semblance of normalcy so that daily rituals, such as the celebration of holidays, observed in the outside world, could also be celebrated here? Bernie's description of this scene became frozen into a tableau in my mind: in the midst of mass murder, grown men drink and celebrate while boys look on.

. . .

I remember that same New Year's Eve of 1944 very well. During the winter, the circle of life had drawn closer around my family in Kleinheubach. Activities became more and more restricted to the immediate environment. Not only did Berlin, the center of Nazi power, seem far away, but even the distances between the villages in the Main Valley increased as the war went on. Five of us, my stepgrandfather, stepmother, two aunts, and I, sat in the living room around a small light fixture that pulled down from the ceiling. Rimmed with a green, glass bead fringe, it cast a dim light onto the table. We drank hard apple cider, a specialty of the region. Very little was said. Before midnight I went to bed in the room next to the living room. I lay there as the clock in the living room struck midnight. The radio was on, and I listened to the first movement of Beethoven's Fifth Symphony followed by an announcement I will never forget. With his hard-edged voice and sing-song pitch, Goebbels, the minister of propaganda, proclaimed that the ground was swaying below us Germans but that Providence and, even more than Providence, Der Führer would steady all of that in the coming year, which was sure to bring a final victory to Germany. I was rational enough to wonder, right there in my village bed, what the metaphor of the "swaying ground" really meant, realistically. The world had grown cold, dark, and dangerous around me— that I knew.

. . .

The year 1945 arrived. The January weather grew increasingly severe. Allied bombing raids multiplied. For Bernie, there seemed to be some minor improvements in concentration camp life for a very short time. But then conditions at Gusen deteriorated rapidly in February. The only inmates that Bernie recalls whose lot improved markedly were two who were assigned to work in the crematorium extracting gold teeth from the mouths of the increasing number of corpses that they processed. Some of this gold was surreptitiously passed on to German guards. If the inmates had been caught keeping any of the gold themselves, they would have been shot. But German guards were glad to pocket some of the dental gold and gave the inmates incentives in the form of extra food rations to participate in these macabre exchanges. Other inmates envied these crematorium workers and would have gladly taken on their job in hell for more food.

For everyone else, including Bernie's group of teenagers, who had remained healthier than the adults, the pace of disintegration quickened. Their eyes grew ever more hollow and sunken. Weakened physiques became skeleton-like, and more of them joined the growing number of walking dead. Lice multiplied on everyone. Corpses began to pile up, and pushcarts came by twice a day to pick them up.

Bernie was transferred to block 5, where conditions were even worse. The huge cavernous brick building was overcrowded, the Kapos were more brutal than usual, and, because of a total lack of discipline, the bullies among the prisoners had unchecked license to abuse their weaker fellows. Had luck abandoned him totally at this point, Bernie probably would have perished. But, fortunately, he ran into the friendly Austrian inmate who had been in charge of block 15. In the meantime, this man had been promoted to *Lageraltester*, in charge of the entire

Lager 1 at Gusen. He gave Bernie some food, and Bernie told him about the terrible conditions in block 5. A few days later the *Lagerältester* paid a surprise early morning visit to the barracks and was appalled by the conditions there. After a heated discussion between the *Lagerältester* and his subordinate *Blockältester*, the lot of the prisoners in block 5 improved somewhat.

In March Bernie was given garden duties in the camp, but he himself began to weaken. The meager bread rations were cut back even further, leaving inmates with little more than one slice of bread and a daily portion of watery, wormy soup that was rendered even more inedible than usual by the fact that it wasn't salted. For a time, Bernie simply couldn't swallow it. But then starvation forced him to do so. There was nothing else to eat. All around him people began to stagger, collapse, and die.

During the second and third week of April—Bernie's usual precise sense of time begins to blur—conditions in Gusen turned even more hellish. The battle zone was approaching; the German army was in disarray and in full retreat on all fronts. The Nazi death machine as well was beginning to lose its smooth, fatal precision. Some of the German inmates who had been imprisoned for criminal activities and who formed the "elite" of the prisoner hierarchy were given military training in order to shore up the sagging front. Other inmates—those who had become visibly ill—were taken to the "Bahnhof" (train station), as inmates dubbed the gas chambers, to be killed.

Victims began to discuss among themselves whether they should save part of their daily bread rations in case rations were cut further. Most of them felt that this was not necessary since the Allies would soon arrive to liberate them. Bernie, although he now believed he would not survive until liberation in any case, still favored the bread-saving strategy in order to prolong life as much as possible.

Suddenly, on April 15, the Jews of the Gusen camp were collected for a march back to Mauthausen, where, for the first time, women and men separated since Auschwitz were brought together again. On arrival they were herded into a makeshift encampment outside the main camp. Only the first to arrive were able to sleep in the few tents available, while the vast majority slept out in the open, on bare soil, without bedding or any other protection from the spring cold. In the absence of the well-organized death machine, with its efficient methods of mass extermination, brutality now became more personal and direct. The bare hands, arms, and legs of the victimizers took over. One particularly vicious guard by the name of Kaduk delighted in placing his victims across a wooden contraption, something like a pair of low sawhorses, and then jumping on their backs, breaking them.

Executions became more frequent. The carts picking up the dead never stopped rolling by. Bernie witnessed an incident in which an inmate being clubbed by an SS guard tried to escape the assault by playing dead. His body was placed on a wagon of corpses to be transported away, and a tarpaulin was thrown over the pile of bodies. But an inadvertent movement he made under the cover was seen by a guard, who took up a wooden board and kept beating on the tarpaulin with all his force until the twitching stopped permanently.

SS guards frequently ordered inmates to evacuate their tents and then took young women inside, where they raped them in relative privacy, before continuing their operations in the killing fields.

Guns could be heard in the distance as the Allies pushed their way through Bavaria into Austria. But as the liberators approached from the west, murderers were still in charge at Mauthausen. Several thousand Jews in the encampment, Bernie among them, were hastily driven out of the Mauthausen camp and forced to march about 40 kilometers in a southwesterly direction beyond the town of Wels to Gunskirchen, a small village that is visible nowadays from the Salzburg-Vienna train. After the war this notorious four-day trek became known as the Death March. Those too weak to keep up with the others were shot or clubbed to death, as were the friends or relatives who stayed back, trying to aid them. Guards left no one alive who dropped or even paused by the roadside. At the rear of the procession, a work crew collected corpses along with the refuse left by the living in order to keep the road clean for the local Austrians. Before the prisoners passed through the village of Ens, guards removed the local population from the streets. Yet marchers could still see some of the inhabitants in the distance who watched their horrendous trek. Of those who had escaped the Nazi death machine thus far, more than 50 percent succumbed during the four days of this march.

Those who survived all the way to Gunskirchen were deposited in a makeshift camp of prefabricated barracks that had been hastily erected in the middle of a pine forest near the village. But in a few days, corpses began to pile up everywhere. Even the barracks themselves filled up with the dead, and the dwindling group of survivors stacked up the bodies to form partitions that demarcated different "rooms" for those still alive in the barracks. The guards began to treat those who still clung to life like refuse. In this primitive camp, the SS no longer had an efficient gas chamber and crematorium at their disposal, complicating their murderous task greatly. At one point, an SS officer wanted to clear corpses and inmates out of the overcrowded barracks in which Bernie was housed to create some space and order. Carrying a heavy log, he began to swing at and hit both dead bodies and living inmates indiscriminately. Some tried to move, but many were simply too weak to comply, so that he only succeeded in knocking them to the ground where they writhed in pain. After flailing away for a time, the officer finally realized his efforts were futile, dropped the log, and left the barracks in frustration.

To relieve the overcrowding, some of Bernie's fellow inmates placed a dying man outside. But to ease his suffering a bit, they moved him under the eaves, as close to the building as possible, to protect him from the rain. Although they covered him with a thin blanket, rainwater dripped onto his body anyway. For several hours, steam rose from the covered body, indicating that he was still alive and warm. But after a while, the blanket stopped moving, and the rain continued to soak into the lifeless pile of fabric and limbs.

Bernie witnessed a reunion that took place at Gunskirchen between one of the teenagers in his group and the boy's father, whom the boy assumed had died after their separation at Auschwitz. Following tears of joy, the son entrusted to the father his precious ration of bread, asking him to save it for him for the following day. But during the night, the half-dead father, overcome with starvation, ate his son's ration. The following morning, the sobbing father confessed his deed to the son. A few days later, the father was dead. Bernie does not know whether the son survived. At the same time, Bernie recalls acts of incredible selflessness, as when an emaciated woman shared her meager piece of bread with a young boy whom she had never seen before.

With virtually no food left, and with the intolerable conditions made worse by an unseasonable cold spell (he remembers that it snowed on the first day of May), Bernie's body gradually joined the growing ranks of the Musulmänner. He remembers standing in a food line when a friend of his, who stood next to him, simply fell over and died. The Allied armies had not yet reached western Austria and Mauthausen, Gusen, or Gunskirchen.

"I am running out of adjectives. What can I say?" For a moment Bernie brought the conversation back to us and the present, but the past pulled him right back like a magnetic field with its two poles, one that spelled death, powerful and ever-present, and one that spelled survival, fragile and distant. "The mortality rate was 50 percent," he said. Half or more of the remaining inmates, who had survived the march from Mauthausen less than ten days earlier, died of murder, starvation, or exhaustion in the camp. Typhus raged, as well as dysentery, and many simply lost heart and gave up. Shortly before liberation, he felt it had become hopeless for him, too: "I truly felt I was not going to make it." All margins for survival were gone. Chaos reigned. Bernie became delirious intermittently. Death accelerated all around him at an ever more frightening pace, while he felt his own life ebbing away. Evidence was later discovered that the guards in this particular camp at Gunskirchen had gradually fed arsenic to the remaining inmates to hasten their deaths. Bernie was told that the Germans had administered three of five planned doses of the poison to the last inmates before fleeing in the face of the American advance. Had all five doses been ingested, presumably few, if any, of the prisoners would have seen the day of their liberation.

One afternoon in early May 1945, while artillery fire could be heard in the distance, a rumor raced through the concentration camp in the Gunskirchen pine forest that the German guards were gone. No raging battle was fought for the camp. No triumphant forces arrived for a jubilant liberation. Rather, there took place a curious, cautious, and gradual confirmation by the inmates themselves that their captors and tormentors had simply disappeared, vanished. Bernie paraphrases T. S. Eliot to describe the end of his captivity. "It came about not with a bang, but a whimper." He describes the initial mood, not as one of elation, but as a stunned sensation, as if the survivors had stepped out of darkness into the sunshine, with eyes unaccustomed to the light and the freedom they barely remembered. There was no energy left to celebrate, only an urgency to find something to eat. Along with most of the other inmates, Bernie headed toward the food storage area of the camp. Survivors stuffed into their clothes and into whatever containers they scrounged up any nourishment they could find, including the dried and vermin-infested ingredients of the soup that had been their only fare during the last days of their captivity. In their retreat, a few German soldiers had failed to get away in time and had been mobbed and killed by inmates. Bernie stripped one of these dead German soldiers of his pants and rolled up the legs, which were much too long for him, in order to replace his own pants, which were in tatters. He told me about this acquisition with a degree of embarrassment, excusing himself by saying that he was so very used to the presence of corpses by then.

Eventually, a Red Cross truck arrived out of nowhere. As Bernie tells me this, he misspeaks and says, "a Bread Cross truck." Out of this vehicle spilled primarily cookies. Even as he consumed some of these "delicacies," as he called the handouts, as he held cookies in his hands, he feared his failing body would not be helped by them. Indeed, they came too late for many who ate them and died anyway, or in some cases because of them. He gave some of the food he collected to an older Hungarian who promised to hide it for both of them in the rafters of the barracks, but the man deceived Bernie and ate it all.

. . .

Bernat Rosner was thirteen years and three months old on the day of his liberation. The Nazi reign of terror had left him suspended between life and death.

. . . .

During February and March 1945, the front moved ever closer to Kleinheubach in western Germany. Air raids increased as tactical strikes and strategic bombings that supported the advancing Allied army filled our days and nights. I remember the two nights Dresden was bombed: February 13 and 14. I had gotten myself a widely published map of Germany and an official military grid that could be superimposed on it. Horizontal and vertical lines were marked by numbers and letters. Then, as I listened to military reports of the bombing raids that were broadcast on the radio, I was able to follow the position of the planes in their paths over Germany. "Anton, Bertha vier" would correspond to coordinates on my map, and I could determine the approximate position of the bombers. I remember that when I tuned in on February 13, the first wave of bombers was already on its way out of Germany near the border of the Netherlands. The last wave was entering Germany over the Eifel mountains, southwest of Cologne. Many squadrons seemed to fly in various directions at first, but in fact all zeroed in eventually on Dresden. The death toll was particularly high—approximately 135,000 people were incinerated during the two nights—because half a million German refugees from the east had poured into the city. Goebbels's total war on the world had finally come home to the Germans themselves. A few Germans, however, didn't seem to have noticed. My teachers in Miltenberg continued to instruct me and my peers without skipping a beat, as if nothing was happening outside the red sandstone walls of our school building.

One day about forty of us between fourteen and sixteen years of age—the older ones had already been drafted—were told by the school principal to assemble in a large classroom. I sensed that something important was up. I remembered the advice my father gave me when he left on his last furlough in case I were ever drafted and saw action. Avoid the front line, he said, where the enemy could shoot you, and the back as well, where the fanatics might kill you. Stay in the middle where nobody would notice you. Now I decided to sit in the middle of this assembly so as not to attract attention. Wearing long overcoats, three SS officers entered briskly, stood in front of the class, and asked for volunteers to become officer-cadets in the SS. They emphasized that anyone signing up at this point, at the time of Germany's greatest need, was sure to advance rapidly in the SS ranks after the war was won. No one volunteered. The officers became frustrated and called us cowards. Then they produced a list of our names and harassed those of us whose fathers were officers in the army. They started in on a schoolmate of mine whose father was a retired captain in the German colonial army of World War I in Africa. Under their verbal pressure and abuse, he started to cry. I was one of the smallest in the group, so I hoped my chances of not being noticed or chosen were better than average. I was afraid they might pick some of us whether we volunteered or not. I was not the only one afraid—the fear throughout the classroom was palpable. Everyone sensed that these strangers had more power over us than our parents did; they could do anything they wanted with us, including taking us along with them. In the end, however, they left in disgust, empty-handed. They failed to persuade us, I think, because our village had a way of categorizing people into two types—those you knew and those you didn't. The simple fact that we didn't know those men remained more important in our assessment of them than the distinctions they tried to draw for us between heroes and cowards or Germany and her foreign enemies.

We sensed that a danger had passed. A few weeks later, our school was finally closed as heavy artillery fire came nearer. Particularly at night, machine-gun fire could be heard from several kilometers down the river. Then, on the morning of March 30, 1945—Good Friday—we discovered that the Americans had arrived at the northern edge of Kleinheubach, about 3 kilometers away. When I spotted one of their tanks in the distance, I felt a strange mixture of excitement and fear. In complete disarray, singly or in groups, German soldiers straggled away from the front, bartering on their way with civilians for food and cigarettes. A Wehrmacht captain tried to assemble a fighting unit from the group of uniformed stragglers, but many of them lacked weapons, and those who were still armed lacked ammunition. I remember some of them trying to enter homes in the Baugasse, to hide in basements from the Americans, but Kleinheubachers refused to let them in. One of the younger women in the village plied them with Schnaps and tried to persuade them to take a stand farther south against the advancing U.S. Army, at a position she claimed was more defensible. But, in reality, she simply wanted them to leave the village. The retreating soldiers had no more interest in fighting, and they quickly dispersed.

Suddenly, perhaps half an hour later, a well-dressed, fully armed SS contingent of about ten men arrived at our main square in squad cars. They had been given orders to assemble the Volkssturm of the village, that is, the people's militia consisting of all the old men and young boys, because they had failed to show up to defend the nearby village of Röllfeld against the American Third Army and its armada of tanks. The SS started up the Friedensstraße, the "Street of Peace" so called, in an attempt to round up the eligible males, most of whom were hiding in their cellars, and ended up ridiculing the first one they found, saying, "We can't fight the enemy by collecting corpses like this." It was the village electrician, an elderly, asthmatic stroke victim who walked with a limp. They sent him shuffling back home and themselves left the village around noon in their car, half an hour ahead of the first American tanks. After the first tank salvo hit one of the stone lions that adorned our main square, I fled along with my fellow villagers into our cellars to await the arrival of the victors, my unknown countrymen by birth.

Everyone was afraid of what the Americans might do to us. Would they rape the women and kill the children, as Nazi propaganda wanted us to believe? I hid for some time with a neighbor family in their cellar. Nothing seemed to be happening above us, and we knew we couldn't just stay there forever. After debating for an hour or so about what to do, a neighbor woman and I finally emerged with trepidation to see our first American. Our fears vanished. He was leaning back in a jeep, feet propped up on the dashboard, chewing on a long piece of straw that twitched up and down to the movement of his lips. He slowly turned his head toward us and just as slowly turned it away with a bored look. Then they came—wave after wave of American tanks. All day long they pushed south through the village, the chains rumbling and grinding their way over the cobblestones. One of them plowed into the rose garden of a house at a corner and turned ninety degrees to get a better bead on the road to the next village. My first impulse was to call the police. After all, the tank had ruined the neighbor's rose garden, his private property. Then I realized what a foolish notion this was. We were now occupied by the Third Army, each member of which sported distinctive triangular emblems in yellow, blue, and red on their upper arms. The gunfire had stopped. The fighting was over.

The same houses that previously had been festooned with red, white, and black Nazi banners on Hitler's birthdays and other Nazi celebrations suddenly sported white flags. Some of these flags were large and painstakingly sewn together from several bedsheets by those foresighted enough to anticipate this moment in history and to hide them until the American tanks approached. Others were merely sheets that would soon again cover mattresses or pillowcases, hastily displayed by more reluctant villagers who nevertheless didn't want to be left out of the general rush to surrender. Village gossip about these flags began immediately, and snickers about the relative political commitments of neighbors, now on display for everyone to see.

Within a week the Americans had built a temporary encampment next to Kleinheubach to house and feed the GIs who guarded a hastily set up prison camp for SS troops that had been captured in the region. Using the scant English I had learned in school, I asked to work in the U.S. Army kitchen. I was hired to clean pots, and at the end of the day I was allowed to scrape out whatever was left in them and take it to my family. We didn't know exactly what we were eating—a light cream sauce with reddish meat floating in it. The flavor was new to us, as well as the name: "shit on a shingle."

The presence of the Americans established a peacetime with wholly new ground rules. Soon girls and young women began to sport hand-tailored red skirts—skirts converted from Nazi flags. But the white circles with the black swastikas in the center were gone.

. . .

I was fourteen years and four months old on the day the Americans entered our village. It was a day of confusion for everyone in Kleinheubach. Some felt relieved, others depressed, and most tried to forget. No one wanted to think about what might be happening east of us in a town called Mauthausen, where the dying, killing, and torturing were still going on.

. . .

When we reached the end of the war in our stories, Bernie remarked to me, smiling, "I could tell who would survive and who wouldn't." The way he looked at me suggested that I would not have been among the survivors. I pressed him several times to confirm my assumption, but he never did. A year later, when he finally gave me a thumbnail sketch of a survivor, I realized that Bernie described himself. I did not recognize myself in this list of characteristics—instincts for the smallest opportunities;

mental toughness; the ability to roll with the punches; the ability not to be anguished by horrible sights, to insulate yourself from your surroundings; when faced with unremitting horrors, the ability to become callous, to armor yourself, to hibernate, to slow your breathing nearly to a halt. You had to hunker down, he summarized, to stick tight like a barnacle to its rock or underwater crevice, to cling to your spot, unaffected, while crashing waves rolled over you.

But then there is the author Ruth Klüger, another Auschwitz survivor, who believes that in reality it was mere chance if you stayed alive.

Fritz and his mother,
Hedwig Tubach, née Sawicki,
San Francisco, 1932.

Fritz and his father, mid-1930s,
Kleinheubach.

Fritz begins the first grade,
Kleinheubach, 1936.

Class photo of first and second grade,
Kleinheubach Volksschule, 1937.
Fritz is fourth from left, front row.

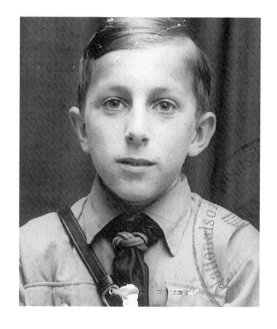

Fritz's father in *Wehrmacht*
uniform, 1941.

Fritz, 13 years old, in *Jungvolk*
uniform, 1943.

Fritz's stepmother,
Marie Tubach, née Zink, 1943.

Members of the German
occupation of Guernsey,
early 1945.
Fritz's father (seated at left) is
the first violinist.

Fritz,
San Francisco City College,
1949.

Bernie and Charles Merrill in
Modena, August 1945 (Bernie's
earliest surviving photograph).

Bernie (right) and Simcha at
Selvino, September 1945.

Bernie (far left) and friends at
Selvino, September 1945.

Group picture of Selvino
orphanage; Bernie is at the top
left.

Bernie's official U.S. entry
photograph, 1947.

Bernie at prep. school,
St. Louis, 1948.

Bernie as a U.S. Army officer
candidate at Cornell, 1954.

Bernie and Fritz revisit the Tab
railway station, 1990.

Ruins of the Tab synagogue
steps, 1990.

Potsdamer Platz, Berlin, 1997;
from left, Fritz, Bernie,
Manuela Bayer, and Sally
Tubach.

Fritz and Bernie, Alpe di Suisi,
Dolomites, 1999.

Letter from Charles Merrill, Sr.,
on Bernie's graduation from Cornell.

MERRILL'S LANDING
580 NORTH LAKE TRAIL
PALM BEACH, FLORIDA
May 11, 1954.

Dear Bernat:

From a member of the Personnel Department of my firm, who visited Cornell University for several days recently, I have learned of the wonderful record you have made at Cornell during your four years there.

This man has written in glowing terms of your achievements -- not only of the favorable impression you made on him, but the fact that you are one of the most popular young men on the campus, and, in addition to your popularity, you are liked, rsspected and admired by all your classmates and Fraternity brothers.

Knowing your history from the time you were a child, when Charles, Jr. first became interested in you, when he met you in Italy, and later had you broughtto the United States as his protege, naturally, I have been interested in you, and your career. The first time I met you I liked you, and I have always admired you greatly for your courage, -. and your ambition to make something worth while of the opportunities offered you.

What you have accomplished at Cornell speaks for itself; you have made an enviable record, and you have a very promising future before you at Harvard Law School. I am sure that Charles, Jr. is just as proud of you as I am.

It is with a great deal of pleasure that I enclose my graduation present to you, and with it go my heartiest congratulations and all good wishes for a job well done, and a happy and successful future.

Sincerely yours,

Charles Merrill

Mr. Bernat Rosner,
Cornell University,
ITHACA, New York.

CEM EK
ENC.

AFFIDAVIT IN LIEU OF BIRTH CERTIFICATE

I, BERNAT ROSNER, declare and swear as follows:

1. I was born in Budapest, Hungary on January 29, 1932.

2. In June, 1944, while Hungary was under German occupation during World War II, my entire family, including myself, was arrested by the German controlled authorities, and deported to a concentration camp in Poland. As part of this process, I was not permitted to retain or was deprived of all personal effects and documents, including any birth certificate or similar document.

3. Following the above events, I was the only survivor of my family (aged 13-1/2), and in view of post-World War II conditions, I did not attempt to return to Hungary. I spent the years 1945 through 1947 in various Western European Displaced Persons Camps as a "stateless person." I immigrated to the United States in January, 1948, and became a U. S. Citizen in May, 1953.

4. During the first 10 years following my departure from Hungary, political conditions made it impossible to attempt to secure any documents such as a birth certificate or copies thereof from that Country. Subsequent to that time, I have attempted to obtain such documents, but was advised by the relevant authorities that, because of the chaotic conditions that prevailed during and following World War II, no records consisting of or the equivalent to a birth certificate or similar evidence regarding the time and place of my birth were available or could be located.

5. In view of the above facts, which I have set forth in affidavits similar to this one, I have been granted U.S. Citizenship and a U.S. passport (which has been renewed several times) without the production of a birth certificate or similar document.

Bernat Rosner
Bernat Rosner

Subscribed and sworn to before
me this 9th day of October, 1986.

Judy E. Kirkland
Judy E. Kirkland, Notary Public in and
the County of Alameda, California.

OFFICIAL SEAL
JUDY E. KIRKLAND
NOTARY PUBLIC - CALIFORNIA
ALAMEDA COUNTY
My Comm. Expires March 7, 1989

Affidavit in lieu of birth certificate.

FIVE

. . .

Roads West

Behold, I send an angel before thee, to keep
thee in the way, and to bring thee into the place
which I have prepared.

— EXODUS 23:20

The war was over, the Nazi death machine was dismantled,
and Germany and much of Europe lay in ashes. Daily life for
most Germans had become a struggle for survival. No one
played the fiddle on the ruins. Lives were lived, not in the head-
lines or in the momentous decisions made far away in Washington, Moscow, and London, but in a bleak everyday full of
deprivations. For me, in Germany, there was hunger — not starvation — and an all-pervasive disorientation. What would the
days to come bring? And the year? And the future after that?
Would the conquerors take revenge for what we had done? The
eyes of the adults around me answered only in blank stares,
gripped as they were by fear and apprehension. For many Germans, everything was chaotic and subject to change at a moment's notice due to any number of things — random luck, individual seat-of-the-pants initiatives, the capacity to hunker
down, the ability to leap onto a train to get away or to go home,
if home was still there.

What of my future friend? The farther east in Europe you went, the more evident the destructive effects of the war became. Right after liberation, life for Bernie consisted of scrounging, scrounging, and more scrounging—for food and warm clothes. The eyes of the adults to whom Bernie might have turned to answer questions about his desperate present or precarious future were no longer there. Those adults who remained were competing with him in their own search for food.

Thus, the dice were thrown for everyone in a new unpredictable game of chance. Two teenaged boys—Bernie and I—in spite of disparities in our fates, stood on new playing fields, more similar now than before, to deal with the roll of the dice as best we could and to act as if we had a hand in determining our future.

During the first day of his liberation, after it became clear that their Nazi tormentors had fled, Bernie and a handful of fellow survivors found some red beets and cooked them up in a soup, just to put something into their empty stomachs. That night Bernie was gripped by a fever and fell very ill. The lice seemed to be winning the battle over his weakened body. Yet he joined the others the next day as the emaciated group spread out over the landscape in search of food. They stumbled upon a field of potatoes, dug them up, and ate them raw on the spot. Between 10:00 and 11:00 that morning a truck full of soldiers, with a white star on its side, arrived. Bernie called them "English." In fact they were Americans, but in Bernie's world at the time, no such fine distinctions existed. The soldiers tossed sweets to the scraggly crowd that clamored in German for *Brot*.

Late that afternoon the rumor spread that there was a German food storage depot nearby. The crowd hurried to locate it and looted it thoroughly. Bernie and Simcha found a can of *Rindfleisch*, or beef, intended for the German army. Bernie believes they must have used a door handle or some other metal object to force the can open. Without hesitation, they devoured its cold, greasy contents. Thus Bernie's first postliberation movable feast consisted of red beet soup, dirty raw potatoes, and greasy canned beef courtesy of the departed German army.

On the third day after liberation, Allied trucks arrived to pick up the aimless crowd of starved survivors and deposit them into barracks at the U.S. air base set up at Hörsching, not far from Linz. Bernie and his fellow survivors, including Simcha, were sprayed with DDT once again, as they had been at their arrival in Auschwitz, to delouse them. Though housed at the base, the survivors continued to forage the countryside for food. Bernie was not always lucky in what he found. On one of his search-and-eat expeditions, he looted a large box from a warehouse and lugged it several kilometers back to the barracks. When he opened it, he found nothing but packets of rough German army toilet paper, a booty with low bartering value.

Although the survivors gradually put more and more days between themselves and their Nazi imprisoners, still their fragile health continued to deteriorate. Bernie himself was getting weaker and weaker, "falling apart," as he puts it. Simcha also became very ill with repeated bouts of nausea. At one point, worried about losing him, Bernie raced down a flight of stairs in the barracks in which they were housed to look for an army doctor, and in doing so he lost his amulet, his prized identification tag that the kind silversmith, the Austrian inmate at Mauthausen, had made for him. Simcha survived. But the one tangible sign of an act of human kindness performed during Bernie's stay in the camps was gone. Even as he told me this, his sense of loss was palpable, and for a fleeting moment I had the irrational desire to get up and help him search for his amulet. I realized once again that Bernie is a man without mementos, without memorabilia or trinkets of any kind. And I think of the drawers and shelves in my home that store photos, letters, and tokens from the days of my youth.

The distinction between days began to blur for Bernie as his condition weakened. During this slide toward death, he happened to encounter a villager from Tab who had survived Auschwitz, including an infernal tour of duty working in the gas chambers. Most gas chamber workers were systematically killed by the Germans because they knew too much. As one of the few who survived, this man confirmed—definitively for Bernie—that his parents had been gassed. This news, along with the typhus he had contracted, the scant food rations, and the effects of the arsenic fed him by camp guards—all combined to make his spirit ebb further. Bernie lost consciousness. He remembers hallucinating about food and having nightmares about specters of death. When he regained consciousness, he found himself in a field hospital run by the Americans. His first thoughts were of Simcha. By now, he and his friend had reclaimed their real names, by which they could be recognized; the concentration camp number no longer counted. Bernie's weight at this time, at almost fourteen years of age, was between 26 and 27 kilograms, or about 58 pounds. I remember that when I was sick with tuberculosis at age twelve and a half I had weighed 70 pounds.

The condition of the two camp buddies gradually improved, and they were finally released from the sick ward and returned to their barracks. Bernie went on an exploratory trip to the nearby city of Linz, where he wandered by mistake into the Soviet-occupied zone. He had picked up some Russian words that he put to use now communicating with the Russian soldiers. Back in camp, rumors were spreading, which turned out to be true, that the entire region was to be incorporated into the Russian occupation zone. Now that the fact of his survival had sunk in, it was no longer just the search for food that preoccupied Bernie. As he began to realize that he might have a future after all, he started to worry about what would lie ahead. He thought about ways to go west, rather than east. He saw little reason to return to his native Hungarian village, and he knew that he would rather be in the U.S.-occupied zone should land swaps with the Soviets be made.

One day during the early summer months, Bernie hung around the Hörsching airstrip where an airplane was being loaded with well-fed and neatly groomed children his age. Shabbily dressed, undernourished street urchin that he was, Bernie observed them enviously and then clambered up the boarding ramp unobserved and hid underneath a seat, even though he didn't know where they were going. But the boy to whom the seat had been assigned discovered and reported him. Bernie was taken off the plane and whisked to an office. He asked for mercy from the officials by pleading with them in his fractured German: "Vater, Mutter kaput. Nicht essen. Wohin kann ich gehen?" (Father, mother dead, nothing to eat. Where can I go?). Bernie was very adept at communicating, and his plea moved the officials to tears. Nevertheless, the airplane departed without him. The American soldiers in charge of the flight gave him some C rations to try to console him.

Something else, however, came along that would transport him to other places. One day, a contingent of smartly uniformed, armed men arrived unexpectedly. Members of the Palestinian Jewish brigade, this trim fighting force had put itself in charge of concentration camp survivors. They wore spiffy British uniforms with the leaping stag insignia. Their goal was to organize the survivors' clandestine exodus to Palestine. The astonished camp inhabitants were told to get ready for transport south. Soon they were loaded onto twelve trucks whose rear canvas flaps were left open as they departed. These flaps were carefully closed, however, as the convoy approached the Austrian-Italian frontier, presumably to avoid a confrontation with border authorities, whom Bernie believes were probably aware of the nature of the transport and allowed its passage unchecked. Except for the border crossing, the flaps were kept open so that Bernie and the other youngsters could see the beauty of the Austrian and Italian Alps as they rolled by. He was "blown away," as he puts it.

After all his suffering for being Jewish, Bernie now came to know a proud group of young Jews not only in control of their destiny but also ready to guide others to a life of self-affirmation and dignity. But more important than pride for Bernie and his fellow refugees was the simple fact of being treated as human beings to be nurtured. He stood in awe before these uniformed Jews who for him were heroes, not victims. He became witness to a new chapter in Jewish history that was being written with their take-charge approach.

The truck convoy through southern Austria and over the Brenner Pass arrived after two days at Tarvisio in northern Italy, where the Jewish brigade set up camp. The young survivors were given medical care and all the nourishing and tasty food they could eat. Bernie felt he had "died and gone to heaven." But this stay was short, as they were soon transferred to a huge refugee camp in Bologna, where they received little attention, skimpy food rations, and none of the amenities enjoyed in Tarvisio. Bernie was forced to sleep on the floor once again. Euphoria changed to depression. The Bologna camp turned out to be a holding pen. Although it was a far cry from Mauthausen, life here was still miserable. After all, they had briefly been shown a ray of hope that was no longer visible. Bernie tried to earn a little pocket money for himself by carrying bags. For one entire day he devoted all his energies to helping an Italian family with their luggage but received nothing for his efforts.

Bernie and the others were moved again, this time to Modena, where they were housed in the Palazzo Ducale. Most of the huge building in the central square of this northern Italian town was occupied by the Jewish refugees, but one wing was used by the American army. After he had failed to earn anything from the Italian family, Bernie tried his luck with the Americans. He hung around with some other boys near the American gate to the Ducal Palace. The GIs passing through that gate in their jeeps represented everything that was enticing and far removed from the hunger and dreariness that still characterized his life. They were also a source of food, candy, and other good things that could be had through begging or performing services for them. By this time Bernie wore light summer shorts given him by an Englishman—a welcome change from the bulky trousers stripped off the dead German soldier. And since it was hot during this early Italian summer, he went barefoot. Several days went by during which Bernie advanced to the self-appointed post of unofficial doorman for the GIs. One day, a staff car drove up with four Americans inside. They turned out to be a team from the 88th Division, Fifth Army, in charge of repatriating prisoners, for the most part Italian civilians who had been arrested on suspicion of having collaborated with the Germans. As he had so many times before, Bernie approached one of these strangers and offered to carry his duffel bag. Entrusted with the bag, Bernie preceded the soldier into the interior of the American quarters. All the owner of the duffel bag could see as he followed behind the boy—as he was to tell Bernie later—was the heavy bag over small shoulders and bare feet underneath. This encounter would change Bernie's life forever.

For the next five days, after he finished his debriefing work, the twenty-four-year-old soldier, whose name was Charles Merrill, Jr., son of the founder of the renowned New York brokerage and banking house, spent several hours talking with the thirteen-year-old village orphan.[1] They spoke broken German together, the one language they had in common. Bernie poured out the story of his life to Merrill, who was deeply moved. On two visits to Hungary before the outbreak of World War II, the young Merrill had developed a liking for its people. He now gave the Hungarian boy food, bought him ice cream, invited him to restaurants, and took him to a boxing match. They took a ride in a horse-drawn carriage together. But most important, they became friends.

As Charles Merrill related to me later, perhaps a thousand survivors ready to show their tattooed numbers from Auschwitz, Mauthausen, Dachau, and other camps were there in Modena under British and American administration, along with some Palestinian Jewish soldiers who boosted their morale. What impressed him about the teenage Bernat was his energy, upbeat personality, and courtesy. He did not see in him so much the lost waif as I had assumed. Rather, Bernat Rosner appeared to the American GI as a youngster ready to take on the world, if only it gave him a chance.

Approximately one year had passed since the train with the Rosners on it had left Kaposvar for Auschwitz. Bernie had passed through the vortex of the maelstrom and emerged alive. And now, in July 1945, his life took a turn for the good. For the first time "since he left home," as Bernie puts it, he experienced a human bond that provided him with warmth and support. But Charles Merrill was transferred in the line of duty, so he and Bernie exchanged addresses and bade each other farewell.

. . .

As he now tells me about his encounter with Charles Merrill, Jr., or "Charlie," as he calls him, Bernie employs the present tense. "Now we'll see what happens next." Only twice before in his recollection had a moment in his past overwhelmed the present so completely by its force: the body search of his mother by Nazis on the day the Jews were forced out of their homes and several months later at Mauthausen when he faced the notorious quarry steps. But this moment from the past in Modena made its appearance in the present tense as something benign and good.

. . .

During late summer 1945, Bernie, along with a group of other youngsters with the same background, was transferred to Piazzatore, a summer camp run by a Zionist organization for Jewish-Italian children. But the camp was to be shut down in the fall, and the refugee children would have to be moved again. The person in charge of the organization was Moshe Z'iri, a deeply committed Zionist, passionate about the fate of his charges and about the destiny of a country—Israel—not yet created. While the teenage Auschwitz survivors from Hungary had no idea what was going to happen next, Moshe Z'iri tried to manage the chaotic postwar situation to their advantage. He assured them that he would find solutions and places for them to go on their hazardous exodus to Palestine. And he did.

Bernie had never heard of the places they would see, Italian towns that became way stations in the refugees' uncertain movements. Moods of hope and despair were measured by the random quality of life these various locales presented. And finally, there was Selvino, a beautiful little town in the Italian Alps north of Bergamo where they arrived in September 1945. Here they were housed in what was originally built by the fascist regime as a resort for tubercular children. The name of this resort was Sciesopoli. An idyllic period ensued, sweet days in beautiful surroundings. Bernie was happy there, and fortune willed that he would stay a long time, almost a year and a half, until February 1947.

Shortly after their arrival in Selvino, Moshe Z'iri arranged a convocation to celebrate Rosh Hashanah with the spiritually deprived youngsters. It was their first opportunity to return to the religious traditions stifled by the Nazis before their internment. For Bernie and his Orthodox family, religious life had come to an end in the brickyard near the Tab railroad station. Moshe Z'iri wanted to lead these orphans back to familiar religious habits. But the service had to be stopped when the entire group of youngsters began to wail and sob. The rituals so long forbidden only brought forth memories of the terrible losses they had suffered, especially the loss of their families, with whom they had practiced their faith.

Despite this failed attempt at religious revival, for the first time since he was taken from his home, Bernie enjoyed at Selvino a predictable daily life, guided by a social order in which activities were arranged both for the good of all and for the benefit of the individual. He also enjoyed something approaching regular schooling. Selvino had a sizable library of Hebrew texts, including translations from European and American literature, and devoted teachers opened up a world of humanistic learning for him. He devoured these books, including a Hebrew translation of Irving Stone's biography of Vincent van Gogh. Another Hebrew translation, of Upton Sinclair's *The Jungle*, made him aware of the existence of social inequalities in the United States. A generalized pro-socialist ideology, which implied a rejection of the capitalism that America stood for, guided the camp's leadership. Yet another kind of America reached the camp as well—the America of glamour. In films like *Sotto il cielo di Hawaii*, Hollywood stars like Alan Ladd and Rita Hayworth moved in a fabulous world of make-believe and wealth. The language of the subtitles did not matter—Italian, English, or whatever. It was the images that made a powerful impression of a magic kingdom beyond the horizon to the west.

The camp language at Selvino was Yiddish, a language understood by all in spite of their different European origins. Hebrew was vigorously promoted by the camp authorities, and Bernie was employed to teach it to his peers. The small group of Mauthausen survivors, six boys including Bernie and Simcha, spoke to each other in their native Hungarian. The mode of this instruction was quite different from the Orthodox rigidity of the Hebrew school way back in the village of Tab. Now Bernie was introduced to secular learning, and he loved it. There were even dances for the growing teenagers, and the forbidden activity of climbing the fence to explore the surrounding countryside. As weeks turned into months, a daily routine, so long denied them, reestablished a sense of normalcy in their lives.

The primary purpose of instruction at Selvino was to mold young minds to the Zionist cause, to inculcate in the survivors the image of a heroic "New Jew" who was ready to take the collective future of the Jewish survivors and make it part of what was to become the nation of Israel. This fervent message was presented with great intensity by their Zionist role model, Moshe Z'iri, who appeared to these impressionable young people as a towering giant. A model of leadership, he inculcated in the young Bernie a deep sense of his own worth. One day the entire camp went to Milan to attend a performance of Bizet's "Carmen." Afterward, they participated in a Zionist demonstration advocating the creation of a Jewish state in Palestine. Moshe Z'iri was everywhere, dealing with the past, organizing the present, and preparing for the future of his young disciples.

It was after his liberation and particularly during his stay in Selvino that Bernie realized that religion had lost its grip on him. In this camp he was imbued with secular teachings and inspired by the tanned, muscular soldiers who discarded the demeaning, submissive behavior of the people in the Diaspora and the blind adherence to the belief that God will provide. God had not done so in Auschwitz. Furthermore, his Orthodox faith had been tied to his immediate family, now gone. Still, he learned that a sister of his mother had survived the Holocaust. Now she wrote him from the land that was to become Israel and exhorted him to return to the rituals and practices of his Orthodox faith. She asked him to join her in the ultraconservative religious enclave, Mea Sh'arim, that had been created in Jerusalem. But return to an Orthodox life held no attraction for Bernie, and he declined to join this aunt.

To the leaders of the camp, Bernie was a bright prospect—energetic, intelligent, able to think on his feet, and, more important, fluent in Hebrew. He also had a working knowledge of German and Italian. Above all, he had survived Auschwitz, Mauthausen, and Gusen, and these sharp survival instincts made him a natural candidate for the exodus to Palestine. Camp chores were performed by the young initiates in such a way as to nurture a spirit of solidarity with each other and with the larger Zionist cause. Bernie was told—many times—that it was his duty to go to Palestine.

Yet he thought of Charlie, who had left him his military address. Bernie had written his GI friend earlier and gotten a reply toward the end of August. He took good care of this precious letter, and he and Charlie started to correspond regularly. To ensure his recovery to complete health, Charlie sent Bernie a box of Puretest Plenamin vitamins as a supplement to his camp food rations. To this day Bernie keeps the cardboard box that contained those pills—one of the first mementos he was able to save. The box now holds photos from the Italian camps.

In the autumn Bernie received the most important single document of his life—a letter dated November 4, 1945, from Charles Merrill, Jr., now discharged from the military and living in the United States. Already a married family man at twenty-four, the former GI now offered the Jewish-Hungarian concentration camp survivor a different alternative and a new opportunity: "Wenn ich Reisemoeglichkeit und Visum fuer Dich bekommen koennte, wuerdest Du dann nach Amerika kommen wollen, um mit uns als unser Sohn zu leben?" (If I can arrange for travel and a visa for you, would you then want to come to America to live with us as our son?). Charles Merrill encouraged Bernie to make his own decision and ended with a generous offer of help, regardless of his decision: "Und ganz gleich, so Du bist und was Du tun willst, lasse mich bitte immer wissen, was ich fuer dich tun kann" (And whatever you decide and are and want, please always let me know what I can do for you). It is a strange irony that this most important letter in Bernie's life was written in German. Although grammatically imperfect, the proposal was a perfect example of humanity.

Even though the war had ended in August 1945 with the dropping of the atomic bomb on Hiroshima, in Europe chaos continued for a long time. In this chaos, a Jewish boy from Tab, Hungary, had to make the biggest decision of his life. On the one hand, he was being urged to commit himself to a collective and follow the call of the Zionist cause to Palestine. Bernie realized that even the utopia of a Zionist future would have disadvantages. To choose Palestine would mean, first of all, an internment camp on Cyprus to which the British authorities regularly consigned "illegal" Jews heading for that country. The thought of being imprisoned in yet another camp surrounded by barbed wire appalled him. And in spite of all the individual attention Bernie received at Selvino, he did not fail to notice that it was a collective force that attempted to mold the young concentration camp survivors. He was torn by an inner conflict between his sense of solidarity with and pride in belonging to a group of Jews who were no longer victims and his intense desire for personal freedom, his need to escape restraints, to not be fenced in physically or mentally. In his childhood, he had dreamed of a beautiful life to be lived if only he could follow the sun.

Now he discovered that certain things sat deeper in him than his pride and newfound solidarity with the Palestinian cause his Zionist mentor had outlined for him. He wanted to have a family again.

When Bernie accepted Charlie's offer, Moshe Z'iri's reaction was swift. In a passionate face-to-face encounter, the "shit hit the fan," as Bernie recalls. Moshe Z'iri could be uncompromisingly brutal in pursuing his cause. Bernie was put under intense pressure to change his mind. He was accused of being a traitor and ostracized as an outsider. A rumor spread through the camp that Charles Merrill was planning to abduct Bernie to America and turn him into a Catholic priest. But Bernie stood by the risky decision that was certain to burn an important bridge behind him. And indeed, the road to a future in Palestine closed for him now. Yet it would take an excruciatingly long time before the American sponsorship could be implemented. It would not be an easy thing, and Bernie's decision to opt for America made life at Selvino more difficult.

By the end of 1946, Bernie was still at Selvino when a large group of Eastern European Jewish children arrived. These children, who had grown up in or escaped to parts of the Soviet Union the Germans failed to reach, had not been in concentration camps. They had different stories to tell than the smaller group of camp survivors whom Moshe Z'iri initially brought to Selvino and who were bound by their common suffering. By then, the total population of the children's home had grown to approximately one hundred fifty youngsters, and only a small nucleus of Auschwitz-Mauthausen-Gusen survivors was left. In late 1946 the time had come to say farewell to his concentration camp buddy, Simcha, who was headed for Palestine via Cyprus. They didn't know whether they would ever meet again.

When Bernie's stay in Selvino ended in February 1947, the roll of the dice was not favorable. He and the other Selvino veterans whose destinations were other than Palestine were moved to a huge, squalid refugee camp at Cremona, where life suddenly took a downward turn. Bernie grew increasingly depressed. By the autumn, however, a way out of the Cremona squalor finally opened up. In a letter, Charles Merrill encouraged him to contact an Italian woman in Lucca who had worked in the underground during the war. She had found an Italian family in Viareggio willing to accept Bernie as a boarder. The bill, of course, was paid by Merrill. This Italian family was welcoming and kind and gave Bernie an enduring feeling of warmth for Italians. Bernie's stay of several months in Viareggio ended his life in the various camps of war-torn Europe, from the Nazi death camps to several postwar refugee camps.

In the meantime, his sponsor worked hard to secure a U.S. entry visa for Bernie. In November 1947, two years after Bernie received Charlie's letter offering to sponsor him, papers were finally approved and Bernie made his way to Genoa to pick them up. Because Bernie possessed no passport, birth certificate, or other papers to verify his identity or origins, a special document for a stateless person had to be prepared by the U.S. Consulate to permit him to emigrate to the United States. He probably would not have been able to enter the United States at all had it not been for Charles Merrill's persistent efforts and the substantial amounts of money he spent to cut through bureaucratic red tape.

Now America started to loom on Bernie's horizon as something tangible. With the Hungarian-English dictionary Charlie sent him, Bernie studied English feverishly. He took up the painstaking task of tackling Robert Louis Stevenson's *Treasure Island* for the next six weeks. It was hard work. By referring to the dictionary, he managed to translate twenty-eight pages of the adventure novel—the best he could do to prepare himself for the next step in his life, a leap across the Atlantic to the United States of America.

Charles Merrill sent him money for the journey. Bernie planned to travel cheaply by freighter to New York, but Charlie wouldn't hear of it. Only a swift airplane flight from Europe to America would do for Bernat Rosner. So it happened that the dice rolled for Bernie once again—winning dice, this time. On January 17, 1948, two weeks before his sixteenth birthday, he checked in for a TWA flight in Rome that was bound for New York's La Guardia Airport via Geneva, Paris, London, and Newfoundland. He had papers in hand, some money in his pocket, and his sponsor, Charlie, in the New World. This time no Nazi thugs, no government officials or any of the myriad authorities, uniformed or civilian, good or evil, that had crossed his path over the years appeared to question his moves or to hold power over him. No one had the authority to prevent Bernat Rosner from boarding the airplane that would take him west.

· · ·

At the end of the war, there were no dice to roll for me, or so it seemed at first. Physical mobility was restricted to the village and its surrounding fields and forests. Life as we knew it changed radically for Germans, Nazis and non-Nazis alike. For practical purposes, the outside world ceased to exist. Village elders went so far as to call a meeting to discuss whether it was possible for Kleinheubach to survive on its own, seceding in effect from what remained of Germany. It was thought that the apple harvest from the thousands of apple trees owned by villagers constituted an important trading asset that might assure economic autonomy. Although the meeting was held in the Gasthaus zur schönen Aussicht, with its appropriately ironic double meaning of "beautiful view" and "promising prospects," nothing came of this village utopia.

The Americans did not permit Germans to bear firearms, with the result that hunting became impossible and wild boars descended from the Odenwald mountains to damage the spring crops in the fields. My grandfather tried to fashion metal bows and arrows in his blacksmith shop to shoot them, but no one organized a posse to go after the destructive foragers. Schools closed, and no one knew when they would open again. Many adult males either had been killed in the war or were missing in action. Most ended up in POW camps throughout Europe and North America. Some were on their way home by foot from the various collapsed fronts of the war. A few had returned before the end, dismissed from the army because of mental or physical debilities. The occupying American army posted a declaration on the village bulletin board that any harm done to a GI would cause the village to be razed to the ground. They displayed another poster nearby: an enlarged photograph of a mass grave in the Warsaw ghetto. That horrifying image of emaciated corpses hanging on the walls of the open pit has never left me.

All weapons and Nazi flags and insignia had to be delivered to the town hall. I decided to turn in my father's officer's dagger, adorned with an ivory handle and a silver oak leaf cluster, which he had left at home during his last leave from his Channel Islands post. As I carried it toward the town hall, an American soldier spotted it, hurried up to me, and ordered me to hand it over to him. He left the scene with this special memento of World War II stashed under his coat.

We, the young, felt an unfamiliar freedom from restraint. No more marching, no more uniforms, and, most of all, few orders from the adults, who were too busy with our day-to-day survival to perform their pedagogical duties. We let our hair grow long. During the first days after occupation, we hung around the American tank parked on the Hirschplatz, the village square, where just a few days earlier the last contingency of the SS had tried to rally the Volkssturm of Kleinheubach to defend the fatherland. Now the GIs sat on their tank and tossed candy to us. When our distinguished grammar school principal, the bald-headed *Oberlehrer* Kahlert, rode by perched high on his old-fashioned bicycle, we automatically raised our arms and saluted him with an accustomed "Heil Hitler." The GIs found this hilarious, and all joined in shouting "Sieg Heil! Sieg Heil!" over and over at our mentor, who pedaled away from the scene as fast as he could. Most of the soldiers were white, but the few black soldiers in the occupation force were especially friendly and nice to us as they tossed candy down from their tanks. While the village and our part of Germany obviously were controlled by the Americans, we, the village youngsters, believed that the streets and nearby fields and forests belonged to us.

Everything American, which until recently had been condemned as decadent, now had an enticing, glamorous aura. Before the collapse, school officials showed us a Nazi propaganda film designed to instill in us a hatred for American "decadence"—a clip of Benny Goodman playing his clarinet while young Americans jumped in the aisles of a music hall to syncopated rhythms. The somber Nazi commentary proclaimed that the Jew, Goodman, was seducing American youth and that we must defend ourselves against such dangers. Now that Benny Goodman's music had arrived, and Tommy Dorsey's band as well, we loved it, particularly because it still tasted a bit like forbidden fruit. We avidly memorized the lyrics to "Chattanooga Choo Choo" and "Hey Bob a-Ree Bob," only half understanding what we were singing but believing that this was truly America. One of the first German postwar hits was a love duet in which the lovers promised each other to move to Arkansas or Arizona and raise green beans together.

The Americans instituted an ineffectual denazification and reeducation program that included a questionnaire with 132 questions to be completed by all adult Germans. As I had the only typewriter in our street, I filled out a lot of questionnaires for our neighbors, who would give me a few details and let me invent the rest. Some questions were easy, such as whether or not an old woman had served in the Waffen-SS. Others were more difficult, for example, when it came to Nazi affiliations and sympathies. Everyone was classified into five categories, ranging from war criminal down to innocent. Most fell somewhere in the middle as sympathizers or activists, or as just plain folk who had kept their mouths shut. I received some food in return for my typing services and in some cases for my inventiveness.

The Americans had a hard time finding Germans politically acceptable enough to teach the young and required prospective teaching candidates to write an essay about the three persons they admired most in history. One of the candidates, whose essay I typed, told me that among the most popular triads were "Jesus Christ, George Washington, and Franklin Delano Roosevelt" and "Jesus Christ, Abraham Lincoln, and Albert Einstein." Apparently, all the candidates made sure that one or two on their list of purported favorites were Americans.

Many Germans wanted to believe at first that the clock had been reset to a "zero hour" (*Stunde Null*). It was a convenient way to forget that this German clock had been running punctually before and throughout the war, keeping time with the Nazi death machine. The fact was, the clock of the Third Reich had merely stopped at the end of the war, and the innocence of a zero hour was a form of self-deception that the Germans maintained for a time. The seductive glamour of America, exciting as it was for the young, could not dispel the general gloom. After all, the American presence had more to do with tanks than with films and music during the immediate postwar years. There was much talk about democracy and what it might mean. At first it was nothing but a term vaguely related in our minds to our collective bad conscience about our Nazi crimes.

A few weeks after the war ended, I was practicing my English with an American officer, a "chicken" colonel—a term I learned from a GI. The epithet derived from the small silver eagle insignia on his lapel. I stood next to the colonel's jeep near our village square. In the middle of our exchange, the American suddenly exclaimed angrily, "You Germans killed the Jews and you all knew about it!" I was shocked and recoiled from his remark. Instinctively, I denied this accusation to the officer's face, but what I was denying was the second part of his claim. I, along with my fellow villagers, had seen the photographs of the mass graves of the Warsaw ghetto that the U.S. Army posted on the town hall bulletin board. From these photographs, we all knew what had happened. I believed that we Germans had done it, but when faced with the accusation, I couldn't believe that people of the village I passed in the streets everyday—let alone members of my own family—knew what had happened in the concentration camps. Along with everyone else, I attributed the atrocities to *some* Germans, not all Germans—to the SS, above all, and, more precisely, to the SD, a specially trained elite within the SS. I had a personal reason to suspect them, because I came in contact with a group of such officers.

When the war ended, the Americans set up a temporary camp of SS prisoners in the park of the Löwenstein castle. Guarded by an armed GI, four of these prisoners were assigned to work in my grandfather's blacksmith shop on odd jobs required to maintain the camp. I inherited an Eisenhower jacket and a pair of U.S. Army boots from the American guard, who hailed from St. Louis—the only boots I had for the winter. I had outgrown the old German pair that had given me frostbite the year before. This soldier would leave his loaded rifle downstairs in the blacksmith shop while he came upstairs to spend time with my family to alleviate his homesickness. That unguarded rifle was within reach of the SS prisoners, all in their twenties, but they never dared to touch it. The anxiety they exuded was palpable.

At this point, ordinary German POWs would have had no reason to be so afraid in American hands. So I suspected that these prisoners were trying to hide something horrendous. They insisted that they had been part of a fighting unit that had had nothing to do with concentration camps. One claimed to have been an ordinary soldier whose unit was incorporated into the SS against its will. But his story did not sound credible to me. In fact, these young men, with abject fear in their eyes, groveled in front of me, a fourteen-year-old, who had no power over them. They oozed guilt and fear. I cannot prove it, but I am convinced they were guilty of atrocities. The world had turned upside down. Just three weeks earlier I had seen their likes, in smart

SS uniforms, cocky and condescending, drive through our village ready to machine-gun anyone who disagreed with them. Now, at sunset and before the evening curfew began, I recall that many villagers collected outside the hastily erected barbed-wire fence in the castle park and threw food over to the SS prisoners, who evidently did not have enough to eat. I don't remember whether we gave anything to the four who worked in our blacksmith shop, but their American guard ordered them to stack our firewood for the winter, and of course they obeyed.

· · ·

The red, white, and black flags were gone, and it was as if the swastika had never existed. Yet my village, like the rest of Germany, had been caught up in the collective madness, in the deadly mix of order and rage that characterized the Nazi movement. Divisions in the village, divided loyalties in families, and even fissures within individual souls characterized quiet struggles behind the scenes, struggles not visible in public.

When the war was over, everyone wanted to believe that no one had been for it. And no one admitted they knew about the Holocaust, or at least not its magnitude. After we all saw the pictures of atrocities, confusion reigned and a wide spectrum of reactions was voiced, everything from "Es stimmt nicht" (It's not true), to the "Ich habe Schlimmes geahnt" (I suspected as much; I suspected terrible things) of my stepgrandfather. Everyone asked, "Now what's going to happen to us?" What I heard most often was, "*Others* did it—the *bad* Germans." The Nuremberg trials of the top Nazi criminals provided average

Germans, imbued with a hierarchical sense of society, with a convenient excuse to rid ourselves of feelings of personal guilt or complicity. This deep belief in hierarchy also allowed even those directly implicated to hide behind the claim that they had only followed orders. I remember that the widely reported trials were received with relief in the village. Here they sat in the dock—fat Hermann Goering, rigid General Keitel, crazy Rudolf Hess, and all the others. *They* had done it. Good riddance. *We* are innocent. Let's go on with our lives.

. . .

Immediately following the war, for those who preferred to deny Nazi collaboration and to embrace the idea of a zero hour, the moment had come not to worry about the past but to start building the next Germany. The voices of those who had opposed the Third Reich were too few in Kleinheubach and too feeble for the most part to tell their story. They also feared they would be drawn into a new political arena they did not understand. And they had failed, after all, to make a difference when it would have counted. So why speak up now? They did not fit into the new social order that was being shaped. But village memories are long and precise. They are particularly adept at fixing on individual behavior that deviates from the norm, in recording and criticizing transgressions, remembered and handed down. For centuries the village memory has provided the backbone for local customs, as perpetuator and enforcer. It is as effective and normative as are the laws of the courts and the state.

For most villagers, politics was like the weather. Since you had no control over it, you accepted it. If hailstones fell on others, it was their problem, but you tried to protect yourself from whatever adversities threatened you. The Nazi movement was generally accepted in Kleinheubach. Many paid their party dues, and some became active collaborators. A few fanatics among the Nazi activists were feared by most people, however. Herr ter Meer, for one, had a nervous tick that contracted his chin and neck in a grotesque manner. Even to the friends he passed in the street on a shopping errand, he would jerk his right arm straight out in front of him and pull the outstretched hand right back to his chest in a rapid Nazi salute. Most people kept their distance, since he reported anyone he suspected of anti-Nazi sentiment, which included, of course, neighbors with whom he had any kind of dispute, political or not.

Among the other extremists were a couple who ordered their two sons to volunteer for the SS as soon as they were old enough. Both were killed on the Russian front, and the parents were proud of the "heroes" they had sacrificed for the Third Reich. It would have made no more sense to argue politics with people like that than to rage against a storm or a drought. They were more feared than crazy Herr ter Meer, because their sacrifice had given them a special legitimacy. The family "inherited" one of the finest Jewish houses on the Hauptstraße, and a question as to how they came into its possession would have put the poser at grave risk.

There were the many low-ranking petit bourgeois Nazis as well, who tried to climb as fast as possible the social ladder the movement provided them. For their eagerness, they were openly ridiculed at times, not because of their politics, which would have been dangerous, but because their behavior was socially unacceptable and could therefore be attacked safely. At one point, all the Nazi youth groups joined with the NSKK (Nazi motorized brigade), the NSDAP, and the SA in preparation for a local parade in the spacious park of the Prince of Löwenstein's castle. When everyone was lined up and the *Ortsgruppenleiter* (head of the Nazi Party) of the village had to leave the premises for some reason, he ordered one of his underlings, a simple SA man, to take over temporarily. This fellow jumped to attention and clicked his heels so hard that he lifted himself off the ground. At the same time, in his excitement he shrieked out a command in which he used the wrong pronoun: "Alles hört auf *mir!*"—the equivalent of saying "Everyone listen to I!" Struck by his ridiculous posturing, we all started to snicker, and decorum deteriorated when giggles spread through the crowd. I know now that this ridiculous figure would have killed anyone, Jewish or Christian, for the sake of a permanent promotion in the party.

Finally, there was my grammar school teacher, Fräulein Gundelfinger, who had given me the anti-Semitic primer when I was in second grade. The morning after the party election of 1938, she entered the classroom to announce that thirteen Kleinheubachers had voted against Hitler. She had us repeat in unison, "Pfui, pfui, pfui!" (For shame!). One of the thirteen had been Hermann Bohn, of course, my buddy Ludwig's father. Hermann Bohn was a devotee of his World War I idol, General Luddendorff, who believed that the Bolsheviks, Nazis, Catholics, and Jews had united in a global conspiracy against Germany and that Hitler was merely the willing tool of these "forces" who wanted to destroy the German soul. Not only did Hermann Bohn believe these theories, he often behaved in socially defiant ways. He carted manure out to his fields on Sundays, for example, because he disliked the Catholic church even more than Hitler. He was someone you did not cross, because he was large and formidable. Aside from that he was the best butcher in the village; he made the finest *Fleischwurst* in the area.

Hermann Bohn's idiosyncratic delusional politics were not typical or representative of anything but his own eccentricity. There was, however, some serious, even if muted, resistance to the Nazi regime in our village. I remember a book printer, well known to me because he lived only two blocks from my grandmother's house. I could still just make out the large faded lettering on one wall of his house during a visit in 1999: "Josef Dier, Buchdruckerei." In 1934, a year after the Nazis came to power, Herr Dier had the courage to publish the pamphlet that the Protestant parson of the village, Pfarrer Gottlieb Wagner, had written about the history of the Jews of Kleinheubach, "Geschichte der Jüdischen Gemeinde zu Kleinheubach a.M." This text chronicled the presence of Jews in Kleinheubach from the first evidence in 1326 until 1933. Herr Dier was imprisoned for more than a year in the Dachau concentration camp for his antifascist beliefs.

During my father's heyday in the party, he once ran into Josef Dier and offered him a ride to the next village in a borrowed official car. As my father told us after the encounter, he wanted to know from someone who had been there about conditions in Dachau, so he asked Dier about his experience during this ride. Instead of answering, Dier insisted that my father stop the car immediately and let him out. Despite my father's repeated reassurances that he meant no harm with the question, that he was only curious, Dier refused to answer and again demanded to be let out. He walked away without a word. My father came home quite upset to have been considered a dangerous informer by a neighbor he had liked despite their political differences.

Years later, in November 1943, during my father's last furlough from the front, I was walking with him to the post office when we ran into Josef Dier. Dier was no longer quite the hunted person he had been before the war. He asked my father, "Well, Albert, do you think you'll win this war?" clearly implying that Germany would not win. Now it was my father's turn to leave the scene in silence. If he had agreed with Herr Dier, which he probably did by then, it would have constituted treason. And if he had reported Herr Dier, he would most likely have caused his death, which he certainly didn't want. I was old enough to know that their brief exchange next to our village post office had contained political dangers for both of them. My father no longer had the psychological upper hand over this brave dissident.

Once the war started, political conflicts that existed in the village became less important as people became more absorbed in daily concerns about the war and how it would affect them personally. The significant stories of resistance, such as they were, were lived out elsewhere, in the big cities—Munich, Leip-zig, Berlin. At the end of the war, there was no time to reflect on what had happened. Josef Dier, however, according to vil-lage lore, waited patiently for Herr ter Meer—who had left with the SS during the German retreat in 1945—to return home. It was said that when the returning Nazi passed by Dier's house, Dier greeted ter Meer, saying, "We've been waiting for your re-turn." Ter Meer was subsequently arrested by the U.S. military police and jailed for several months. But it wasn't long until he was freed, and he rapidly blended into postwar village life along with the rest of us.

. . .

In the first months after the war, everyone was caught in the consequences of the Third Reich, which produced within the shattered country an all-pervasive silence and a dull search for food, for lost relatives, for housing, for firewood, and for some-thing with exchange value on the black market. A cold feeling gripped both body and mind, and the darkness inside mirrored the darkness of the winter nights.

Like many other families, the Tubach family was distraught. My grandmother cried every day for her missing sons and for grandchildren not yet found in the destroyed cities. Her house at the edge of the village was slated to be occupied by the Ameri-can army, but when they saw my grandmother, my nearly blind grandfather, my aunt who was ill, and her daughter in the lat-ter stages of a pregnancy, the Americans let them stay. The con-fusion was less profound in the home of my stepmother. None of the immediate members of the Zink family had ever participated actively in the Nazi cause, as some of the Tubachs had. There was no shattered faith. No political dreams had been destroyed with which they had identified. The Zink family's opposition to Hitler provided a sense of continuity to their lives. And there was work to be done in the blacksmith shop, horses to be shod, fresh wooden wheels to be enclosed in iron hoops, and, most of all, fields to be tended in the spring. The oddly comforting motto, "If you want to eat, you have to work," helped to guide me through the chaos. I still remember the deep satisfaction I felt at the end of one autumn harvest day in 1945 sitting, tired from work, on the cow-drawn wagon that was filled with sacks of potatoes we had hoed up from our fields all day long.

School started again shortly before the onslaught of a bitter cold wave. In the unheated classrooms, the frost that stuck to the inside of the window panes when we arrived remained for hours before it thawed from our collective body heat. My "new" GI boots were also too tight for my frostbitten feet.

Despite denazification, the same teachers returned to take up instruction where they had left off before the collapse of our thousand-year Reich. Although the principal, an avowed Nazi, was no longer in charge of the *Gymnasium*, he returned as a regular teacher. German was his subject, and he regaled us with themes such as "What needs to be nourished in society must start in the family"—themes that resembled those of the Nazi period. They were just as irrelevant to our current reality as they had been before.

The history teacher returned as if nothing had happened since he stopped teaching nine months earlier. But the "Heil Hitler" greeting on his entry into the classroom was dropped in favor of a snappy "Grüß Gott," followed by a prayer in Latin. In spring 1945 he had ended our survey of European history with the Germanic invasions of the Roman Empire, having arrived in our slow trek through European history at around the year 100 B.C. We had learned that morally pure Teutonic tribes, the Cimbri and Teutonici in particular, had swept in from the north to free the enfeebled Romans from their decadent ways of life. Now, at the end of 1945, the same teacher described the same Germanic invasion and the same battle of Aquae Sextiae, but this time he instructed us that the cosmopolitan Romans were defending civilization against the onslaught of the barbaric Teutons from the north. Where did he stand? I asked myself. He had switched sides without breaking his pedagogical stride. He lost all credibility in my eyes at that moment, and from then on, I devised ways of interrupting classes just below the threshold of detection. I brought an assortment of discarded cogwheels and bolts from our blacksmith shop and furtively rolled them on the floor under the desks toward the front of the classroom. They made a satisfyingly disruptive noise, but after several days the trajectory of these subversive bullets was traced to me, and I was nearly expelled.

Disorder held a fascination for me. I enjoyed it as a response to the monomania that had held most Germans in their grip: "Ein Volk, ein Reich, ein Führer." As a native-born claustrophobic, the word *ein* had always bothered me, even before that "oneness" was shattered at the end of the war into millions and millions of individuals, all trying to escape the very unity that had been an essential element of the twelve years of mass hysteria. I had always felt different from my schoolmates, moreover, in a way that was visceral, not ideological. For one thing, as a small child I had lost my mother, this mysterious woman always described to me as *die Amerikanerin*, who was said to have exhibited her sense of humor at inappropriate times. She laughed, for instance, as I was told, the first time she saw a parade of goose-stepping soldiers. What's more, I kept on repeating to anyone who would listen that I was born in San Francisco, California. At the beginning of each school year we had to give our name, date, and place of birth, and I always was pleased that I could point to a birthplace far away from the Main Valley.

The first postwar winter was not only cold, it was also dark at night. Two weak electric lightbulbs hung in our house—one in the living room and one in the kitchen. Our dwindling supply of candles was reserved for power outages. There was little to do, and everyone was involved in his or her private world. Only the laments of the women for their men who had not returned from the war punctuated the drab monotony of village life. At Christmas time we sat around the lamp in the living room making papier mâché stars. The radio still stood in its customary corner. One year earlier, Goebbels's voice had blasted from it, exhorting the Germans to make greater sacrifices for greater glory. I looked for some guidance—very tentatively—because, young as I was, that shattering poster of the mass grave in the Warsaw ghetto that was mounted on the bulletin board of our town hall had planted a seed of caution in me about commitments to any cause, big or small. Ever since I came face to face with that picture, I have remained suspicious of collectives larger than a glee club or a soccer team and all institutions in which the levers of control are not visible and the controllers far removed. I am also deeply suspicious of individuals who are totally convinced of the correctness of their causes.

In this low-key chaos, some adults, those who had not compromised with the mass hysteria, began to stand out, providing me with a sense of continuity. There was my indomitably optimistic grandmother Tubach, who was the first to dry her tears. She kept on telling the rest of us that after years of anxiety, years of joy would surely follow. Her expressed belief that "soon carnival will come around again, and young people will start enjoying life," still rings in my ears. And then there was my step-grandfather Zink, who did not crow over his avowed anti-Nazi stance once the political hyperventilation had come to an end. He continued to work hard and generally fell silent about anything outside his domain. And at school there was my fierce, partially lame English teacher, Herr Molitor, who drilled us in the English language. He was convinced that high academic standards were good for us and that English was the key to our future, if we were going to have one. I did not interrupt his classes as we struggled through Shakespeare's "Richard III," barely making out the plot of the drama. We also learned Scottish and American songs, from "D'you Ken John Peale?" to "Way Down upon the Swanee River." Every day he added several new phrases to our vocabulary, such as "to make a beeline for." Even in those cold, dank classrooms of the Miltenberg *Gymnasium*, he made sense to me.

In the months after the war ended, mysterious strangers moved in and out of our village. Most of them had agendas we did not understand, and even if we had, we certainly would not have rendered up to them our newfound freedom from constraints. Some were church people who were trying to save our souls; others were Esperanto teachers who promised to teach us a lingua franca that would provide a gateway to the world, after, of course, we paid our dues in the form of edibles or goods with some exchange value. One day a civilian appeared out of nowhere and called the teenage boys together in one of the few elegant villas of Kleinheubach to persuade us to join his organization. He promised us uniforms, open-air activities, and practical skills. We retreated from the villa as fast as we could and only later learned that he was a representative of the international Boy Scouts, trying to transform our marching habits into harmless and useful endeavors.

In my free time, far away from school and grown-ups, I developed my own escape into a fantasy world that no one could touch. I appropriated some of the literature I had read, with Schopenhauer's mystic pessimism at its core, into my very own, private world of reflection and make-believe. My *Meyers Lexikon* atlas (volume 12) provided the geographic map for many an imaginary trip that I would trace with the pin of a needle to faraway mountains, rivers, and cities. I shared my private ruminations with very few friends. We agreed that the world around us was too stupid and brutal to get very close to it. Minimal work in school kept me from flunking out.

In spring 1948, when I was seventeen, my father returned home from the British prisoner-of-war camp where he had been held since the end of the war. He climbed off the train in Klein-heubach tanned and overweight. The suitcases he brought home were full of presents, including a box of English magic tricks for me as well as items valuable for bartering on the black market, such as cigarettes and flint stones. It was obvious from most of his stories about the war and the POW camp that he had taken his transformation from counterintelligence officer in the German army to British prisoner of war in stride, even made out like a bandit. With the violin that had served him well back in San Francisco's Golden Gate Theater in the 1930s (the instrument never left his side), he organized a POW orchestra that was invited to perform all over northern England. He delighted in telling how his orchestra used to play the melody of "Deutschland, Deutschland über Alles" from Haydn's "Emperor Quartet" in a minor key and with slightly altered rhythms so that the British audience wouldn't notice they were performing a surreptitious dirge for the Nazi national anthem.

When I asked him about concentration camps, he told me that the British made the German POWs watch a film depicting atrocities. Some members of this audience of German officers shouted "Lies," as my father reported, and one officer sprang up and covered the projector lens, complaining that they didn't want to be subjected to such things. Apparently, so had

Heinrich Himmler, the top henchman of the Gestapo, who did not like to witness the very horrors he had ordered. Later in life, when I returned to the question of the Holocaust with more insistence, my father repeated this same anecdote, adding almost ritualistically, in sentences that remained unchanged: "It was the most terrible crime committed in history. But hardly anyone believed it. I was an intelligence officer and I didn't believe it." Every time he produced this answer, it seemed as if he were formulating it for the first time and that it represented once again the whole truth and nothing but the truth about what he knew or did not know. At other times, when he was in a more defensive mood, he liked to point out that soon after being put into the Haltwhistle officers' camp, the British intelligence service arrived to inquire who among the German officers had fought on the Russian front. When two SS officers stepped forward, they were taken away "to serve Great Britain," as my father put it, thus ending their war guilt (these officers were most likely going to be useful to the Western Allies during the incipient stages of the cold war). He believed that this bit of recall spoke for itself, and he never elaborated on it. But it was clear to me that with it he rationalized and exonerated the role he played during the Third Reich.

At home again, my father assumed his role as my guide and educator. As his first act, he rummaged through all my drawers when I wasn't home and found the secret diary that I had kept since I was twelve years old, into which I poured all my confused adolescent emotions. I discovered his perfidy when the diary showed up among my schoolbooks during a Latin class.

He had read every line, marked up the pages in red ink with his own critical commentary, and added after the last entry, "If you were not my only son, I would call you the black sheep of the family." It was obvious that he then planted the diary in my book bag, so that I would come across it during school hours. I felt violated and devastated. I destroyed the diary before I returned home. Since the notion of privacy as a personal privilege had not been developed in my generation of Germans, I lacked arguments with which to defend myself and remained silent in the face of his authoritarianism.

He finally provided me with a list of friends I could keep and others I would have to drop. I ignored the list. In my mind, he had become an intruder whose guidance I did not accept. His unchanged authoritarianism lacked legitimacy for me. The adult women with whom I and my peers had lived—mothers, grandmothers, aunts—had shown courage and tenacity. Even more important, we had seen them suffer hardships and mourn the dead. Most important, we had seen them weep. But my generation of young Germans was still hurt by and angry at the fathers and uncles who drifted back from the POW camps of Europe. What was there to emulate in them? Many of us felt that they had lost their moral authority, because they had been seduced by an evil regime. Some saw their returning fathers simply as defeated losers. Most of the returning men were disoriented, ill, and spiritually dead. Not so my father, who came on as strong as ever.

I could not communicate with him. He and I were ridiculed in the village when for a time we wrote letters to each other and mailed them through the post office while we lived in the same house. I could not raise with him the most important problem in my life that ran like an ever-present undercurrent at the time but now in the retelling seems oddly abstract and distant: I couldn't make sense of the world around me. Knowledge of the enormous violence that had happened just a few years before—bullets ripping open bodies, women gasping for their last breaths in gas chambers, planes dropping phosphorus bombs on children—that was now enveloped by silence, as if nothing had happened, robbed my life of purposeful direction. All I had was my inner world of daydreams, my friends, and sexual escapades and parties that formed an inchoate rebellion against the "infamy of what was."

My father pushed my gentle stepfamily Zink—grandfather, mother, blacksmith shop, and all—aside. I felt trapped in my family, in school, and in my childhood village. Soccer matches and countless evenings of training to become a top-notch goalie did not add up to a life with a future. But with the arrival of the Americans, my dreams of escape had gotten a boost. The threads connecting me to my place of birth had never been completely severed. We had a collection of American comic strips, some sheet music for the piano, including pieces by Fats Waller, the silk American flag with which I had played my private games of concealment in the Jungvolk, and a whole stack of unwritten postcards depicting an early-twentieth-century train ride from the East Coast across the western plains to San Francisco. A picture of a train crossing the Utah salt flats was one of my favorites. And now America had come to me. By law I was eligible to return to the United States. But what would I do there? I had no skills beyond farmwork and no professional goals. My schooling at the *Gymnasium* had no marketable value, and my average grades as much as my lack of funds would preclude university study. Besides, what would I study? Schopenhauer? It all seemed far-fetched. But I had a great-uncle in San Francisco, a musician by profession, who had become a special delivery messenger for the U.S. Post Office after the demise of the theater orchestras during the depression. Aside from this job, he managed an apartment building on Shrader Street near the "panhandle" of Golden Gate Park. I wrote this distant uncle and asked if he would sponsor me. After a month I received a positive reply. Now I was propelled. I *had* to go, never mind the absence of goals. After all, for years I had been tracing maps on my world atlas for amusement. The one subject I excelled in was geography. The time had come to trace a path west, not with a pin on a map, but with my own body, all on my own.

I went to the American Consul General's office in Frankfurt, where I met my first American government official not directly connected to the U.S. military. A vice consul, he was so myopic that his glasses seemed to me like the bottoms of Coke bottles. Later I wondered whether his shortsightedness was symbolic of U.S. policy on screening German emigrants at that time. In front of this vice consul in Frankfurt, I affirmed my U.S. citizenship based on my place of birth, and I relinquished my German citizenship, which, according to German law, was determined by "blood." My *Gymnasium* education unfinished and with no money, I tore myself away from my family and village to make my way to an "uncle" in San Francisco, a half brother of my grandfather, whom I knew only from hearsay and our brief correspondence.

While we waited in the railroad station in Aschaffenburg for my overnight train to Bremen, my father handed me an empty notebook. He looked sad. I had always been told that in appearance I could have been his younger twin. I boarded the train and found a seat at the window. My father stood on the platform as the train pulled out of the station, and I stared at him until his figure vanished in the distance. When he was out of sight, I opened the notebook and leafed through the empty blue-lined pages. He intended it to be my new diary for the future. He knew that I had destroyed the diary I had kept since age twelve, after he had marked it up with his critical comments. He wanted me to start with a "clean slate" that would be filled by his expectations. He probably thought that to wipe things out was the best way to move through life without moral qualms and hindrances.

It was not the last I would see of him. A few years later he decided, over my strenuous objections, to immigrate once again and join me in California. I had grown apart from him during the war and during his years as a POW, and in the year we were together in Kleinheubach after his return, we became increasingly alienated from each other. He came back from camp as if the Nazi years had never happened. I believe he did not care who he worked for as long as it brought him personal rewards. Once in America again, he married a woman thirty years his junior and had three children by her. He leased a popular beer hall in the Sonoma valley, called "Little Switzerland," where, microphone in hand, he loved to sing "Sur le pont d'Avignon" to the accompaniment of his band. After a few years, he decided that Germany was a better place for him after all, and he returned in the early 1960s to raise his family and to teach German to American GIs stationed near Nuremberg.

But restlessness drove him to yet another twist in his picaresque life. After a number of years in Nuremberg, he befriended an American Baptist church group and persuaded them to sponsor him and his family to return to the United States once again. To this end, he decided to become a Christian. Not that he pretended to be a Christian—this would seem an obvious inference, but it is too simple an explanation. Since pragmatic opportunism and personal belief were inseparable to him, being a Christian was a natural and sensible thing to do; it facilitated his return to the United States. Eventually, he settled down in Lubbock, Texas, and grew very old as a respected member of the church community that sponsored him.

During his Texas years, he never visited me in California, but I saw him once in Lubbock. When he was eighty-nine, he fell ill and seemed to be dying. He wanted me to come see him to "make up." Reluctantly, I flew to Lubbock. When my half brother picked me up at the airport, he reported that our father was feeling better and didn't want to make up with me after all. I spent two days in his house passing the time in polite conversation. I departed thinking that I would never see him again and relieved that he had not wanted to "make up." Indeed, I never saw him again.

Three years later, in 1992, surrounded by the wife and children of his third marriage, he died in Lubbock at the age of ninety-one, a person without a moral compass. He was a man too weak for the strong times he lived in; too eager to be someone important at all costs, even at the cost of his soul.

Yet as a child I had loved him. He made up adventure stories of a fictional hero who fought lions in Africa, looked for gold in South America, and almost died of thirst in the middle of Australia. My love of geography comes from those tales that he invented for me. Throughout his life he loved his violin, and he often claimed that playing it kept him sane. When I was a small child in Kleinheubach, he enjoyed telling me about California and what a wonderful place it was. He often said he regretted having left in 1933. I believe this to be true, since I remember him saying so, even early in my life, when the Nazis were at their height. How to reconcile his positive cosmopolitan American experience with his overriding opportunism and ambitions in the Nazi Party and the German army was surely the major inner conflict he had during this fatal period of his life. When I was an adult, he told me that he had suffered a recurrent nightmare in which he found himself the only person left on earth frantically searching for human company in empty streets. I hope that this dream came from some better part in him that he failed to heed in the way he decided to lead his life.

．　．　．

My trip from the Aschaffenburg train station to northern Germany on my way to faraway California was slow, since the train stopped frequently. The compartment was crowded with passengers who planned illegal border crossings into the Soviet zone of Germany, an undertaking that was becoming more difficult as the Iron Curtain grew increasingly impenetrable. These were, for the most part, people who had made an illegal visit to the West and were returning home. The conductor made his way wearily through the dimly lit compartment to advise them where to get off for the safest passage across the East-West divide. He asked everyone their destinations—Halberstadt, Magdeburg, Schwerin. Everyone was tired, laden down with bags and full of worries as they listened to his advice. When the conductor came to me, I replied matter-of-factly, "San Francisco." People bestirred themselves to look my way. The conductor advised me, deadpan, that I should stay on a while longer before getting off. Everyone broke up laughing as the train continued through the night. I stayed on board until the end of the line.

On June 8, 1949, I left Bremerhaven on a converted freighter, the *Marine Shark*. Ten days later it arrived in New York Harbor.

· · ·

Almost a year and a half ahead of me, on January 17, 1948, Bernat Rosner debarked at La Guardia Airport, after a two-day flight from Rome. He forgot his exhaustion, since he was about to greet his American friend, the GI he had met in Modena, Italy. Bernie got off the plane and entered the airport terminal to look for Charlie. While the other passengers were warmly greeted by family or friends and headed purposefully for the baggage area,

Bernie searched for the one face in this huge country that he should recognize. Would he, indeed, recognize him? And would his sponsor still recognize Bernie? Gradually, all the passengers, as well as the people who had come to meet them, moved away, and Bernie was left alone at an empty gate. He looked around and confirmed the fact—nobody was there to meet him. Standing in the terminal at La Guardia, Bernie started to cry. And for fifteen endlessly long minutes he continued to cry, until suddenly Charles Merrill hurried up to the gate and Bernie's life was transformed.

He had gotten stuck in New York traffic, Charlie explained to Bernie as they boarded a curbside taxi that transported them to downtown Manhattan. When the first skyscrapers came into view, Bernie could see only their upper stories lit up and thought they were mountains. The taxi ride through the canyons of this megalopolis brought them to Charlie's stepmother, a warmhearted, welcoming southerner, who received the Hungarian teenager in her elegant apartment on the Upper East Side. The following morning, having noted Bernie's shabby clothes, Charlie took him shopping at Brooks Brothers and outfitted him with a new wardrobe appropriate to his new station in life. Now Bernie donned his first vest and was decked out in the finest men's apparel. When they returned to the stepmother's apartment, he looked every bit the preppie that he was neither in spirit nor in training but would soon become.

Bernie's English was so minimal that Charlie had to translate their German conversations for the rest of the family. During one of their first meals together, Charlie's stepmother offered Bernie a huge dish of vanilla ice cream. Never having seen ice cream in that quantity before, Bernie thought he was facing a large gob of lard. He politely refused, to the surprise of his friendly host. But it didn't take Bernie long to figure out that lard was not consumed in this household and that his European tragedy had turned into an American fairy tale.

Charles Merrill took Bernie to St. Louis to meet his wife, Mary, and two daughters. In Merrill's family Bernie had, for the first time since his childhood days in Tab, the comforts of a home. For a moment he was able to experience them almost as his own. After his English was good enough, Bernie would tell the Merrills' eldest daughter, Catherine, the story of Ali Baba and the forty thieves, a story she still remembers to the present day. Years earlier Bertha Rosner had told this tale from the *Scheherezade* to her small son in Tab; Bernie carried it in his memory through Auschwitz, Mauthausen, Gusen, and Gunskirchen to pass it on in St. Louis.

Yet the transition from an epistolary friendship to a face-to-face relationship on a daily basis was hard on everyone, particularly on the Merrill family, which had to adapt to the newcomer. So, after a few weeks, arrangements were made for Bernie to live in a dormitory of the Thomas Jefferson School in St. Louis, a prep school founded by Charles Merrill in 1946. Bernie's class was made up of boys primarily from Tulsa and Dallas, but there was also a Pole, a Belgian, and a Japanese, the latter probably the first postwar Japanese student to come to any American school, as Merrill pointed out to me. Bernie's fear of having been rejected by the family was short-lived, as his loyal sponsor spent many hours with him, tutoring him privately. Bernie quickly felt at home in the nurturing environment of the private school, which sent boys on to prestigious Ivy League universities. During his first summer in the United States, he also met the patriarch of his new family, Charles Merrill, Sr., at his luxurious summer estate in Southampton, New York. As Bernie puts it now in his understated way, "I was used to adapting to new environments, and this one was by far the easiest to take."

The time had finally arrived for Bernie to develop his intellectual gifts to the fullest. No hostile forces, no dangerous circumstances, no mortal enemies stood in his way. Within a few months he was well established in his studies and fully integrated in his academic setting. He remembers a particular moment one early evening in March or April 1948 at the Merrills' home. He was engrossed in John Steinbeck's *The Moon Is Down* when he suddenly realized, "My God, I'm reading English fluently!" By the time he graduated from prep school, he won the school prize for creative writing. From that moment on, he said, "I never missed a step." Thus was his American persona born.

. . .

My road into American life was slower and less predictable. My first day in New York was spent at Grand Central Station, where I hung around the Traveler's Aid office waiting for the check my uncle in San Francisco had promised to send me. With a quarter left in my pocket and several German marks, I held my breath until the money arrived at Traveler's Aid via Western

Union: $113—$83 for the train ticket to California and $30 for expenses. I ventured out into the streets of New York and for a time was gripped by the fear that if I were to collapse they would sweep me into one of the huge garbage trucks rumbling by. I wore old knickerbockers from our family's prewar wardrobe, a Tyrolian hat, and a German version of the Eisenhower jacket that my stepmother had tailored for me, based on an American original. I felt quite snazzy until I became aware that people stared at me, obviously finding me much stranger than a turbaned Sikh who walked in front of me, whom they ignored but who was one of the most exotic sights I had ever seen. I was upset that I didn't pass for an American. I fled into the nearest Foster Cafeteria and tried to regain my composure. Once I arrived in Chicago the next day on the Twentieth Century Limited, I headed for the public baths in the railroad station, threw my hat and knickerbockers into a trash can, and put on the only other piece of apparel I owned, an old, dark blue pinstriped suit, a discard from one of my uncles. After that, no one took notice of me anymore.

I had a six-hour wait at Chicago's Northwestern Station before the California Zephyr was scheduled to leave on its two-day journey to Oakland. These hours, as I walked around the city streets near the train station, defined my early years in America. I saw both the incredible poverty, the alleys with broken wine bottles and broken people, and the elegant automobiles that glided along carrying well-dressed passengers only a few blocks away. Everyone was absorbed in their individual pursuits and no one seemed to care about anyone else. The lesson was clear to me. I would either move up or down on this scale that distributed people according to their achievements and failures—and luck. On the train again, someone asked me what I was going to do in California, and I made up a story: "I'm going to study at the University of California in Berkeley." Fat chance, I thought to myself, since I had neither money nor academic qualifications, not even an American high school diploma in my pocket. All I had was one address that I hoped would provide me with a good job—that of Agnes Albert, a San Francisco socialite, whose German husband my father became acquainted with in the POW camp in Great Britain.

The dice were rolling, but I had no idea how they would land. At least I was here, and on my way west, on an endless train ride through the vastness of the plains. In Nebraska, the North Platte River went on forever. Looking out of the window at another point, everything appeared to be covered with snow, right in midsummer. I realized I was staring at the salt flats west of Salt Lake City. On the morning of the last day, the train stopped in the middle of a town festooned with neon lights. I looked out the window and saw just a few yards away a sign arched across the main street that read, "Reno, the Biggest Little City in the World." By the time the train reached California, I was overwhelmed by what seemed to me the emptiness of it all. There had been no villages, church steeples, or cow pastures passing by outside every few minutes as on a German train. As we passed Sacramento, it no longer sounded like the city I had read about in adventure stories of the west; it sounded like a curse to a villager who had been condemned to live in distant exile. Once in the Bay Area, I felt I had reached the end of the earth—*finis terrae.*

When I stepped off the train at the Oakland station thirteen days after I had left Bremen, my uncle was there, standing right in front of my Pullman car. He recognized me immediately, because he, like all my relatives, thought that I looked just like my father. It was June 21, the longest day of the year, and as he drove us across the San Francisco Bay Bridge in brilliant sunshine, it was a relief to be with someone who did not regard me as a peculiar foreigner.

My uncle provided me with room and board, but it was obviously up to me to make something of myself. My first move was to make an appointment with the socialite at her Lyon Street mansion. Agnes Albert was pleasant enough in her elegant taffeta dress, and she recommended me to a cousin of hers, the president of the Hibernia Bank. When this polite gentleman realized, however, that I possessed no marketable skills, he recommended me to one of his friends, who ran a good downtown restaurant. But this friend, in turn, didn't have a job for me at the moment. When he recommended me to a greasy spoon at the beach where they needed someone to flip hamburgers, I decided not to pursue this downward spiral any further. Instead, I helped my uncle cleaning the apartment building. For pocket money, I scrounged around and came up with an assortment of odd jobs: digging roots from gardens, cleaning a warehouse on Bryant Street on weekends, and, at one time, distributing discount tickets for the Roller Derby to stores in the East Bay. On this job I walked from one end to the other of East

14th Street and then, a few days later, the entire length of San Pablo Avenue from downtown Oakland all the way to the town of San Pablo.

My uncle decided that without additional education I would get nowhere. He was a widower without children and something of a bohemian. He had never particularly liked my father, but one day he sat me down after several bottles of beer and said he had made up his mind that to spend some of his extra money on my education was probably a better investment than spending it at John Murio's bar up at the corner of Shrader and Haight. I readily agreed. Two years were going to be mine at San Francisco City College to earn an A.A. degree. When I began at City College, my English was so imperfect that I was required to take a remedial class. Toward the end of the semester, I was given a chance to demonstrate what I had learned, so I carefully prepared an oral presentation on the topic of German music. But I couldn't understand why my classmates broke out laughing when I began to discuss Beethoven's haunting "Moonshine Sonata."

Embarrassed but undaunted, I passed Subject A and signed up for English 1A in the fall semester of 1950 with Ruth Somers, the teacher with the fiercest reputation at the junior college. When Mrs. Somers entered the classroom the first day, everyone was sitting around in a relaxed manner, paying only cursory attention to her as she placed her books and purse on the desk. Ruth Somers was a large woman with a booming voice. Suddenly it rang out: "So shaken as we are, so wan with care, / Find we a time for frighted peace to pant. . . ." The room fell silent in startled surprise as she brought us face to face with

Henry IV, Part I. As I found out years later, she had been an admirer of Sarah Bernhardt and in her youth had wanted to become an actress. She had made it as far as some male roles in classical plays presented at the University of California's Greek Theater back in 1915.

She was the first authority figure I truly admired. I devoured English literature as fast as Mrs. Somers offered it to us, from Shakespeare to Hemingway. For the required term paper, I chose to write on Thomas Wolfe's *You Can't Go Home Again.* I was so engrossed in this composition that for two nights I didn't sleep, and it didn't dawn on me that the title was an answer to my situation in life. Then the defining moment came, my big break, my own "miracle of Modena." Toward the end of the semester, Mrs. Somers returned all the term papers to the class except for mine. Instead, she devoted an entire session to reading it out loud as a model of a good term paper. After a few weeks, as that marvelous incident of recognition settled in, I began to believe in myself and developed the desire to study. To the extent finances would permit, I would study foreign languages, different cultures, and perhaps even psychology and anthropology to find out what motivated people. I began to believe that if you knew the causes of things, you would overcome fear. And perhaps I would one day teach at the very school where my mentor taught—San Francisco City College. It slowly dawned on me that I had found my calling. Now I devoted all my time to doing as well in my classes as I could in order to become eligible for admission to the University of California. When I succeeded at this, I felt that the dice had rolled me right into my new niche at the university in Berkeley across the San Francisco Bay. And, after all, my mentor had once been a student there. I had finally found someone whose footsteps I could follow safely, a good and moral person whose passions had to do with insights into people not with power over them.

. . .

As immigrant teenagers, Bernie and I began our new lives at different levels in the social and economic hierarchy. Yet in the end, we both were given an opportunity, no more and no less, to define our own futures and to succeed, based on our talents rather than our backgrounds. We only had to be smart and to work hard. The steps in Europe: some had led up and many down; some had led toward extermination and others nowhere at all. Here the steps were of a different sort, namely, steps forward, steps across and over obstacles, moves sideways around dead ends, steps and leaps into new adventures of the intellect and of the heart, as if a giant hopscotch matrix had been superimposed over the New World just for us. As we embarked on our American lives, both Bernie and I sang with Walt Whitman, "My ties and ballasts leave me . . . . / I am afoot with my vision."

SIX

. . .

Careers:
An American Story

> As the weaver elaborated his pattern for no end
> but the pleasure of his aesthetic sense ... so
> might a man look at his life, that it made a
> pattern.
>
> W. SOMERSET MAUGHAM

That first summer in America, Bernie—or Bernat, as Charles
Merrill called him—became acquainted with wealth and luxury. From St. Louis, Merrill took his family, including Bernie,
to the East Coast to attend the Amherst graduation of his brother,
Jimmy. Then they proceeded to Charles Merrill, Sr.'s opulent
estate, known as The Orchard, in Southampton, Long Island.
The family accepted the odd addition of this young Hungarian
to its summer gathering as one of those idealistic quirks to which
Charles Jr. was prone. Given his cultural and social background,
the elder Merrill treated Bernie with a remarkable degree of tol-
erance and courtesy. The same was true of Charles's other relatives, particularly his sister, Doris Magowan, and her husband,
Robert (the latter, when chairman and CEO of the Safeway corporation, was to be instrumental in launching Bernie on his
business career). For Bernie, one wondrous experience piled on
another. He had walked into an enticing world defined by new
rules for living and working. With algebra lessons from Charlie,

a summer cottage on Cape Cod, and his first American girl-friend, Bernie was all set, with many opportunities laid out before him.

He worked hard at becoming a typical American teenager, even adopting a midwestern accent to highlight his permanent residency in St. Louis. He was competitive but at the same time guided by a mind-set that was adaptive. Ever ready to adjust to his social environment, he had a great need to be accepted, to fit the mold that offered him a good life. He was committed to the kind of success he saw around him, and he gladly conformed to the standards of this upper-class milieu. His survival skills honed in Europe were transformed into a sharp sense for this new world of possibilities, but at this level of American society there was no room for a Jewish survivor of Auschwitz, Bernie believed. He perceived his past as baggage that would weigh him down, socially and emotionally.

Still, the past did not let go of him easily. The state of Israel came into existence on May 15, 1948, and a few months later he received a letter from Simcha Katz. His old concentration camp buddy described the struggle for national survival, including the ordeals and deaths of Selvino comrades in the battles for the emerging nation. The news tore Bernie apart. It left him confused, tormented by guilt and, to a certain degree, by regrets as well. For a time he became preoccupied with this other life that he had rejected in favor of America, but soon he shifted his concentration to goals rather than the past.

Bernie likes to see himself as a tough person, as one who can move ahead without looking back, if necessary. So he surprised me one day several years into our work together when, during an everyday conversation, he remarked out of context, "You know, in one of the letters Simcha wrote me in June 1948, he told me how a girl with whom I'd had a romance in the Selvino camp whispered my name as she lay dying from her wounds." Barely able to control his tears, he quickly changed the subject to regain his composure.

Should Bernie have followed the call to go to Israel? One might ask who was the more consequential—Simcha Katz, the survivor who participated in shaping a new collective identity, or Bernat Rosner, who opted for American individualism, with its already established playing field. Ever since, Bernie has wondered what his fate would have been had he decided to go to Palestine. But in his early days in America, in the life opening up before him, there was no time for tears about the past.

Bernie graduated from high school and was accepted at Cornell University in fall 1950. On his way to Cornell, he was joined on the train from St. Louis by another preppie bound for Princeton. This traveling companion warned him to beware of fraternities that accepted Jews. Bernie thanked him for the advice.

Once at Cornell, Bernie threw himself into his undergraduate studies. Literature and history were his favorite subjects to begin with, but as time went on he was more and more attracted to courses in business administration. In his social life he did everything he could to be one of the boys. He joined the "right fraternity," which was, among other things, non-Jewish. The American college creed of the 1950s dictated conformity, and Bernie embraced it. He even came to believe, along with his fraternity brothers, that "typical Jews" were not "his kind of people." Although his sponsors, Charles and Mary Merrill, both traditional New Deal liberals, were at best ambivalent about Bernie's determined efforts to become a member of the "fifties generation," he remained focused on his goal of total assimilation.

Calculating as this attitude might seem on the surface, in actuality it provided Bernie with an effective way to shatter the last vestiges of his victimhood—wherein murderers had branded him for extermination because of his religion and ethnicity. In the Auschwitz barracks he had jumped across a wall to become part of the slave labor group destined for transfer out of the camp, leaving behind the group marked for extermination. Now, at Cornell, he made another escape across a wall, this time the invisible wall of racial and religious prejudice, into the safe haven of a prestigious, upper-class fraternity that was integrated into the mainstream of American campus life. By doing so, he had, without giving it much thought, joined those to whom the Holocaust and its horrors had no particular significance. With my German upbringing, do I have a right to a moral judgment? After all, like Bernie, I also followed a fashion of the fifties. I insisted on my individuality to shield me from what Germans had done to the Jews and to the rest of Europe.

Bernie wanted to conform to the course followed by most of his fraternity brothers at Cornell. He also wanted to finish his college education without being drafted into the Korean War, so he joined the ROTC. When, during his subsequent military service, he was promoted to the rank of first lieutenant in the

U.S. Army, he thought back with pride and satisfaction to the resplendent Hungarian *second* lieutenant who had so impressed him as a boy in Tab, whom he now outranked. Aware of his unique background and his success at Cornell, college authorities chose him during his senior year to give the keynote "Personal Value Speech" to entering freshmen. Prophetically perhaps, he drafted this speech on a paper shopping bag.

This evolution toward traditional conservative values, coupled with his growing interest in business courses, caused tensions between Bernie and the Merrills. Though nominally Episcopalian, already in his youth Charles Merrill, who has jokingly referred to himself as a "semi-Marxist," was less interested in mainstream religious observances than in ethical standards and social activism. He had worked for ten cents an hour as a store clerk in a mixed-race, Christian-socialist cooperative farm in Mississippi in 1941, long before civil rights activism became fashionable. Bernie's talent for accommodation and his lack of idealism in favor of a self-interested pragmatism came up against Charlie's progressive liberalism, or rather his unbending moral stance—terms the young disciple used to compare his sponsor to the stern posture of an Old Testament patriarch. Their warm relationship suffered a chill for a number of years.

While in college at Cornell, Bernie became an American citizen, and on graduation in 1956, he was accepted at Harvard Law School. Aside from his law courses, a work by Henry Steele Commager, *The History of the American Republic*, confirmed for him the secular principles of individualism that now guided his new American life. He had resisted committing himself to the collective called Israel that came into being on the basis of secular Zionist principles, and he had lost his faith in the Orthodox religion of his family.

But Bernie has always maintained that his early study of the Talmud influenced his interest in the law, particularly constitutional law—which captivated him more and more. A respect for the precision of the written word was not merely a learned professional reflex but an important part of his cultural background. Half jokingly, he explained how his decision to attend law school was influenced by an 1861 legal case he came across while researching his senior thesis at Cornell on the subject of the ex post facto clause of the U.S. Constitution. *Hartung v. the People of the State of New York* involved a woman sentenced to death for having poisoned her husband. At the time of her crime, a person sentenced to death in the state of New York was to be returned to jail and executed within a fixed number of days following pronouncement of the sentence. After Hartung's commission of the crime, the law was changed to require condemned prisoners to be put in solitary confinement and to be executed only on specific orders from the governor. Through an oversight, the legislature failed to include the usual "savings clause" making the old law applicable to those to whom the new law could not be applied. Mrs. Hartung's lawyers argued that the new law imposed a severer punishment than the old law and that application of the new law to their client would violate the ex post facto clause, which, among other things, prohibits a retroactive increase in punishment. Further, since the old law was automatically repealed by the new law, there was *no* law under which Mrs. Hartung could be executed. Amazingly, the highest court of the state bought this argument, and Mrs. Hartung was permitted to go free. Bernie felt that a profession that gave scope to such creative use of logic and argument was worth pursuing.

He used the terms "ingenuity" and "elegance" to describe the outcome of this unusual case, and it became clear to me that the formalistic playfulness of the legal maneuvers struck a deep cord in him. On the face of it, I had a hard time accepting that this case may have had a bearing on his choice of the law. But since neither he nor I have much faith in psychological cause-and-effect reductionism, I at first let the matter rest with his straightforward, legal account. Only later, when I went over his story again, did I realize an odd coincidence that had escaped both of us.

During the Holocaust, Bernie came closest to death—from starvation and from the arsenic administered by the departing Germans—shortly before the arrival of the Allies. At this point he existed between two laws, the laws of the murderers who had fled and the laws of the liberating armies who were just arriving. Chaos and the closeness of death marked this suspension in his life between two worlds that operated under radically different rules. When he evoked this dangerous, transitional period for me, his fear of death became more palpable than in any other time of his storytelling. Did the New York murder case represent an existential step for Bernie beyond one of the most traumatic moments of his life? Was this simply a coincidence, or did it indeed constitute a matter of cause and effect? I believe it represents one of those random confluences of events that shapes recall, memory, and the writing of history. But when I mentioned this to Bernie, he thought it was one of my academic speculations, intriguing perhaps but lacking the rigor of proof.

After completing his Harvard law degree in spring 1959, Bernie entered into the "right marriage" when he wedded Betsy Baylies, the daughter of an East Coast Brahmin family. He admits that he decided to marry a girl from the upper class after reading Maupassant's novel *Bel Ami*. As it turned out, Bernie was deeply devoted to this kind woman, who was "non-Jewish," as he told me, and also Episcopalian like the Merrills and Magowans. Quite aside from being a dynamic part of Bernie's trajectory up the economic and social ladder, Betsy was friendly and warmhearted. For a wedding present, Charles Merrill gave the Rosners a new Vauxhall automobile, in which they drove west on both a honeymoon and a move to a new home. They settled into a happy suburban marriage in Lafayette, California. As Merrill recalls, there were no signs of his Jewish background in Bernie's new home. Indeed, he kept the fact of his Jewish upbringing even from his wife for a time.

At first, Bernie told me that he hadn't told Betsy about his Jewish background because it belonged to his now-irrelevant "first life." Later on, he divulged a detailed and compelling explanation for this peculiar fact. When he chose to come to America rather than Palestine, he was determined to break with the past, both in terms of religion and in terms of Jewish nationalism and loyalty. Not just in the concentration camps, but even during his childhood in Hungary, the outside world, the "establishment," as he put it, drilled into him the notion that Jews were inferior, hateful, and repulsive. That kind of treatment and atmosphere generated self-hatred and feelings of inferiority. The war and its upheavals offered him a new life. Thus, in America, he believed he needed to become a new person, free of his former identity. The upper-class, Ivy League milieu that he entered gave him a powerful incentive to assimilate and conform. Already in St. Louis it became clear from the attitudes of his classmates that being Jewish was not an asset. Bernie drew a parallel between the nonchalance of the beautiful young people he admired in Tab as they strolled to the tennis courts and the tales of his preppie American schoolmates about their adventures at last Saturday's debutante ball. This time, he was determined to end up in the right crowd.

Although Bernie says that he never denied his Jewish origins outright, among his friends and acquaintances he played down the fact. When he talked about his concentration camp experiences, he usually explained that the authorities discovered that his family had listened to the underground Allied radio. The fact that "there was some Jewish blood" in his lineage, he mentioned only as a reason incidental to their deportation. His strategy was to avoid mentioning his deeply Orthodox family life and upbringing altogether.

Charles and Mary Merrill knew, of course, his true background and history. But after leaving for college, then the service, law school, and his career, his contacts with them were less frequent, especially because they spent much of the 1950s in Europe. But the Merrills returned to the United States and settled in Boston in 1957, the year Bernie entered Harvard Law School. Mary then became quite close to his fiancée, Betsy, and discovered the "sanitized version," as Bernie called it, of the past he had told her.

Following this discovery, Mary Merrill confronted Bernie in harsh terms. When I asked Bernie what he meant by "harsh terms," Bernie related that Mary had strong feelings against Germans and their war crimes and reminded him that his parents had been killed because they, too, were Jewish. She implied that he was being untrue to himself and admonished him to tell Betsy the truth. He did. He knew that by then it would make no difference to her. He told me that he was "surprised and humbled" by the fact that Betsy's family accepted him for what he was. He has maintained a warm relationship with them ever since.

The conflict with Mary, however, caused some estrangement with the Merrills that stretched over many years. The first step in the healing of this rift came in 1980 when Mary learned that Betsy, at the age of forty-five, was dying of cancer. Innately compassionate, Mary abandoned all reserves and rushed to comfort Bernie's afflicted family. The ultimate reconciliation came in 1999 when Bernie visited Mary as she lay on her deathbed. In wide-ranging conversations they were able to reminisce about how the Merrills had taken Bernie into their family long ago, and he was able to thank them for their generosity. And Mary absolved him of his past "sin of omission."

As one of the amazing twists in my friend's life, I interpret the odd fact that Bernie, the orphaned refugee with his Orthodox Jewish background, was rescued and given a future by liberal American Protestants as something of a disincentive to seek out involvement with Jewish organizations in the United States. Had he done so, he might have shared his camp experiences with other survivors or found a measure of emotional support and solidarity. But it was his decision not to. He coped with his wounds on his own, drawing the legitimacy he needed to grow and function in the new world solely from his own extraordinary inner strength. He traveled a long road before deciding to reconcile his first with his second life.

After he and Betsy moved to California, the issue of his Jewish background became moot. California culture was more open than the circles in which he had moved on the East Coast. Moreover, the insecurities about his past gradually faded away as he gained in self-confidence and realized that the world in which he now lived accepted him. When his three sons were old enough to understand, he told them the "unvarnished truth." And since he had lost his emotional ties to Judaism, he raised no objection to Betsy's desire to have their children raised as Christians. Two of them were baptized and christened. But the Rosners attended religious services only infrequently at the Lafayette Episcopal church.

. . .

Bernie's marriage to Betsy was the culmination of what he set out to achieve in America, both in his private life and with his public persona. It represented a triumph over a past he had overcome. It was toward the conclusion of our work together before

I understood how this fact was connected to the drunken, anti-Semitic diatribe Bernie and Betsy suffered at the Tab railroad station in 1971, and the devastating effect this encounter had on him. We were going over this episode once again when he startled me by breaking into tears. It was the only time during our sessions when he was unable to hold them back. Now I finally came to understand the implications of the wrenching afternoon in Hungary. He had assumed he could manage this visit to his Hungarian village from the sovereign distance of a successful American businessman with his wealthy and loving wife by his side, maintaining the separation from his former life as a hunted Jew. But during the awful moments the drunk assaulted them verbally, his defenses against the past collapsed. He told me, "All I had done with my life since being deported to Auschwitz from this railroad station at Tab seemed to vanish. I felt back at where it all had started for me and my family."

. . .

In California, Bernie began his professional career in June 1959 at the Safeway corporation, which was originally co-founded by Charles Merrill, Sr., and later run by his son-in-law, Robert Magowan. During college and law school, as tensions developed with his sponsors, Bernie's growing admiration for the "know-how" of American capitalism on the highest levels had drawn him more and more to the Magowan side of the family. Charlie's sister, Doris Merrill, had married Robert Magowan. The Magowans realized that Bernie was more than the human flotsam that Charlie had picked up in Europe, as they had first viewed the young immigrant; Robert Magowan admired his determination, courage, and adaptability. Bernie began work in the legal division of the company and became assistant general counsel in 1980. He rose to become senior vice president, general counsel, and corporate secretary in 1984. By then, Robert's son, Peter, was chairman and CEO of Safeway, and Bernie considers his close personal and professional relationship with both father and son a measure of his success and a source of pride and satisfaction.

As legal counsel for Safeway, Bernie played a central role in a number of prominent cases that made headline news starting in the 1960s. While he battled with all his skills for the interests of the food chain, my sympathies, as an activist professor at the University of California at Berkeley, were with the "anti-establishment" voices on the other side of the political divide. In one memorable case, Safeway was accused of price gouging inner-city customers in Washington, D.C. Bernie told me that he checked out the accusation in person, found the claim to be untrue, and defended Safeway out of both personal conviction and professional obligation. The year was 1967, a time when political activism in American universities defined the values of the young and disaffected against the social order of Johnson's Great Society. Students reacted, not only against American involvement in Vietnam, but also against what was perceived to be an impersonal set of oversized institutions. Safeway, the giant food chain, was for them a perfect symbol of corporate insensitivity.

Also in 1967, cattle growers accused Safeway of violating federal anti–price fixing laws. Represented first by Joe Alioto, Sr., and later his son, the cattlemen alleged that they weren't receiving a fair share of meat profits, because Safeway was involved in a conspiracy with packers and other retailers to manipulate prices. Following a Supreme Court decision concerning price fixing, Safeway "won" the case when it was finally dismissed in federal court in 1984.

Then came the case of the California grape pickers, led by their charismatic spokesman, Cesar Chávez, who accused Safeway of abetting the exploitation of farmworkers for the sake of corporate profits. Anyone even marginally involved at the time will remember that boycotting Safeway because of its refusal to stop making grapes available to its customers became a moral litmus test for progressive political behavior. For a long time I ate no grapes. I did not know my friend Bernie at that time, but if I had known that he was one of the principal figures defending impersonal corporate America against the exploited Chicano grape pickers, I am sure I would have participated in a sit-in in his office. *Tempora mutantur, et nos mutamur in illis* (the times, they are a-changing, and we are changing with them).

In the major case of his career in the mid-eighties, Bernie told how he became an expert on hostile takeovers and leveraged buyouts in the same way a person who is hit by a high-speed train becomes an expert on kinetic energy. He and I already knew each other when he had to defend Safeway against an attempted takeover by the corporate raiders Herbert and Bobby Haft. Considered all-powerful by grape pickers, cattle ranchers, and university students and their professors a few decades earlier, the Safeway corporation was now threatened by a father and son team of entrepreneur-adventurers. The attempted takeover and its consequences became the most significant single event in Safeway corporate history and the main battle of Bernie's professional life. He slept little and kept inhuman working hours, but Bernie and Safeway's management emerged the victors in this particular game of high financial stakes.

In overseeing the operations of Safeway's legal division, Bernat Rosner proved himself a formidable attorney. Beyond that, his career was dedicated to the family that had given him a start in America. His was not just the labor of a conscientious employee but also the gladly rendered gift of a grateful adopted son. It would be wrong to view a career such as Bernie's as merely a series of "after-the-fact" events, following the great traumatic moments of the twentieth century in which he was trapped in the role of victim. He played the role of an insider at a major American corporation and enjoyed it very much. Once, when Bernie noticed my critical reservations about his business career and the gusto of his engagement, he stopped in midsentence and interjected, "I guess this is not the way an Auschwitz survivor is supposed to feel." I didn't say anything at the time, but I believe, after all, that a survivor has earned the same right and freedom as anyone else to choose a path from among all the possibilities, whether or not his choice conforms to a particular ideology.

In the middle of his career, Bernie suffered a major blow. Betsy contracted cervical cancer. An operation at Alta Bates Hospital in Berkeley failed to stay the disease. A few months before her death, Bernie and Betsy celebrated their life together on a vacation in Hawaii. She died on January 13, 1981. Bernie was now alone with their three teenage sons—Michael, 18, Andy, 16, and Owen, 11. He went into a deep depression, and, as he said, "never since the concentration camps" had he suffered such anguish—sleeplessness, anxiety, chest pains, loss of physical energy—all the while knowing that he had to keep up his side of the bargain in his professional life. With Betsy's illness and death, he once again suffered exposure to a world of deadly chance, to the dark abyss with which he had become all too familiar in his youth. He had climbed out of it before. On the tennis court, Bernie's most common habitat next to his office, he met his wife-to-be, Susan, who helped him out of his depression in summer 1982.

Celebrated as a successful corporate lawyer involved in key legal cases, author of articles in the *Antitrust Law Journal*, lecturer at numerous antitrust conferences and seminars, executive committee member of the Antitrust and Trade Regulation Section of the State Bar of California, and vice chairman of the American Bar Association Section of Antitrust Law, Bernat Rosner retired in 1993.

. . .

The steps that led to my career were much more modest than Bernie's. After my uncle subsidized my junior college education and my English instructor, Ruth Somers, encouraged me to study for the sake of my "inner development," I was able to enroll at the University of California at Berkeley as a transfer student from San Francisco City College. To me, acceptance at Cal was a step of liberation from the village in which I had grown up as well as from my personal fears about the jarring contrasts between rich and poor I encountered at the Northwestern train station in Chicago. At the university I would be encouraged to advance on the basis of an established set of norms, and it was up to me to live up to them. Consequently, I tried, at least at the outset, to blend in to the general conformism of the 1950s.

Walking through Sather Gate onto campus was like walking through the looking glass into an intriguing world with an immense intellectual buffet spread out before me. I immersed myself in a great variety of subjects and rarely took time out for social life or recreation. In fact, Sundays, a time for relaxing, depressed me. I was consumed by a curiosity without limits; at the same time, my studies constituted a grimly determined escape from the "world outside," which I deeply feared for its hidden dangers, sudden violence, and unpredictability. After General MacArthur returned from Korea to more than half an hour of wild applause at the 1952 Chicago convention, I was convinced that the United States was heading for a dictatorship. But when in the final balloting for the Republican presidential nominee he garnered only three votes, I received my first lesson in American democracy. I felt reassured.

McCarthyism, rampant in the 1950s, lay outside my horizons. I was more aware of the psychological meanness of the televised hearings than of any menace these witch-hunts presented to democratic values. For me, the American pursuit of happiness lay within the well-protected walls of the university. Berkeley represented an intellectual haven, an all-absorbing focus that required no engagement in society at large, at least not during the decade known for its introversion. Some time passed before I realized that the loyalty oath demanded of the faculty had been an assault on the academic freedom that I, the newly arrived immigrant, took for granted.

The Department of German counted among its students and faculty many refugees from Nazi Germany. Most of them brought to America an intense devotion to German literature and culture. Among these academics was Frau Strauss, a heavy-lidded, well-coiffed, and meticulously dressed woman who had escaped before the Nazis had a chance to exterminate her. Her past never came up in our conversations. She was able to recite by heart the entire first part of Goethe's *Faust* in German. Despite a large age difference between us, I felt close to her, and we prepared for several final exams together. She seemed to have the kindness of my grandmother.

Later on, I teamed up with another graduate student, Franz Bäuml, whose Jewish father and Gentile mother had escaped Austria in 1938. Known to everyone as "Fritz and Franz," a German version of the Katzenjammer kids, we worked through the graduate program together. We both became medievalists, and when it came to job hunting in a tight market, we decided not to compete against each other. Instead, we each drew straws for five of the top ten universities from a list we had drawn up and applied to them for instructorships. He ended up at UCLA, where he had a distinguished career, and I started my academic life at the University of Michigan but was recalled to Berkeley after one year. I believe we learned more from each other than from all our required courses. Our different ethnic and social backgrounds and the war only a decade behind us never played a role in our friendship. The only tensions we had involved manners. He sported a slight British accent and once tried to teach me how to hold a glass of wine without leaving fingerprints. Having grown up in a village with peasant ways, I objected to his uppity condescension, and we got into an argument over the rules of etiquette.

The only instance when my youth in Nazi Germany came into view in graduate school was in an advanced class on German style required of everyone, native and non-native. I thought this class would be easy for me, but the instructor, a refugee from Nazi Germany, handed back one of my written assignments early in the semester with a grade of "C." She underlined some expressions she claimed contained echoes of a Nazi mentality—not in content, but in syntax. I was deeply shocked by her accusation and defended myself to her. But privately, to my chagrin, I began to understand what she meant when I reviewed her comments in detail. I trace my enduring interest in the relationship between language and ideology to this incident.

In postwar American universities, the popularity of existentialism well suited my intense introspection. I started to study symbolism in European poetry—Baudelaire and Rimbaud in French, Rilke and George in German. I read Sartre, Camus, and Kafka, staples of the postwar student generation. The text itself counted in the humanities in those days, while the social import of literature was left to the sociologists. That Hannah Arendt was a guest professor at Berkeley in the mid-1950s had no effect on the foreign language departments. In one of my French seminars while still an undergraduate, I spent an entire semester studying one poem—Rimbaud's "Les voyelles"—a sonnet about vowels in which the mad, seventeen-year-old genius of French poetry tried to reveal the deeper secrets of synesthesia, to discover a hidden core in the psyche where all human senses were supposed to be one. Coupled with a course on Nietzsche by Hans Wolff, a refugee from Berlin who committed suicide at the end of the semester, my introverted search for what I considered deeper truths hidden in the language of poetry and philosophy led me up against an impenetrable wall of silence. There were no answers, because I had not articulated the right questions. For several months during the last semester of my senior year, I fell into a private hell of high anxiety and panic. Something unknown in my life had caught up with me, but I didn't have a clear idea what it was, this nameless dread without content. For guidance and hope, I pinned Virgil's tribute to Lucretius above my desk: "Happy the person who could learn the causes of things and who would put beneath his feet all fears." I had become a person without a skin.

Shortly before graduation, I was able to crawl out of this disastrous state of mind. And soon after I entered graduate school in 1954, I began to be attracted to an ever-widening circle of facts, figures, historical events, and ideas that no longer fed the intellectual introversion of my confused undergraduate period. I enjoyed deciphering difficult texts in older European literatures that represented a fascinating cultural substratum. Luck had it that Archer Taylor, a leading figure in international folklore studies, took me on as one of his last doctoral candidates. He had an encyclopedic memory of historical facts, and he pitted this legendary gift of recall against the invincible force of forgetting. With Professor Taylor's encouragement I embarked on a ten-year study of medieval religious tales that was finally published by the Finnish Academy of Sciences under the forbidding title *Index Exemplorum*[1]—a collection, summarizing 5,400 religious tales with 44,000 variants. But this devotion to the tangible material of cultural and religious history never quite put to rest the skepticism I had developed about the validity of historical studies. Later on in my career, I became increasingly concerned with methodological premises; these concerns were reflected in conference papers and in a book on medieval German poetry.

Throughout the 1950s and on into the 1960s, German literature at Berkeley was taught and studied as if the Nazis had made no difference to the culture and the language. Even the Jewish immigrants, most of whom were culturally conservative, wanted to surround the literature and culture they so loved with an aura of immunity from the forces of barbarism and preserve its traditional respectability. But by the end of the decade, I was no longer satisfied with exclusive absorption in the study of literature for its own sake.

My dissatisfactions came to a head in spring 1959 as a result of an exchange that took place at the home of a fellow graduate student in German who lived in Mill Valley. Fred, a German

Jew who had fled Berlin, married a Danish woman, and emigrated to the United States, was showing me some of his German books when I stopped in front of a photograph of his mother near the door of his study. She had snow-white hair neatly parted in the middle, and she smiled with a kindness around her eyes that Fred had inherited from her. I asked him what had happened to her. At the time, and in this pleasant house, the Holocaust was far from our minds. He didn't answer but led me on to another book and tried to change the subject. I repeated my question, "Fred, what happened to your mother?" Another refusal, but I persisted. "Fred, come on, for God's sake." He finally told me in just these words: "She died in Theresienstadt." Several moments passed between us in silence while I sought in vain for an adequate response. It suddenly seemed to me that the literature we had studied in common made no sense. Finally, I asked him why he was so reluctant to tell me about his mother's fate, and he said, "Look, I didn't want to embarrass you."

I was thunderstruck. *He* had wanted to protect *me* from the facts surrounding his mother's death in a German concentration camp. I was stunned by his consideration for my feelings. As I stood there in his home, a deep anger rolled over me against Germany, the country where I had grown up. I remembered the photographs of the atrocities: mass graves, emaciated bodies, and twisted limbs of the victims of Nazism. These images had been both overwhelming and at the same time strangely abstract and incomprehensible when I had first seen them after the war. Now, standing enraged in my friend's study before the picture of his mother, they suddenly became real and tangible for me. At that moment I woke up from the political somnolence that had enveloped most Germans since 1945 in their rush to rebuild their shattered economy and to forget the past, and for me, to build a life in America. It was a moment that defined the end of the conformist 1950s for me and had a profound effect on my political and social ethics.

A year later, in 1960, I was asked to read a paper at an international conference of Germanists in Copenhagen. At one point, the West German embassy invited conference participants to a cocktail party, while at the same time the East German contingency competed with a bus trip to a memorial honoring Nazi victims. I was the only Westerner at the memorial, showing my solidarity with this antifascist demonstration.

The student revolution that started on the Berkeley campus in fall 1964 while I was on a sabbatical in Munich finally brought together my private values and political convictions. Having already advocated student representation on faculty committees a year earlier, I had a pro-student reputation and was asked to chair the faculty Senate Committee on Student Affairs on my return to California. This new committee assignment put me right between the "firm principles of university governance" articulated by the administration and the conservative wing of the faculty and the "non-negotiable demands" of the radical students and their faculty supporters. It was deeply disturbing to me to see uniformed policemen hitting students with clubs to enforce law and order within the walls of the academy. My sympathies shifted more and more to the side of the students, who began to represent for me a justified attack on the status quo, that is, an attack on the established powers of large, impersonal institutions, even one as devoted to intellectual matters as the University of California. I had come to believe that the university was not just a safe haven for academic study and research, but that it also helped to sustain the corporate structure of the nation, without much concern for humane values—if necessary at gunpoint. Beyond that, the war in Vietnam raised the stakes for all of us. It was no longer sufficient to articulate political objections in committee meetings behind closed doors. One day I confessed to my colleague Bluma Goldstein this discrepancy between my private beliefs and my lack of public commitment. She was an articulate member of the radical wing of the Berkeley faculty, a strong personality who had been raised by her single mother, a worker in the New York garment industry. Bluma said there had been a lot of good Germans who had the right thoughts in private but did nothing in public to prevent the rise of Hitler. That hit home. When I asked what I could do, she told me to join the march to Oakland the following week to protest the war in Vietnam. When she noticed my hesitation she added that I shouldn't worry, since there would be a large crowd. I decided to go.

We congregated next to Harmon Gym, where Allen Ginsberg stood on a flatbed truck in front of us and blessed us with chanted mantras. As it turned out, there wasn't as large a crowd as Bluma had predicted—only about seven thousand, by our own optimistic estimates. As we trekked through Berkeley and Oakland marching in pairs, onlookers jeered and called us communists. I spotted Registrar Gilliam in the crowd and noticed the surprise on his face on seeing me in this company, as if to say, So, you too. It was my first political march since the Nazi youth rallies twenty years earlier. No one wore a uniform, except for the police watching us, and we didn't march but ambled. Most important, the majority was against us and did not cheer us on to "bigger and higher goals." This march was for a good cause, but I felt distinctly uncomfortable by the exposure and by the political commitment it implied for all to see. Ideally, I would have liked to have carried a sign saying that I was for this march but with certain reservations. It became clear that in this political arena you were either for or against. This became even more obvious as time went on and the political struggle intensified. It was not easy to climb up Sproul Steps to sign a faculty-sponsored call against the draft while a government helicopter whirred overhead, presumably to record proceedings. My strong antifascist beliefs had finally found a focus.

Although I remained cautious at heart, events forced me to make choices, not only as an individual, but also as a faculty member. One evening in fall 1966, I was sitting down to dinner at home when an urgent call came from the administration. The campus was in an uproar. Students were rioting and police were chasing them. The administration asked me, as chair of the Student Committee, to join them on campus in Dwinelle Hall. I didn't go home that night.

At issue was a recruiting table set up by the ROTC that the majority of students didn't want on campus. Chancellor Roger Heyns was in New York, and two of his assistants—both of whom became distinguished scholars and administrators in their subsequent Berkeley careers—had decided to call in the police. When I asked one of them, John Searle of the Philosophy Department, what they wanted to achieve, he started to pace back and forth in the Dwinelle Hall office with the large steps characteristic of him when he was agitated. "We have to transform the revolution of the students into an evolution," he said. That seemed reasonable on the face of it, but I was doubtful of their power as administrators to manipulate the dynamics of this uprising. Without being entirely aware of it, however, I actually agreed with them. For me, it all came down to the problem of violence, for as much as I sympathized with the students' anger, I was convinced that violence from either side would achieve nothing.

When the student leader, Mario Savio, came to my office a few days later on a mission to muster faculty support, I asked him what his objectives were. He answered frankly, in his usual stammer when speaking in private, that he wanted to break the campus up into smaller units to create a humane community for our studies. As far as the faculty was concerned, he wanted to bring about a clear split between the reactionaries and the progressives, or the conservatives and the radicals, as my colleagues on the right would say. I was instinctively against that. Whatever the University of California represented as an institution of the state, the campus community was too fragile to have it transformed into an arena for dialectic struggles. Consequently, I devoted much of my time to efforts to create a faculty consensus that would neutralize both political extremes and that would in time bring about conditions favorable to far-reaching educational reforms.

Michael Heyman, chair of the Faculty Senate committee, was a master at formulating language that incorporated politically disparate positions. A small group of us joined him in creating a faculty consensus on a centrist position that combined language from the opposing camps—the administration and the conservative faculty on one side and the students and their faculty supporters on the other. When a lopsided vote of 795 to 28, with 143 abstentions, supported us in a major faculty convocation on December 5, 1966, with students and police milling around outside Wheeler Hall, a newsman from San Francisco congratulated us on the "slick job" we had done. It was Caspar Weinberger, who was to gain prominence during the Reagan era. I didn't like the words "slick" or "job," and for a moment I thought of calling Mario Savio to apologize. Behind all the opaque language contained in the faculty motions was a real and contentious battle over the governance of the academic community. The faculty, split as it was, was caught in the middle and ultimately lost power it never regained.

The student revolt at the time was unfocused and hectic, and all the factions did a good deal of political improvising. Some members of the faculty, however, had clear political objectives in mind. At one point I was asked to present myself for a conversation with one of these highly political colleagues, rumored to be a follower of Mao. I knew his name, but I had never met him, and I did not know what he wanted from me. In his campus office he more or less interrogated me for fifteen minutes before thanking me for my time. I asked him what the purpose of this meeting had been, and he replied that he just wanted to get acquainted with me. I didn't like this meeting. It had political power written all over it that seemed to derive its legitimacy from no obvious context. Since my childhood in Germany, I had developed a sensitivity for personalities with totalitarian traits.

While the student upheavals spread, I began to worry about their consequences throughout the United States and Europe. I wondered whether academia was strong enough to deal internally with political conflicts outside its boundaries. Once, on my way out of the Berkeley campus with Czeslaw Milosz, the Polish author, who later won a Nobel Prize for literature, we found Sather Gate blocked by a demonstration. When I began to wax poetic about the function of such disruptions as a prod to rethink established institutional routines, he looked at me under his bushy eyebrows and grumbled in his Slavic accent, "These are the spoiled children of the American bourgeoisie." It reminded me of the radical student leader who, after having advocated bringing down the university and society, asked the assembled students on the main floor of Pauley Ballroom whether anyone had found the term paper he had lost in the library. Yet our serious commitment to help bring about an end to the war in Vietnam never wavered. A sympathetic liberal Republican friend helped to arrange a meeting with the newly elected senator from Oregon, Mark Hatfield, an avowed opponent of the war. With Carl Schorske, now a professor at Princeton University, I flew to Washington, D.C., to try to enlist

Hatfield in our cause. As we approached the Senate building, Schorske said to me, "You know, to succeed, we on the left have to be a lot smarter than the people on the right." We were well received by the senator but left without a promise of support. Perhaps the gulf between a liberal Republican senator and two Berkeley professors was too great to be bridged.

A year later, underrepresented minorities organized the Third World Strike to the end of combining community work and activism with university research and studies relevant to their particular needs. Clearer in their objectives than the "value"-oriented rebellion of the white student majority, minority strikers demanded a college of their own. I noted that hardly any of the white student leaders who had enjoyed high profiles in the past now played roles of any significance. Through the Third World Strike, Chicanos, African Americans, and Asians began to define educational objectives that included community building and economic opportunities as an integral part of the academic enterprise. I felt a great deal of solidarity with the minority groups, because it was so obvious that they had legitimate needs not addressed by the university.

While the strike was on, I teamed up with a graduate student in English who had extensive connections with African American, Chicano, and Asian students. They, in turn, together with their faculty sponsors, helped to formulate the content of new courses. With my experience as former chair of the Course Committee of the Academic Senate, I was able to offer my know-how in writing proposals acceptable to faculty committees. It was obvious to me, however, that the university would not move in the direction of the striking students unless it was under duress. Minority student leaders had a finely honed sense for power and its consequences as well as for the lack of power and its disadvantages. One of them advocated burning down the library. When he saw I was horrified, he argued that burning down the library would put the white majority and the minority students on equal terms. I considered his comment hyperbolic speech uttered in the heat of the moment. Yet a few weeks later Wheeler Hall went up in flames. The library remained unscathed, because the administration took extra precautions to protect it.

The unrest seemed to be turning into a full-fledged revolution of the minorities, when, pressed into a corner, the administration finally made some concessions in regard to minority programs. There were people hard at work behind the scenes — white professors who had supported minorities in the South, leaders from the African-American community, Chicano churchmen, even the Republican Berkeley mayor, Wally Johnson — to channel the dynamics away from violence toward obtainable academic goals.

In the middle of this turbulence, personalities came to the fore, most of them now forgotten, like my English graduate student named Sewell, who had extensive contacts in the various minority groups. The great-grandson of the hanging Judge Sewell of New England, he was also an official U.S. Frisbee champion. He could throw a Frisbee over the roofs of two suburban houses only to have it return to him like a boomerang. And there was a tough and brilliant African-American student leader with the improbable name Charlie Brown. An extremely gifted speaker with a keen mind, he once passed me a handwritten note during a faculty meeting to which he had been invited. To my astonishment, his handwriting and English were that of a child. At one point during the revolt, he and other strike leaders admitted me into the Third World Strike Center on Bancroft Avenue. When I asked him why they had let me in, I was stunned by his answer: because I had a German background, my prejudices would be against Jews and not blacks.

My period of political involvement came to an end with the People's Park unrest in 1969. I found the strange mix of flower children and political ideologues, of drugs and revolution, beyond my sense of what was important, and by the early 1970s the student revolution had run its course. Its surplus energy and utopian impulses were reined in by the then governor of California, Ronald Reagan. I left Berkeley for almost three years to become director of the University of California Education Abroad Program at Göttingen, where the politically focused German student revolution, which had considerable support among the general population, was at its height. For me, the American decade of upheaval had brought together private beliefs and public commitments. It also had a permanent effect on my academic career.

On my return from Göttingen, I joined the fight against institutional orthodoxy in the foreign language departments in favor of interdisciplinary studies. These internecine fights, of little obvious consequence to larger social issues, deepened my skepticism about the role of traditional departments of humanities that would rather prove the cohesiveness of a specific field of study than interpret the cultural history of Europe as a larger social and moral enterprise. I came to see teaching, more than research, as my primary purpose. The treasured gift Berkeley gave me was to allow me to instruct and know some of the brightest students of several generations, each with its own set of questions and priorities. I was particularly attracted to undergraduate instruction, since the interactions on that level are less deformed by the power relations so evident in graduate seminars, where students are preoccupied with their own academic careers. On the graduate level, I devoted most of my energies to medieval lyric and epic poetry in order to decipher cultural codes of a mentality other than our own. In undergraduate courses and in a coauthored book on German cultural history from the rise of Hitler to the early 1990s,[2] I became more and more involved in trying to understand the rise of Nazism within the larger context of German cultural history of the twentieth century.

In the middle of my career, I was struck by a fate similar to Bernie's. My wife, Muriel, died of leukemia on April 23, 1975. The disease showed no symptoms until a week before her death. A cold developed rapidly into bronchitis and pneumonia, followed by coma and death. Her hidden disease had rendered antibiotics ineffective. I went into shock. I experienced her loss as if my family had fallen victim to sudden violence. My two children, Karen, 13, and Michael, 11, lost their mother. When they woke up the morning after she died in the hospital, and I had to tell them the news, my daughter first thought it was a cruel joke played on us by the hospital, while my son fell to the living room floor and wept. I knew I had to pull myself together to raise the children, particularly when I was awakened by them early one morning a few days after their mother's death. Frightened, they had come to my bed to make sure I hadn't died, too. I swore to myself that they would never come home from school without my being there to greet them. I arranged my schedule at the university accordingly. Bernie and I hardly ever talk about this strange coincidence of losing our wives in midlife, but it is part of a deeper understanding we have of each other.

. . .

What made it possible for Bernie's and my paths to cross and for us to make our return to the past a joint enterprise? Whatever similarities in rural childhoods we shared, the divide that Nazism drew between us was absolute. We came from the opposite sides of the Holocaust. And after the defeat of Germany and the victory of the Allies, we continued to move in very different worlds, both in postwar Europe and after we came to the United States. In spite of the ballast we left behind in Europe, the values that guided both our lives in the New World were nevertheless shaped in part by what we had experienced and learned in the Old. Having suffered as an outsider during the violent years of Nazi totalitarianism, Bernie made himself into an insider in America. I, however, having lived my early life within the Nazi regime, having been surrounded and deceived by it, found the role of the outsider to be the only morally defensible one to play in its aftermath.

So why did we become friends despite the odds against this happening? There was, of course, the chance meeting of our wives. Then, the casual suburban nature of our early friendship made it possible for a crucial factor to come into play, namely, the sharing of our common European cultural heritage in terms of music, the arts, philosophy, and literature. Beyond that, there was the Bay Area, this great crucible for new ideas, experiments, risk taking, and daring IPOs of all sorts, not only financial, but also of the creative and cultural type. So we came together, and why not us, and why not in this form? Why not explore how two divergent paths might be made to cross?

For Bernie, the freedom that America provided was all the more personal, because it stood in sharp contrast to the totalitarian violence that almost took his life. This explains his cherished belief in reason as a shield against the mythology of Cain and Abel. To be able to enter our friendship with a remarkable degree of ease, he had to travel a long road from Auschwitz to our brotherly dinner table in California. I, in turn, learned that freedom was not just handed me as a gift but something that had to be earned. The Orthodox Jew from Hungary and the Hitler Youth candidate from Germany had become Americans—the fact that made a true crossing of paths possible. In America, working and playing together—and breaking bread together where the ghosts of the past no longer loomed up to join us at our table—finally became normal, everyday facts of life.

SEVEN

. . .

Germany:
Fifty Years Later

The web of our life is of a mingled yarn, good
and ill together.

— WILLIAM SHAKESPEARE

Early in the writing of our stories, Bernie and I planned a trip to
Germany for spring 1997 as a way to complete our recall of the
past. We decided that our trip should start in the Austrian city of
Mauthausen and the forest near Gunskirchen where Bernie had
nearly died at the end of World War II. We met at the Dom Hotel
in nearby Linz. Somehow it surprised me to see Bernie move
around Austria with the same self-assurance that he had at home
in California. I felt an unfamiliar twinge of self-consciousness at
being with Bernie in German-speaking Europe.

In the morning we drove east along the north bank of the
Danube through the peaceful, green Austrian landscape toward
the Mauthausen concentration camp, now a museum. It stands
on top of a hill behind the small town — a cold, gray, forbidding
prison with massive stone walls. You enter through a large gate
that displays a round opening near the top of its arch, where a
swastika had supported the eagle of the Third Reich more than
half a century earlier. Sally and I were confused for a moment

to see the letters "KLM" displayed at the entrance, as if the Dutch airline were advertising at this locale, until Bernie explained that in this case it stood, of course, for Konzentrationslager Mauthausen. He said he had found it amusing after he learned what those initials meant to the rest of the world.

A ticket booth manned by an Austrian government employee is located well within the walls in front of the barracks area. I found it perverse that Bernie should have to pay to revisit the camp where he nearly died. As a matter of fact, why wasn't this monument free of charge to everyone? Why shouldn't the Austrian government pay to maintain it? I tried to persuade Bernie that he already had paid his entrance fee years earlier and that we demand free admission for him now, but he wouldn't hear of it. At least Sally and I insisted on paying for him. Bernie suggested with a grin that he and I take advantage of the senior discount, which we did. At 10 schillings, the fee was less than a dollar.

Once inside the barracks area of Mauthausen, you face a huge elongated asphalt square framed by long rows of parallel one-story barracks on the left and a row of larger buildings on the right. This area, nearly empty in the morning sun and stretching about half a kilometer to the far end, reminded me of the Nazi rally site in Nuremberg. Both spaces had been designed to move human beings around easily—to mold the masses, as Hitler had said.

Bernie's barracks, block 21, was no longer there, but others remained and were open to visitors. We entered one, and Bernie pointed out some typical features: the narrow wooden bunkbed frames on which four people shared a platform hardly large enough for one, the round stone washbasins installed between sleeping quarters, the hooks for hanging clothes. Outside, he showed us the chimneys of the kitchen and crematorium, one not very far away from the other. Many other camera-toting tourists had purchased tickets and roamed through the barracks and the museum and past the memorial statues. Now, of course, the camp provided well-marked, clean rest rooms, but it went too far, I thought, in providing an on-site café, which we shunned. I felt like shouting out to the strangers around us that there was someone here who had been an inmate fifty years ago. But Bernie would not have liked that kind of attention. He was engaged in his own search.

In front of a glass vitrine that displayed a pile of identification bands—some of them crude, provided by the Nazi authorities, and others more artistic, fashioned by the inmates themselves—I noticed Bernie fingering the glasses case that hung from a belt loop at his side throughout most of our trip. From it he retrieved his reading glasses to get a better look at the displayed identification tags. Now he stared intently at the contents of the vitrine. He tried to locate, by some wild chance, the bracelet with the number 103,705 that he had lost, the one that the silversmith inmate had fashioned for him, but to no avail.

We moved on to the kitchen in which he had worked for several weeks. Then he led us across the area where the dreaded morning *Appell* took place during all types of weather, even on the coldest winter days. We asked Bernie what the prisoners did during the day after roll call if they weren't working in the kitchen or the quarry. He said, "Nothing. We just milled around." I realized that this contrasted with his description of his days at Auschwitz-Birkenau. I had once compared the devastation he felt on Betsy's death to the depression he must have felt in Auschwitz, but he objected to the use of the term "depression." Whereas he fell into a depression after the death of his wife, he actually experienced a near-absence of emotions at Auschwitz, because there was no time to reflect. His days there were filled with "ducking, weaving, and motions to stay alive."

In the auditorium next to the museum, we watched a graphically detailed film about the history of the camp and its horrors: for example, stripping and chaining prisoners to a wall outside the barracks and hosing them with cold water before leaving them to freeze to death overnight in winter. These bodies were frozen stiff and encased in ice the next morning. The film also documents one of the messages scrawled on the wall of an isolation cell: "If there were a God, he'd have to beg forgiveness of me." After the film, we slowly made our way out toward the quarry, located a short distance from the barracks. As we walked, Bernie mentioned how he hated to take showers at Mauthausen. Once a week the inmates were marched naked, no matter how cold the weather, to the showers in another building. The water was usually cold; but once in a while it was lukewarm. He showed us a small scar on his right hand from a "cold sore," as he called it, that wouldn't heal while he was at Mauthausen. He had avoided seeing the camp doctor about it for fear he would have been sent to the hospital, from which many never returned.

Bernie remarked about the balmy spring weather and the beauty of the idyllic landscape that we could see all around us outside the concentration camp walls. He was always struck, while a camp inmate, by the unbelievable contrast between the picturesque landscape just outside and the horrendous suffering within. As we approached the quarry steps on rough cobblestone pavement, Bernie admonished Sally and me not to stumble. I recalled his account of the day he had been assigned to this sadistic hell.

Once we reached the bottom of the quarry, the sheer stone cliffs surrounding it seemed hopelessly high. We knew from the film that some inmates had committed suicide by leaping from the cliffs, to smash against the walls or to drown in the ponds below, while others had been murdered when guards forced inmates to push each other off of them. It was an uncanny setting on this muggy day in late spring—brownish ponds, reddish cliffs, lush vegetation. We were the only tourists to have descended the stairs at the time. Unlike the camp above on the plateau, it was not an ugly place. But it is one you don't want to remain in very long, for fear that the walls could close in on you. I wondered what voices might echo back from the cliffs if one were to start shouting. As we headed back toward the steps to climb out of the quarry, Bernie reiterated what the film had said—that during the war there had been a different number of steps because they had been built of uneven heights to make the work of carrying stones up them more grueling. He recalled them as having been narrower, so that when one prisoner toppled down backward, he couldn't help but take others with him. This cruelty had been a deliberate part of the original design.

Bernie and I slowly ascended the safer, reconstructed steps together, counting in silence. We fell into a lockstep, as if we wanted to invent our own wordless commemorative ritual. When we reached the top and he said, "Hey, we made it," we both had to laugh. And we both had counted 186 steps. Leaving the camp felt like crossing an invisible border between the past and the present, between the camp and the gentle Austrian hills. History has marked off this place of horror forever, even though there is now no transitional space between the inside and the outside.

We continued east along the Danube past the bright village center of Mauthausen. All of us felt the need for some comic relief to shake the oppression of the evil place we had just left. I quipped that Bernie had obviously lived on the "wrong side of the tracks" during his stay in Mauthausen. If he had only resided in "lower Mauthausen" and not "upper Mauthausen," he would have been all right. We were amused and scandalized at the same time to note the prominent golden arches of a McDonald's restaurant at the edge of the village, and Bernie asked to stop so that he could photograph the "McDonald's Mauthausen" sign. And we, in turn, took a picture of him taking the picture.

That afternoon, we traced in our car the path of the Death March between Mauthausen and the village of Gunskirchen, the four-day march during which half the concentration camp inmates perished. We knew that those who dropped or straggled behind had been executed. Now Bernie told us that he, like most of the others on the trek, did not look back to watch the executions, but they all heard the shots. When a family member or buddy stayed with someone who fell, they heard two shots.

Now we drove on well-paved roads beyond Wels, one of the towns they had passed on the way to their final destination in the pine forest of Gunskirchen. Wels, with its car lots adorned with colorful flags, has grown so that it is now merged with Gunskirchen. We paused at the church that still stands in the center of Gunskirchen across from the Hänsel und Gretel Brautmoden boutique that displays bridal gowns in its window. From there, we drove out of the village center and crossed the main road to enter the pine forest where Bernie remembered the camp to have been located.

The forest was honeycombed with small paths and dirt roads partially overgrown with vegetation. An occasional clearing strewn with old rotted logs and a new growth of trees allowed for a glimpse into deeper parts of the forest. We parked the car and started to search on foot, to forage around for telltale signs that might remain of the tragedy that had unfolded there over half a century ago during the last weeks of the war. But nothing was left of the makeshift camp of prefabricated barracks. Or perhaps we couldn't find the exact site. (Recently, we met a Czech survivor of the Death March who told us that a small memorial has been erected near the site; but we did not find it.) No voices of the past echoed in the trees—the desperate father who died after having devoured his son's meager rations, the old woman who shared her last scrap of food with a young boy, the corpses piled on corpses, the SS guards who administered arsenic to the remaining victims—all were gone. No traces remained. We only heard the wind in the trees. This absence, this nothingness increased our determination to find something, anything, that would allow us to link the past with the present. So we carefully retraced our steps and drove deeper into the forest, until the road narrowed and almost vanished in the underbrush where branches scraped the sides of our car so badly that we feared getting stuck altogether, or at least ruining the paint job. So, with Sally at the wheel while Bernie and I held the strongest branches away from the car, we slowly backed out of our trap, and out of the pine forest of Gunskirchen altogether. Bernie laughed, "Well, we got through that scrape too." It was getting late in the day, so we decided to return to Linz. This forest, filled with horror for Bernie, revealed nothing more to our eyes—all the more reason to tell our stories.

Back in Linz that evening, we wandered through the town center in search of a restaurant, stopping here and there to read the posted menus. At one point we entered an inner courtyard with an open-air restaurant, where a youth orchestra entertained a crowd of diners. As it finished playing a Viennese waltz, an athletic young man, about twenty years old, appeared out of nowhere, dressed in a sweat suit and running shoes. He stationed himself in front of the band, raised his hand in the Nazi salute, and barked with military precision, "Im Namen des Führers!" (In the name of the Führer!). The crowd fell silent. After his verbal assault, the young brute pranced provocatively from table to table with a hostile smirk on his face. No one stirred, but an older corpulent man standing next to me muttered in German, "Swine!" We left the disturbing scene to search elsewhere for a place to eat. In my mind, I pitted this neo-Nazi thug against a young man of his generation whom Sally and I briefly encountered on our way to Linz to meet Bernie: a father on roller blades, a Walkman on his head, a knapsack full of groceries on his back, pushing a baby stroller containing his infant down the sidewalk. Friendly and curious, he was happy to give directions to two foreigners—just outside the town of Dachau.

Our trip to Austria and Germany, which was to last a week, had been carefully planned. It was Bernie's first trip to Germany. On his other trips abroad, Germany had never been on his itinerary except as a transit stop at the Frankfurt airport. But since I had been to his village of Tab in southern Hungary, we agreed he should visit my village of Kleinheubach on the Main River. And, since the wall separating Germany and Europe into two parts had crumbled and Germany was unified, we were all curious to take a glimpse at Berlin, its future and its past. We realized that as Berlin becomes Germany's new capital, the concern Thomas Mann articulated after World War II takes on new relevance—whether the future will be shaped by a European Germany or a German Europe.

As we crossed the border into Germany, I wondered how Bernie felt. We were discussing contemporary American politics, and he seemed more engrossed than I in our conversation. Content to stay in the right lane, we joined the high-speed race on the Autobahn in the direction of Kleinheubach. On the way we passed by Nuremberg, with its old Nazi rally parade grounds and its former tribunal where the top Nazi criminals were convicted after the war. For Bernie, Nuremberg had an ominous ring, but I have always liked the city. For him, it was the city of Gothic tales, predating Nazism; for me, it was the big city of my youth where my favorite cousin lived.

Although its population has doubled in size since World War II to more than three thousand, my childhood village is not set up for tourism. So we stayed nearby in an idyllic resort hotel, the Paradeismühle (Paradise Mill) in the Spessart mountains. I debated with myself about whether to mention to Bernie that these pine- and beech-covered mountains played a role in the medieval German heroic epic of the Nibelungs. This is where the perfidious Hagen is said to have stabbed Siegfried, the Germanic hero, in the back, giving rise to the stab-in-the-back mythology that was so important in the Nazi ideology about the Third Reich and its "cowardly" enemies. Our peaceful, two-night abode nestled in the forest displayed six flags of neighboring European countries and really had nothing to do with Germanic myths. And, after all, except for students of German medieval literature or the music of Richard Wagner, who cares anymore about these connotations that crowded in on me? Perhaps I should have mentioned them just the same, but I felt it to be too one-sided an introduction to contemporary Germany.

Unlike our slow walk through Tab a few years earlier, I first showed Bernie my village from the car, with brief stops at the blacksmith's shop, my grandmother's house, the English gardens of the baroque castle, the Main River, the village walls, and the ochre-colored Protestant church, where in my youth I had suffered through many a long-winded sermon during Sunday morning services. The pulpit was still adorned with the same gold-trimmed, white pelican who opens her breast to feed her young with her own blood. Nothing had changed in this church since my childhood. A stone plaque on the wall still lists the names of the village men who died in World War I. There is no stone plaque for those who died in World War II. Constructed in the late Middle Ages and never destroyed, the church stands on level ground. The bells were removed during World War II for the purpose of turning them into cannons, but it never came to this. After the war, they were returned intact to the bell tower. Not far from the Protestant church, near the river, I showed Bernie the various high-water markings that indicated levels of the Main River over the centuries.

I was able to show Bernie numerous places where my early life, the life of my family and its friends and acquaintances, was inscribed, tangible evidence of a human geography that continued to the present day, in spite of the twentieth century's upheavals. By contrast, during our visit to Tab, Bernie had been able to show us only a few sites from his past, as he came up against closed gates, razed houses, and the crumbling steps that no longer led to the synagogue where he had sobbed and prayed. Only the train station and gravestone inscriptions in the grass-covered cemetery provided tangible links to all he had been forced to leave behind in 1944.

The nephew of my stepmother Zink, Manfred Zink, had arranged for us to meet with both the former and the current mayors of Kleinheubach in the town hall (Rathaus). Just the year before, in 1996, the former mayor, Bernhard Holl, published the two-part history of the Jewish community in Kleinheubach from 1677 to 1942 on which I have relied for historical background material in these memoirs. Together with the current mayor, Kurt Schüssler, we toured the town hall and met some of his colleagues.

Both mayors accompanied us on a walk through the village and showed us the reconstructed facade of the synagogue in the Judengasse, which had been ransacked during the Kristallnacht of 1938. Herr Holl gave us some historical background. Following the Kristallnacht, the fanatic *Ortsgruppenleiter* had reported the destruction of the synagogue to his superiors in Miltenberg as an act of the "seething soul of the people" (*ein Opfer der kochenden Volksseele*). Then, in 1940, the village purchased what was left of the synagogue for 600 reichsmarks and used it to store fire department equipment and a hearse.[1] Although it later came into private ownership, it was eventually declared a historical monument, and public moneys were used to restore the roof and facade to their condition before the Kristallnacht. The inscription in Hebrew over the door now reads, "This is the door to God.... The righteous should enter."

From the synagogue, we walked to the restored *Mikva* (bathhouse) that Kleinheubach Jews had used for purification rituals. It had been conveniently constructed next to the brook that ran from the nearby mountains, then along the edge of the village and down to the Main River. One of a very few extant *Mikvas* in Bavaria, public moneys also restored this protected monument. It was dedicated during a Kristallnacht memorial ceremony on November 9, 1992, commemorating the Jewish victims of Nazi violence. A red sandstone marker carries the star of David and a German inscription: "To the victims of National Socialism and of all forms of tyranny" (*Den Opfern des Nationalsozialismus und aller Gewaltherrschaft*). We also visited the old schoolhouse of the once-thriving Jewish community and found that it, too, had been restored. Then we drove up to the Jewish cemetery, where 485 Jews have their last resting place, witness to centuries of Jewish life in the Main valley.

Bernie and his German namesake, Bernhard, the former mayor, made their way through the rows of graves. About 186 stone markers were still standing; the rest have deteriorated or sunk into the ground or were used for new grave plates. On the backside of the upright stones are inscriptions in German, while the fronts carry names and dates in Hebrew that Bernie deciphered for Herr Holl. Herr Holl pointed out the grave of the last Jewish inhabitant of Kleinheubach to be buried in this forest cemetery, Julius Sichel, who died on October 10, 1941.

It was clear that this former mayor, who on our arrival introduced himself as a "German patriot," saw the Jews who had lived in the village as an integral part of his own local heritage, as a source of pride. What he did not tell us was that a controversy had raged as to where to place the red sandstone that commemorated the victims of Nazism. Some villagers felt, as I found out later, that it should be placed in the main village square, others that it should be located near the *Mikva*. During its installation ceremony at the *Mikva*, police were present to prevent any potential neo-Nazi disturbances. Although to date none had occurred, Herr Holl confided to us that he feared vandalism there and in the Jewish cemetery. Were it to happen, an incident would besmirch the name of Kleinheubach, of which he is so proud, in newspaper reports "from Kiel to Konstanz," as he put it. He went so far as to fret about the fact that some gravestones had sunk and tilted over time. If they were to topple over one day on their own, it might be mistaken for vandalism. We realized how hard it was for a citizen of goodwill, such as Bernhard Holl, to be a German patriot.

About fifty years old with curly red hair, the current mayor of Kleinheubach, Kurt Schüssler, belonged to a different generation of Germans than his predecessor. While respectful of Bernhard Holl's intense relation to village history, Herr Schüssler was primarily concerned with issues of the present. He talked to us about the governance of a contemporary German community on the local and regional levels, within the context of the modern democratic institutions that Germany has developed since World War II. His focus was clearly on translating grassroots issues into practical solutions. Bernie was quite taken with Herr Schüssler's presentation and, with his customary legal precision, posed myriad questions about the operational level of village governance that left the rest of us listening passively. Typical of his focus on the here and now, Bernie was just as interested in this information about the village's current infrastructure as in the touching ways in which the town memorialized its vanished Jewish community. When Bernie asked him about the chain of command from the federal level down to the local level, Herr Schüssler replied simply, "I'm the boss here," meaning that he was not there just to take orders from above. With his evident expertise and quiet self-assurance, he was a good example of grassroots democracy in a country where power has become decentralized. This was as important to Bernie's assessment of Germans as any devotion they might show for the Jewish presence in the village's past. Here he found reassurance that there is little chance for a revival of Nazism on a grand scale.

We ended the day with a large meal at the Gasthaus zur schönen Aussicht, where, right after the war, villagers had discussed secession from Germany. Seated between the two mayors, Bernie tried manfully through the hours of eating and drinking to keep up with the conversation that lapsed at times into the local dialect. It was his first social event in Germany, and his German, though serviceable, was not always up to the brisk pace of the verbal interaction. Sally and I translated as much as we could, and after a couple of beers his German became more fluent.

At one point in the evening, knowing that I had started first grade in 1936, the proprietor of the inn produced a class photo taken in front of the grammar school in 1937 in which I was seated on the ground in the front row. I recognized most of the faces in the photo. Many of the children I still remembered by name, or at least I knew where they had lived in the village. I handed the photo across the table to Bernie and thought about his mournful examination of the glass vitrine at Mauthausen, where he searched in vain for his number on the displayed ID bracelets. It was not fair, of course, that I could share this photo from my youth in this familiar locale while he had nothing comparable to show from his childhood in Tab. We passed the faded picture around the table, and people remarked about what had happened to this or that person, but soon it was put away as the conversation moved on to other subjects. Several hours after it had begun, our merry party disbanded with warm farewells.

On the drive back to our resort hotel in the forest, Bernie marveled at the degree of continuity that existed in my life. My first reaction was to dispute it. I had emigrated, after all, as an eighteen-year-old to make my way in an American university and in an urban setting that bore no resemblance to the rural world I left behind. But Bernie countered that it was all a matter of degree and perspective. Fundamental breaks had characterized his life, and when he mentioned it in this context, I realized that I had never had to reinvent myself as totally as he was forced to do—from a boy in Tab to an orphan in death camps to a teenager in Italian refugee camps and, finally, to an adopted son in one of America's wealthiest families. I was completely taken aback when, as we said goodnight to him outside his room, he looked straight at me and said, "You know, that SS-Mauthausen entry of my arrival there on September 20, 1944, is the only written proof I have of my early life."

Later, when I reflected on his comment, I realized how easy it had been for me to arrange a get-together with my childhood buddy Ludwig Bohn, who happened to be visiting his parents' house once when I also happened to be in Kleinheubach—this in contrast to the difficulties Bernie had finding Simcha during his trip to Israel. Some of Bernie's difficulties were of his own doing. Early in our memory work, in the first version of his reunion with Simcha, Bernie had only described the encounter itself. Later, another story regarding Simcha emerged, namely, of the barriers Bernie had to surmount before being able to locate his friend in Israel after almost fifty years. The trail leading back to Simcha had vanished. The Jewish agencies he contacted in the United States led nowhere. In Israel, he consulted the database at the Yad Vashem Museum but didn't come away with any concrete leads. He found an oral history of the Jewish children's survivor camp at Selvino, where he and Simcha had been taken after the war. Although Bernie recognized some of the names in this account, Simcha Katz was not among them. By coincidence, during his brief stay, Israeli television aired a documentary program on Selvino. A museum docent Bernie met had been so moved by this documentary and by this American visitor trying to locate his old Mauthausen and Selvino friend that she promised to do everything she could to help bring about their reunion. The docent managed to locate the widow of Moshe Z'iri, the Jewish leader of the Italian camp. Z'iri's widow consulted the archives of the Selvino group that Z'iri had kept unofficially and was able to locate Simcha, who lived in a small community near Tel Aviv. Thus the meeting was arranged. Had it not been for the documentary film and a determined museum employee, the contact between the two former concentration camp friends wouldn't have come to pass.

. . .

As we left Kleinheubach, Bernie said he was very impressed by what had been done in this corner of Germany to remember the past and the former Jewish inhabitants of the village. Bernhard

Holl had given both of us copies of his recently published book on the history of Kleinheubach's Jewish community. This local history, along with the restoration of the synagogue, *Mikva*, and school, stood in sharp contrast to Tab, where, except for the abandoned cemetery, there is no trace of the hundreds of Jewish families who lived there for many generations. Bernie remarked with irony that, during his earlier postwar visits to Tab, its Christian citizens killed during World War II had been equally ignored. But since 1990 and the fall of communism in Hungary, that had changed, and a splendid monument now stood in the middle of the village honoring the fallen "heroes" of that war. As for the Jews, it is still as if there had never been any. Bernie came back to this point many times during our trip. The extent of Germany's interest in the Holocaust touched him, but he also thought that it was time now, fifty years after the war, with a different generation in charge, not to forget the past, but to move on.

The first night Bernie spent at the home of a German family was anything but routine. We had been invited for dinner and an overnight stay 50 kilometers up the Main River by Alfred-Ernst, Prince of Löwenstein-Wertheim-Freudenberg, and his wife, Princess Ruth-Erika, daughter of the Prussian Junker family von Buggenhagen. Our host happened to be a descendant of the Protestant branch of the house of Löwenstein, whose Catholic branch owned the Löwenstein castle and park down the Main River in Kleinheubach. In the eighteenth century, both houses had provided *Schutzbriefe* (letters of protection) for numerous local Jews that guaranteed them certain rights and freedoms, including residency, practice of trades and com-

merce, and participation in civic life. A *Schutzbrief* also constituted a warning to others not to assault the Jew's privileges or to
mistreat him. These letters of protection were a common ar-
rangement at the time for which protected Jews paid annual
sums to the prince and obligated themselves not to provoke or
seduce Christians or to utter blasphemies.[2]

As soon as we arrived in the late afternoon, the large, jovial
Prince of Löwenstein ushered us through his baroque château
to the parlor for a welcoming tea. I turned to Bernie at an op-
portune moment and asked him whether he had ever spent a
night in such splendor. To my surprise, he replied that in its own
way, Charles Merrill, Sr.'s mansion in Southampton was comparable.

Dinner, prepared by servants, was served in a spacious dining
room. After eating, our hosts and their son and daughter-in-law
strolled the expansive grounds with us and gave us a tour of their
castle. When the zu Löwenstein's stately daughter-in-law sat
down beneath a turn-of-the-century oil painting that portrayed
two of her great-grandmothers, we felt time stand still through
the generations. Quick as ever, Bernie volunteered the flattery
that family beauty had survived throughout the century, while I
kicked myself for not having thought of it first. No one had
taught me such gallant manners down the river in my village.

The evening might easily have seemed like a moment removed from the twentieth century. This landed aristocracy had
survived wars, revolutions, social upheavals, and Nazi mayhem.
But aside from their gracious manner of living, the zu Löwensteins have been deeply involved in their times. On a bookshelf

near the door, I noticed a first edition of Hitler's *Mein Kampf*. I opened it and found that the father of the present patriarch had penned marginal annotations, now faded, in old German script, such as *Phrasen* (empty words), which expressed his disapproval of the Austrian ex-corporal's politics.

After the war, the zu Löwensteins became one of the focal points for an active German-American friendship society. They have traveled extensively in the United States, and even today bemoan the departure of the American army. They belong to the war and immediate postwar generation of Germans that is deeply grateful for the American presence in Europe, for the civil society and the political stability we helped to create there. Toward the end of the evening, the prince produced an early-sixteenth-century volume that described life in colonial Virginia. We ended the evening poring over this tome and its lithographs of the New World. Accustomed as he was to an upper-class milieu, Bernie had moved through the evening with great ease.

We said our good-byes after breakfast the next morning. Our host opened his gate and directed us out into the traffic in the direction of Berlin. Through the rearview mirror, we saw him wave farewell to us with large gestures so characteristic of this generous spirit.

We organized our stay in Berlin with the help of two friends, an "East" German artist and a "West" German physician. To a great extent we depended on our friends, with their disparate political ideologies, to show us parts of the city they thought would interest us.

Our physician friend, Manuela Bayer, showed us the side of West Berlin that we all have known as the "showcase of democracy" during the years of the cold war. Bernie had not experienced Berlin as the divided city it then was. At one point he asked us whether a small retaining wall we passed by was a remnant of the Berlin Wall, not realizing how massive the cut through the middle of the city had been. But since his first view of Berlin was untrammeled by the major effects the cold war had had on it, he gained a much clearer view of the present-day metropolis and its progress toward the future than we did, caught as we were with our experiences of the city during its period of postwar division.

We decided to visit Plötzensee, the high-walled prison where Germans who had opposed Nazism were murdered. It is a stark place, hidden away and hard to find, and very much in line with the understated approach Germany takes today in speaking of Germans who resisted Nazism. It is widely known that the failed coup against Hitler of July 1944 led to the execution of the conspirators. Less well known is that more than sixteen thousand people were sentenced to death for political resistance and treason against the Third Reich from 1933 until the end of the war. About a quarter of them were hanged or beheaded at Plötzensee in a chamber that looks like a wholesale butcher shop with its iron hooks and troughs to catch the blood.[3]

Bernie and I lingered a long time over the official Nazi documents pertaining to a particular German housewife who had merely expressed a personal dislike for Hitler. She had been denounced by a neighbor. After a trial and several appeals, on display at the museum, she was condemned to die and was guillotined at Plötzensee. Almost wordlessly, the four of us made our way through this prison, as did a handful of other visitors. To date there is no morally convincing narrative about Germans as victims of Nazism, because such a narrative might sound like an attempt at balancing the scales. Our German guide, Manuela, stayed in the background during this part of our return to the past. It had not been her recommendation to visit Plötzensee, but mine, with Bernie in agreement.

In digging up the ground and removing the last debris left over from the final battles of World War II at the center of Berlin a few years earlier, the Germans had unearthed the SS Headquarters and had converted them into a permanent exhibit called Topographie des Terrors. As we approached the museum, Bernie discovered that his ever-present glasses case, with his glasses in it, was missing. We had joked about the funny red case and the dime store reading glasses before, but now he seemed very upset, almost panicked over their loss. Everything stopped while we retraced our steps and finally discovered them under the table in the restaurant where we had eaten lunch. I realized how very hard on him it was to lose anything—in this case, something he needed right away.

We entered the Topographie des Terrors at the so-called Prinz Albrecht Site, where the remains of the Gestapo, SS, and Reich Security Main Office are located. On the walls of the restored cells, Nazi crimes are documented by photographs of victims and victimizers, documents ordering mass executions, and posters of anti-Semitic propaganda. We made our way slowly through the extensive underground labyrinth. One photograph showed Hungarian Jews being transported to Auschwitz in summer 1944. Two boys—who could have been the Rosner brothers—in heavy coats, with dark caps drawn over their ears, stared back at us with frightened faces. I was stunned by its obvious evocation of my friend's past. But, to my surprise, Bernie passed by it without showing any special interest. This black-and-white image, fixed on white museum walls, didn't stimulate a memory or a response; it provided no emotional bridge to the past for this survivor. If anything, it seemed to draw him, the onlooker, and the boys in the picture apart. I asked him about his apparent disinterest in this photograph later, and he replied with one word, "Overload."

We came to a picture of Adolf Eichmann that showed the very same four stars on his lapel that Bernie had drawn for me in his living room in northern California. Bernie stared at this photograph and then announced, "He patted me on the head in Tab when he was there." Sally and I knew what he was talking about, but our German friend looked puzzled. I told her the story of Eichmann's visit to Tab in spring 1944 and how Bernie had come face-to-face with Hitler's notorious henchman, who called him "Kleiner Bube." I don't think Manuela understood what she was hearing.

Bernie spent the most time in front of a document that spelled out in detail for the top SS echelon the "logistics problems" a high-ranking SS officer had disposing of the corpses of more than a thousand Lithuanian Jews whom he and his troops had executed. Bernie has always been more interested in Heinrich

Himmler than in Hitler, since Himmler claimed to the British army after his capture and before his suicide not to have known about the systematic extermination of the Jews. But here in this exhibit, Bernie came across proof that Himmler was lying, in the form of this Lithuanian SS officer's report. He moved up close to the exhibit and read every line. His satisfaction was evident, and he often came back to this point later—an authentic Nazi document in a German museum that constituted irrefutable evidence of Himmler's knowledge of the genocide.

I had always thought that Bernie's worry about these surrealistic claims of innocence by the upper echelon of the Nazi hierarchy, or even the contemporary extremists' claims that German extermination camps did not exist, represented one of his few irrational streaks. But I began to realize that the extraordinary nature of the Holocaust makes it seem incredible on the face of it, and thus open to exploitation by neo-Nazis. The huge discrepancy between the unprecedented horrors in Auschwitz and the apparent normalcy of the German everyday before and after the Nazi years leaves room for the ill-willed to spin their delusionary yarns.

We emerged from this subterranean realm of past Nazi tortures squinting in the bright sunny day. Not far away was a large, fenced-in area that appeared to be an old construction site, with pieces of broken concrete strewn about in the weeds. Why was such prime real estate in the heart of Berlin abandoned? It turned out to be the location of Hitler's bunker, and the Germans didn't know what to do with it. I suggested that perhaps the memorial to Nazi victims, so hotly debated in Berlin, should be erected on it. Bernie suggested with irony that perhaps a plaque be installed at the location that read, "Adolf Hitler slept here." He made it increasingly clear during the trip that he was suspicious of any continued collective breast-beating about Germany's past crimes. For him, it was the reverse of the collective hatred once directed against the Jews; to attribute collective guilt to all living Germans was to do the same thing Hitler had done to the Jews. I knew that this had not always been Bernie's attitude; rather, it had evolved over time. In 1956, for instance, after he learned about the Czech "ethnic cleansing" of Sudenten Germans, he remembers having commented sarcastically to Charles Merrill, "It couldn't have happened to a nicer bunch."

But the question remained: what should the Germans do with the grassy piece of real estate that covers the remnants of Hitler's bunker? Should they dig it up to see what they find? We finally agreed that we would sell this prime property to the highest bidder, who could then erect on it whatever he saw fit—hotel, restaurant, tennis club, or amusement park. Our German friend did not venture an opinion.

We then drove to the Potsdamer Platz, the largest construction site in Europe, where history unfolds before your eyes. A forest of cranes marked the horizon of this cityscape. Huge machines in motion, they swung in all directions, giving Berlin an aura of determination and unbounded energy. None of us had ever seen anything like it. Mountains of excavated earth, cement, and building materials were piled up everywhere. A network of dirt roads provided access to various sites for heavy vehicles. Groundwater was being pumped out of cavernous holes;

office buildings were going up everywhere, with edifices for Mercedes and Sony leading the way. Huge buildings to house the federal government, scheduled to move to Berlin, were being constructed and old buildings renovated. An entire metropolis was being reconstructed and the contours of a nation changed. You could sense that this new capital not too far from the Polish border was far to the east of Bonn. It remained to be seen what this new seat of power would mean for the future of Germany and of Europe.

Manuela told us about the recent concert that celebrated this new beginning in the heart of Germany, when Daniel Barenboim and the Berlin Philharmonic performed Haydn's "Creation," the mass celebrating the biblical story of Genesis. The orchestra and concert-goers had been seated right in the middle of this enormous construction area. Our German friend was critical of the event, saying that this so-called beginning had little to do with her Germany but much to do with Mercedes, Sony, and other international corporations that were footing the bill for the monumental enterprise, including the musical performance. Bernie defended these investments for the future of Germany and Europe. He found the financial support of the corporate sponsors for the concert a brilliant idea. After all, as he concluded, hadn't it always been the rich who contributed to great art that benefited everyone? Renaissance culture could not have flourished without its wealthy patrons. Today's wealthy and powerful, moreover, have brought benefits to many more layers of society than did the elites who ruled the Italian Renaissance cities.

We climbed the stairs to the top of the Info Box, a temporary observation platform from which we could see all of Berlin's center. Computer screens provided a view of how the city will look when construction plans are completed. Also visible from this vantage point were remnants of the Berlin Wall that reminded us of the Iron Curtain that had split Germany and Europe into two parts. History crowds in on this old divide, juxtaposed to the new and not yet born: Hitler's bunker, the SS chamber of horrors, the old Reichstag building, with its turbulent early-twentieth-century history, and, nearby, the Museum of Modern Art, which during our visit housed an exhibition that included precious works from as far away as St. Petersburg and New York. Architectural monumentalism in the heart of Berlin is inescapable, and given the amount of reconstruction, unavoidable.

Ancient Rome, with its many archaeological layers, was for Sigmund Freud a metaphor of the human psyche. Contemporary Berlin, with all of its demolition, sifting of debris, covering over and building up, appeared to us as a metaphor of modern history.

. . .

The following morning, the three of us took the subway to the enormous Alexanderplatz, the largest square in Berlin, to meet our East German guide, Ursula Strozynski, who was well connected to the grassroots artists' colony that flourishes in East Berlin. When we got off our train, we asked two uniformed police officers with a fierce-looking Doberman in tow how to get to the

Weltuhr (world clock)—our meeting place. They were happy to give us directions. As we emerged onto the windy square, I asked Bernie whether these police brought back memories of other German police and other guard dogs. Not at all, he replied, with characteristic rationality. He had no problem seeing these contemporary German police as his protectors.

We walked through the working-class neighborhoods not far from the Alexanderplatz with Ursula. Well versed in the current debates about the representation of the past in the new Berlin, she proudly held on to her socialist creed and the moral conviction that Germans should try to "reexperience," as intensely as possible, the suffering the Nazis caused their victims, particularly the Jews. Although we detected some of the prefabricated slogans of the socialist past in her speech, we were nevertheless taken by her goodwill as she opened our eyes to some of the subtler cultural differences between what used to be East and West Berlin.

We wandered through streets with sooty brick facades, broken windows and peeling paint, dingy back alleys, courtyards, and weed-filled lots strewn with abandoned junk. Our artist guide saw in run-down things the traces of human activities and of times past that needed to be recalled. For her, this kind of respect for the past was a moral imperative. She related with pride the struggle of the Communists against the Nazis that took place in these streets in the early 1930s.

She then led us to the Beth Café in the Tucholskystraße, a Jewish restaurant that served simple kosher food. To prevent attacks by neo-Nazis, a German police officer stood guard outside the entrance of the modest establishment. Few customers patronized the café, perhaps because the food was mediocre and served by a glum waitress. Some of the other guests probably were tourists, too. All of us, perhaps with the exception of our German friend, would rather have eaten somewhere else. When the four of us left, the police officer no longer stood immediately outside the door but had repositioned himself at the corner a short distance up the street. From this discrete new vantage point, however, he continued to keep a watchful eye on the café. The Beth Café seemed to symbolize a Jewish way of life that no longer existed in Berlin, and what we ate seemed more like "virtual food" of an age that had been erased in Germany. Some things are irrevocably lost, and all the goodwill of those left behind is of no avail to recover them.

With one particular sight, however, Ursula managed to build a bridge between us and her way of seeing things. She led us to a well-kept playground, with sandboxes, swings, and slides, in the Koppenplatz, a quiet residential square. A short distance from the playground stands a bronze memorial consisting of an old kitchen table, one chair placed at the table, and another chair nearby, toppled over onto its back. These everyday objects in somewhat larger-than-life size invite the visitor to sit or lean on them while pondering their meaning—a simple scene that has been violently interrupted. A family argument? An interrogation? A deportation? The four of us wove stories to fit the evocative sculpture. Bernie said that his parents had had a table just like this one back home in Tab, and Ursula told us that the kitchen table in her present house in Pankow was also of the same type. Here we all found emotional access to an unnamed act of violence.

Our East German friend described some of the heated debates among German intellectuals, politicians, and artists that surrounded the construction of monuments to the past, especially to the Holocaust. She believed that those who were for pompous, large monuments only wanted to assuage their consciences. Bernie agreed, remarking that the simple tableau of the disrupted kitchen touched him deeply. He felt it to be a more eloquent symbol of the human devastation wrought by the Nazi terror than any monumental memorial could ever be. Size, he said, shouldn't be assumed necessarily to reflect the degree of guilt of those who erected a particular monument. An increasing number of Germans opposed the construction of a huge Holocaust memorial in the center of Berlin for another reason. They simply didn't want to have a monument to the greatest crime in the country's history in the center of the capital.

In the late afternoon, we parted from Ursula and boarded a streetcar. We moved to the back as it pulled away from the stop, and we looked out the window to see our artist friend running full speed around the corner. What was her hurry? To finish one of her paintings of somber urban cityscapes in her atelier? To catch up with the future that the "East" Germans still defined differently for themselves than the more jaundiced "West" Germans? On our way back to the Kurfürstendam, Bernie observed that in the half-hidden corners of the eastern side of Berlin lies an inventive spirit that will well serve the Germany to come. At first, I was surprised to hear this from my staunchly capitalist friend, but then he has a keen eye for potentials, no matter what their political context. Finally, he turned to us with an amused smile on his face and said how glad he was to have recently invested some money in the New Germany mutual fund.

I had been apprehensive about introducing Bernie to Germany. After all, there was more to this common trip to Germany than Bernie's reciprocity for our visit to Tab, Hungary, in 1990. He had avoided this part of Europe for decades, although his frequent travels to neighboring countries brought him close many times. Throughout our trip, Bernie was engrossed in what he saw and heard, yet somehow quite self-absorbed and contemplative. I wondered whether part of his easygoing interaction with the Germans he met was the learned response of someone who liked to be accommodating and who had learned to be a polite guest. I also knew that he shied away from conflicts and that his training and personality gave him a reserve that prevented him from expressing his feelings spontaneously or with hyperbole.

A year and a half after our trip, Bernie articulated his position about Germany in a speech to a German organization of businesspeople, academicians, government representatives, and other professionals (*Wirtschaftsgilde*) who have been meeting for more than forty years to discuss the social and ethical implications of the German post—World War II market economy. During their annual midwinter meeting, we were invited to read and discuss excerpts from our memoirs in light of the ongoing debate in Germany about adequate forms of remembering (and memorializing) the Holocaust. In carefully articulated phrases, and speaking slowly so that this largely bilingual German audience would understand his English, Bernie made his key points: "I want to be as open and forthright as I can.... What do I think of Germans and Germany? I totally reject the concept of mass and national guilt.... Everyone, not just Germans, should be aware of the first signs of a drift toward the abyss, and stand up against it."

While the differentiation he made between guilt and responsibility is known, what made this moment so important for everyone present was the fact that in the audience were former members of the German World War II military. Bernie was the first concentration camp survivor most of them had ever met. At the conclusion of his speech, the audience sat in stunned silence, not knowing whether it was appropriate to applaud. The brutal fact of Nazi crimes had come home in the form of an individual victim standing before them who appeared, not as an accuser, but as one who sketched in the simplest terms a blueprint for civilized behavior that should guide us all.

Even days after our presentation, conversations with conferees frequently drifted back to Bernie's speech. I was touched by how the participants, all of whom were highly successful in their careers and most of whom had developed a sense of their own worth during the period of Germany's postwar reconstruction, were receptive and ready to communicate about their past. Our presentation opened up a way for many of them to tell their individual and family stories. One man in his sixties stood out for me. His father had been an SS bureaucrat in Prague, selecting Czechs for slave labor in the German war machine. After the war, a Czech court sentenced his father to life imprisonment without parole. The son of the storyteller (the grandson of the war criminal) is at present politically active in a German anti-fascist organization. While the family history of this successful German businessman is extreme, to a lesser degree many members of the audience shared the fate of having lived between two radically different times and between two generations with radically different political beliefs. As a catalyst for bridge building and open sharing of the past, throughout this conference Bernie embodied his often-expressed faith in rational, civilized behavior.

. . .

Coda

While writing our stories, Bernie and I became more aware of our common belief in Euro-American cultural traditions, not just as a set of static principles, but as something alive and evolving, with inherent moral and intellectual resources for problem solving and bridge building. This creed has provided us with the cultural playing field—far removed from ethnic determinism, moralistic breast-beating, or psychological make-believe—to understand and to deal with each other's pasts, their similarities and radical differences.

One evening during our weeklong journey through Germany, Bernie became moved as he described the architectural simplicity of Thomas Jefferson's home, Monticello, near Charlottesville, Virginia—its modesty and understatement in contrast to the affected pomposity of Nazi structures. I could readily identify with what this architecture of the Enlightenment meant to him. Many years ago, at the Acropolis in Athens, I was overcome by the sheer perfection of the Parthenon, that architectural marvel of classical antiquity. Those two monuments encapsulate for both of us a sense of what should be the guide in human affairs—a spirit of rationality.

We know that both the Greeks and Thomas Jefferson owned slaves, and we know that the Enlightenment principle of reason has been instrumentalized to justify violence and to shape ideologies of mass movements. But these distortions have only been possible by rending the principle of rationality from its universalistic moorings. Our stories imply, for Bernie and me at least, a simple affirmation of what has become hackneyed to many, namely, the universal idea of a common humanity. Who would know better than Bernie and other survivors that the extermination camps were the greatest challenge to this idea? This gives us all the more cause to cling to these principles, even if this has a fundamentalist ring to it. Such principles, we believe, will provide a productive context in which a reconciliation between Germans and Jews, who shared so much in building European civilization before the midcentury descent into barbarism, will finally be achieved.

Soon after the Berlin Wall and the Iron Curtain crumbled, the world watched the Germans celebrate the collapse of their division when the Jewish-American conductor Leonard Bernstein conducted Beethoven's Ninth Symphony not far from the ruins of Hitler's bunker. Perhaps our joy over this performance was no more than a leap of faith, an ephemeral *acte imaginaire*, but one that we nevertheless embraced. Yet is such a leap justified? For why would a past moment from Bernie's story— when the dwindling group of survivors at Gunskirchen stacked up corpses to form partitions in their barracks—crowd in on me?

Shortly before the Holocaust befell Europe, Freud described, in *Civilization and Its Discontents*, the life and death instincts as equally powerful forces. Was he right? Or can we cling instead to Thomas Mann's dictum from the *Magic Mountain* for guidance, as an underpinning for our act of faith: "For the sake of goodness and love, man shall let death have no sovereignty over his thoughts."

On our last evening in Berlin, we attended a performance of Mozart's *Die Zauberflöte* at the Staatsoper located on the main boulevard Unter den Linden, in what used to be the center of East Berlin. Mozart's music floated in the air, a perfect symbol of freedom and order, and the story of the opera unfolded with both its dark night and its illuminating path, with its trials and its victories. During those few hours, we experienced, within the magic circle of music, the transformative powers that are inherent in all of us, if we only have the courage, faith, and luck to let them come forth to guide us. We left the opera house to say farewell to Berlin and to Germany, with Sarastro's words still reverberating in our hearts: "In diesen heil'gen Hallen kennt man die Rache nicht" (In these sacred halls, revenge is unknown).

CODA

· · ·

Notes

1. Gottlieb Wagner and Bernhard Holl, *Die Geschichte der jüdischen Gemeinde zu Kleinheubach*, ed. Markt Kleinheubach u. Heimat- und Geschichtsverein Kleinheubach (Kleinheubach: Zehe-Druck, 1996), 165. The first part of this volume is a republication of archival work (originally published in 1934) of the Protestant pastor of the village, Gottlieb Wagner, covering the early history of the Jewish community. An individual Jew, "Sisle von Heubach," appears in records as early as 1326; but a single Jew did not constitute a "community." That no more Jews appear in Kleinheubach until 1677 is explained by the witch-hunts and persecutions of Jews in the intervening period, which discouraged Jewish settlers (27–28). But by 1677, the requirements for a Jewish community in Kleinheubach were met, namely, ten Jewish males, a synagogue, a rabbi, a teacher, a school, a *Mikva*, and a cemetery (126).

In the second part of this volume, Bernhard Holl, a former mayor of Kleinheubach, brings the history of Jewish life in Kleinheubach up to date. I am indebted to the work of these good men for much of the historical information about the Jewish community in Kleinheubach.

2. Wagner and Holl, 76–90.

Notes to Chapter 3

1. Wagner and Holl, 188–91.

2. Bernhard Holl's work enabled me to determine that Frau Sichel was either Ida Sichel (born May 9, 1886) or Klara Sichel (born March 1, 1888)—two unmarried sisters who owned a shoe shop and lived at Baugasse 20. Following their deportation from Kleinheubach, their names appeared on a list of people transported to Poland on May 10, 1942. No further information exists on them. Wagner and Holl, 76.

3. Wagner and Holl, 193–207.

4. Wagner and Holl, 41, 134, 137.

5. Wagner and Holl, 81, 89, 163, 180.

6. A few Kleinheubach Jews who survived the war later made claims for reparations, among them, Theodor Weil and Klara Sichel in 1959. Wagner and Holl, 78, 82.

Note to Chapter 5

1. For Merrill's account of their meeting, see Charles Merrill, *The Journey: Massacre of the Innocents* (Cambridge, Mass.: Kenet Media, 1996), 127 f.

Notes to Chapter 6

1. Frederic C. Tubach, *Index Exemplorum: A Handbook of Medieval Religious Tales*, 2d ed. (Helsinki: Academia Scientiarum Fennica, 1981).

2. Gerhart Hoffmeister and Frederic C. Tubach, *Germany, 2000 Years: From the Nazi Era to the Present*, vol. 3., 2d ed. (New York: Ungar, 1992).

Notes to Chapter 7

1. Wagner and Holl, 111–12.

2. Wagner and Holl, 30–40.

3. Brigitte Oleschinski, *Plötzensee Memorial Center*, trans. John Grossman (Berlin-Charlottenburg: German Resistance Memorial Center, 1996), 5, 7. Of course, the Nazis persecuted many more than were sen-

tenced to die. The Protective Custody law called for the arrest of "enemies of the state and the people." Under this law, not only Germans, but Poles, for example, were also arrested (after May 1943), and most were sent to concentration camps. After 1934, lists of those in "protective custody" included the first letter of the inmate's last name plus a number. One of the last known lists indicated 34,591 prisoners whose last name began with the letter M alone. See *Topography of Terror: Guide to the Exhibit*, trans. Jerry Gerber (Berlin: Berliner Festspiele, 1987–96), 10.

Text : Electra

Display : Electra / Frutiger for ORN

Design : Steve Renick

Composition : Impressions

Printing / binding : Edwards Bros.

Heterick Memorial Library
Ohio Northern University

DUE	RETURNED	DUE	RETURNED
1.		13.	
2.		14.	
3.		15.	
4.		16.	
5.		17.	
6.		18.	
7.		19.	
8.		20.	
9.		21.	
10.		22.	
11.		23.	
12.		24.	

WITHDRAWN FROM
OHIO NORTHERN
UNIVERSITY LIBRARY

OHIO NORTHERN UNIVERSITY

3 5111 00683 1477

Heterick Memorial Library
Ohio Northern University
Ada, OH 45810